Becoming Citizens
in the Age of Television

David Thelen

Becoming Citizens
IN THE
Age of Television

HOW AMERICANS

CHALLENGED THE MEDIA

AND SEIZED POLITICAL

INITIATIVE DURING

THE IRAN-CONTRA

DEBATE

The University of Chicago Press
Chicago and London

David Thelen is professor of history at Indiana University and editor of the
Journal of American History

The University of Chicago Press, Chicago 60637
The University of Chicago Press, Ltd., London
© 1996 by The University of Chicago
All rights reserved. Published 1996
Printed in the United States of America

05 04 03 02 01 00 99 98 97 96   5 4 3 2 1

ISBN (cloth): 0-226-79470-9
ISBN (paper): 0-226-79471-7

Library of Congress Cataloging-in-Publication Data

Thelen, David P. (David Paul)
    Becoming citizens in the age of television : how Americans challenged the media and
seized political initiative during the Iran-Contra debate / David Thelen.
        p.   cm.
    Includes bibliographical references and index.
    ISBN 0-226-79470-9 (cl : alk. paper)
    1. Iran-Contra Affair, 1985–1990—Public opinion.   2. Television and politics—United
States.   3. United States—Politics and government—1981–1989.   4. Public opinion—
United States.   I. Title.
    E879.T465   1996
    973.927—dc20   96-10544
                                                                                    CIP

⊗ The paper used in this publication meets the minimum requirements of the American National Standard for Information Sciences—Permanence of Paper for Printed Library Materials, ANSI Z39.48-1984.

For Esther

Contents

✦ ✦ ✦ ✦ ✦ ✦ ✦ ✦ ✦ ✦ ✦

Contents

A gallery of photographs follows page 64

Acknowledgments

* * * * * * * * * * * *

From the moment eight years ago when I first read what Americans wrote Lee Hamilton as they watched the Iran-contra hearings, I knew first that I wanted others to hear how Americans were struggling to make themselves seen and heard in a media-made age and second that the letters touched major issues in the theory and practice of culture and politics. For access to the basic primary sources, as I report in the Essay on Sources and Methods, I received essential help from Congressman Hamilton and his staff, from staffs of both the House and Senate committees that conducted the hearings, from staffers for individual senators and congressmen, and from the Library of Congress for providing a place for me to examine the letters. Back in 1987, when the letters and telegrams were in the physical possession of the House Select Committee and Congressman Hamilton, our daughter Jennifer came to Washington to help me choose and photocopy the letters I would later analyze in more detail. Since then Greg Sumner, Paul Murphy, Julie Plaut, Patrick Ettinger, and Scott Stephan have helped me with research in Bloomington.

As I struggled to make a framework for the letters that could combine the immediacy of the letters with the historical significance of what their writers were trying to do, with the voice in which I could write while still respecting their voices, I have asked many people for advice, including by asking them to read various drafts of various chapters. While some of these readers expressed reservations, they invariably helped me to figure out what I was about, how to do that better, where to find relevant writings by others, and how I should treat in this text the kinds of skepticism I expect the book will raise in some readers. At various points colleagues at Indiana University provided essential encouragement and criticism: Casey Blake, John Bodnar, Nick Cullather, Lawrence Friedman, David Nord, Michael McGerr, and particularly for reading many drafts and talking about it on many occasions, Steven Stowe. I am also indebted to several people for reading and critiquing the whole manuscript: Paula Baker, David Blight, Harry Boyte, Jacquelyn Hall, Michael Schudson, and above all Michael Frisch and, for other advice, George Lipsitz, Joyce Appleby, Tiziano Bonazzi, Maurizio Vaudagna, Rhys Isaac, Greg Dening, Patrick Brantlinger, Roy Rosenweig, and George Mitchell. Beside inspiration and wisdom, I learned a lot that informs this book from my father, Herb Thelen, including from many conversations about the letters that are the core of this book. In the final stages of figuring out what I wanted to say and how best to say it I had an extraordinary experience with the University of Chicago Press and particularly Senior Editor Doug Mitchell and copyeditor Diana Gillooly. For perspective on opinion management I am indebted to David Gergen and James Carville.

From start to finish this book is inseparable from my life with Esther, though there were times when both of us wished it hadn't been so. After 33 years of marriage I can't describe precisely how her love, criticism, faith, and reality checks contributed to this book, but the book (and much else) would have been impossible without her. And it was an additional bonus to develop the framework for this book while she was developing a parallel framework in her own field of developmental psychology.

Introduction

❖ ❖ ❖ ❖ ❖ ❖ ❖ ❖ ❖ ❖ ❖

The most disturbing complaint of our times is that politics and governance have moved beyond the reach of the concerns and conversations of Americans in their daily lives. This book explores how this has happened and how Americans have fought to reclaim government for themselves.

The presidential election of 1992 was a vivid illustration of how the forum for political discussion looked differently to politicians and citizens. By October of that year President George Bush was clearly following the first rule of modern campaigning. Trailing Bill Clinton in the polls, Bush tried during the campaign's first televised debate, to find and hit the lowest common denominators of viewers by attacking Clinton's patriotism and character. Running up Clinton's negatives, the experts said, was Bush's best hope to win. But Americans did not exist only in the common denominators where the Bush strategists imagined them, and at the second televised debate, four days after the first, they revealed their very different vision of politics. At that second debate, in a University of Richmond auditiorium, a panel of 209 citizens replaced journalists as the questioners of the candidates. Early into the questioning Kimberly Usry, twenty-eight years old and recently laid off from her job as marketing director for a traffic control company, challenged Bush and the other candidates: "The amount of time the candidates have spent in this campaign trashing their opponents' character and their program is depressingly large. Why can't your discussion and proposals reflect the genuine complexity and difficulty of the issues?" She insisted that the president of the United States and the other candidates talk as seriously as citizens did in their everyday lives. Bush, in what the *New York Times* called "an inaccurate reading of the audience mood," answered Usry with a renewed attack on Clinton: "It's wrong to demonstrate against your own country or organize demonstrations against your own country on foreign soil." At this point moderator Carole Simpson of ABC News asked the audience panel: "Are you pleased with how the campaign's been going?" "No!" came the thundering response. Denton Walthall, a thirty-seven-year-old domestic mediator, upbraided Bush, "Can we focus on the issues and not the personalities and the mud?" He demanded of the candidates, "Could . . . you make a commitment to the citizens of the United States to meet our needs, and we have many, and not yours again?" From then on the candidates stuck more closely to the issues. The second televised debate, its terms set by ordinary citizens, was a remarkable event, observed Maureen Dowd of the *New York Times:* "The voters blew the whistle on mud wrestling and had a civilizing effect on the often feral 1992 campaign."[1]

Bush and Walthall stood a few yards apart in that Richmond auditorium, but both knew that their exchange was flashing simultaneously on tens of millions of American television sets. Bush was counting on television's capacity to compress individual viewers into a faceless mass held together by low common denominators and inspired to do the same thing, register disapproval of Clinton at the ballot box. But Americans watch television in many different ways, sometimes passively, but often actively—cheering, modifying, dismissing, or ridiculing what they see there. Walthall and Usry challenged Bush to quit appealing to common denominators and instead converse with them the way people do when a subject or a relationship really matters to them. They credited their fellow citizens with the desire and the ability to see something real on television, something they could discuss and interpret with people who shared their lives.

The debate that evening in Richmond was about much more than who would be elected president in 1992. Walthall and Usry brought into view the concerns and the anger that Americans have come to feel when engaging politics as it appears on television. Usry and Walthall insisted that the citizens, not the candidates and their handlers, should decide how people should talk and what they should talk about in the public forum. The immediacy of that moment in Richmond, with Walthall and Usry face to face with the candidates, inspired them to speak out and rebuke Bush instead of just ignoring or dismissing him as they most likely would have done had they watched his remarks on television. And Usry's statement set off a kind of chain reaction, first empowering other members of the audience and then Moderator Simpson to take charge of the debate, then inspiring people at home to talk among themselves. In the process they brought to life the basic issue that Americans face as they try to take possession of their government in the age of television: how to find and talk with each other and in the process become citizens.

To explore this issue I will focus on a conflict that exploded between citizens and leaders in the summer of 1987 as three-quarters of Americans were watching a televised congressional hearing. Through that window we will see how citizens rejected the voices constructed for them according to practices of opinion management and instead asserted their right to speak for themselves. And as they claimed that right they returned us to the dilemma of democracy in our media-made age: Ordinary citizens seem increasingly to shape what we see and hear in public, but they feel more powerless than ever. And politicians seem increasingly eager to appeal in sound bites to citizens, but they find citizens less responsive than ever. Both citizens and politicians agree when they see and hear each other on television that the current public forum prevents their conversations from doing what each wants them to do: solve real problems and sustain relationships.

We live at a time when popular influence on political discourse appears to be greater than ever. Candidates and officeholders champion low common denominator issues that they expect will appeal to many voters. Sound bites blur into laws. Republicans in the House of Representatives overwhelmingly passed a constitutional amendment to prohibit burning of the American flag—something that happens five or six times a year—in what conservative columnist Charles Krauthamer called "cheap populism and easy patriotism": "How would you like to be called soft on flag-burners in a 30-second spot at the next election?"[2] Meanwhile, at the other end of Pennsylvania Avenue, Bill Clinton launched his reelection campaign with advertisements that trumpeted his law-and-order war against crime—senior White House adviser George Stephanopoulos explaining, "This hits people where they live"—in his latest attempt to find the common denominator of the moment. Democratic congressman David Obey (Wisc.) complained, "if you don't like the president's position on a particular issue, you simply need to wait a few weeks."[3]

At the same time that citizens seem to be shaping more than ever before what appears in public, they report feeling less influence than ever on the outcome. By a 65–22 percent margin, eligible voters told a pollster in 1994 that "public officials don't care much what people like me think." The percentage of Americans who told Gallup that they can "trust Washington to do what is right all or most of the time" fell from 78 percent in 1964 to 19 percent by 1994.[4] Citizens may be more visible, but they believe that no one is listening to them. The voices they hear in the public forum belong, not to individual citizens, but to "the people" as abstractions—Bubba, Year of the Woman, yuppies, Joe Six-Pack.

The 1994 congressional election provided particularly rich opportunities for the management of opinion, as the different parties interpreted the results not as a way to listen to popular concerns but as a way to advance their own agendas. Democrats invented a category that permitted them to avoid listening to any voters who had wanted to rebuke the Clinton administration; they pronounced the Republican victory to be the work of "Angry White Males." While more men than women voted Republican in 1994 (as in earlier elections), male voters specifically rejected—by margins of between 70–30 and 79–21—the label "angry" when it was presented to them in three polls.[5] By characterizing (and dismissing) voters as "angry," however, the administration had relieved itself of any responsibility to listen to them.

Republicans found their own abstraction that allowed them to dismiss what real people thought. The new House Speaker, Newt Gingrich, proclaimed that the 1994 election "was clearly a historic election which clearly had a mandate" in which victorious Republicans "represent the vast majority of Americans" who supported Gingrich's legislative "Contract with America." In fact, the 1994 vote was anything but an unprecedented popular endorsement of Gingrich's measures. First, the election attracted no more than the usual popular interest in off-year elections. The turnout rate of 38.7 percent slightly topped the record low rates of 36.5 percent in 1990 and 36.4 percent in 1986, while it fell below the 1982 rate of 40.1 percent and far below the turnouts of 47.6 percent in 1962, 48.6 percent in 1966, and 46.8 percent in 1970.[6] Second, it is hard to portray the election as a mandate on a Contract that more than two-thirds of voters had not heard of by the time they voted in 1994 and that 62 percent still had not heard of by April 1995.[7] Third, neither the margin of Republican victory in the House of Representatives–51–47 percent—nor the decline in the proportion of voters choosing Democrats for the House (from 51 percent in 1992 to 47 percent in 1994) marks a massive shift in opinion.[8] In truth, the size of a candidate's campaign coffers correlated far better with success than did the candidate's party label. The better-financed candidates won in 85 percent of the races.

All these efforts to understand individuals in the abstract have created a widening chasm between where citizens really stand and where they are perceived to stand when viewed through the lens of opinion management. The failure to see citizens where they really are has distorted not only public debate in elections but, even more tragically, policymaking between elections. During the 1993–94 debate on health care, interest groups purchased television advertisements in an attempt "to frighten members of Congress into believing there's a groundswell of support out there" for their desire to kill reform, explained Darrell West, who had studied the effects of the health care advertisements. The strategy exploited policymakers' fundamental unwillingness to listen to real Americans talk about their needs and experiences and their preference instead to believe that mass marketing appeals would create political support. The industry's advertisements, which portrayed a fictitious yuppie couple, Harry and Louise, complaining about

Clinton's health care proposal, were later credited with the defeat of that proposal. In fact, the Harry and Louise ads had no measurable impact on the opinions of viewers. In the self-contained world of opinion management, however, journalists and politicians believed that the ads had persuaded voters to oppose change in health care programs and that, therefore, responsible politicians should oppose health care reform, as well.[9]

The basic challenge for democracy then is to find and listen to people where they are, not where opinion management can place them. In an age of television, this challange is inseparable from the difficulties posed by television as the place where citizens and politicians alike expect the forum to come into view. The difficulties arise because viewers experience television both as a narrowing compression toward common denominators and as a widening invitation to conversation with those around them. Viewers treat television as a separate, make-believe world of selling, entertaining, and pontificating, but they also choose to enter that world when they want escape, information, or diversion. They can, when they choose, bring television back into their own lives. Broadcasting messages that are assembled to appeal to a mass but received and interpreted in millions of isolated and intimate settings, television provides the experience that increasingly shapes how politicians and citizens talk with each other.

The starting place for exploring what people take from television and how they imagine starting conversations with people they meet there is in the personal relationships where people talk about television with their families, friends, neighbors, and coworkers. This book tells the story of how in 1987, with help from people around them, Americans scrutinized what they saw on television to form their own conclusions. They saw a process that seemed to divide manipulators from manipulated, and they faced a terrible choice between resignation and rebellion. Either ignore politics as a kind of background noise irrelevant to anything real or, like Kim Usry, fight to reclaim government, to speak and to make the conversation as meaningful as when individuals talk and listen to people around them. The citizens rebelled. This book tells the story of the vital and creative ways they went about interpreting the outside world as they built relationships with other people and how they hoped to remake politics in the spirit of those relationships.

Such rebellions have taken shape when conversation on television has blurred with conversation in everyday life: viewers talked about what they saw on television with the people around them, and they became so troubled by public officials or journalists that they felt compelled to interrupt them, to add their own voices, and to try to make talk on television more nearly resemble everyday talk. The rebellions have begun when arguments over basic principles were personified in conflicts between individuals. Oliver North's activities and testimony opened a fundamental debate on heroism, foreign policy, and democratic government in the Iran-Contra hearings of 1987. The conflicting testimonies of Anita Hill and Clarence Thomas became the core of a public debate on sexual harassment, character assassination, racism, and sexism during the Senate's confirmation hearings in 1991. And the televised hearings (1994) and trial (1995) of O. J. Simpson for double murder started conversations about race, wealth, and the police, and the relative claims of victims and accused and prerogatives of celebrities in criminal trials.

Televised congressional hearings, in particular, provide remarkable opportunities for opening real conversation among citizens and with lawmakers. By taking issues from the hearings and making them part of everyday conversation, voters take back from politicians and journalists the capacity to define and manipulate the issue or promote partisan agendas. By conveying conclusions from conversations with people around them through phone calls and letters to congressional committee members, viewers force politicians to talk and listen more in the language of everyday life.

The Senate Judiciary Committee, for example, triggered a popular uprising in 1991 when it televised the testimony of Anita Hill and Clarence Thomas. Citizens joined senators in judging whether Hill's charges of sexual harassment provided grounds for denying Thomas confirmation to the Supreme Court. Viewers bombarded congressmen, newspapers, and talk shows with their observations. Some insisted that the Senate send a clear message to all Americans that sexual harassment was unacceptable; others demanded an equally clear pronouncement that character assassination was wrong. "Never has a national issue felt so personal," a woman from Laguna Beach, California, wrote Illinois Senator Paul Simon, as she recounted the harassment she had experienced. The line between citizens and politicians dissolved in the bond of remarkable intimacy that television could create. A woman in Douglas, Arizona, had felt so traumatized by sexual abuse she had suffered that she had never confided it to anyone—not to her parents, husband, sons, or closest friends—but now, as she listened to the Senate debate, she confided it, including the name of her tormentor, to Paul Simon, a complete stranger: "It is with much pain and revulsion that I put these personal thoughts on paper. I hope that they will be read and understood by you." To a woman in Western Springs, Illinois, the Senate's vote to confirm Thomas "made me physically ill—the same feeling I experienced thirty-six years ago when I was sexually assaulted." A woman from Chicago thought that she had successfully put aside her experience with harassment a decade earlier, "but these hearings have dredged up feelings I haven't experienced for nearly a decade and I am now forced to relive the entire episode." Even so, the hearings could "prove beneficial to our nation" because "men and women have got to wise up. . . ; they'd better learn to believe that this does happen, and that it ruins lives." In a beauty parlor in Elmhurst, Illinois, or in the homes and offices of Freeport, Illinois, the Thomas-Hill debate was "all anyone is talking about these last few days," a woman told Simon. Senators had to hear their experiences and conclusions. A woman from Albany spent $60 for phone calls and telegrams over four days and, because she had "dialed the phone dozens of times and did not get through," she wrote Simon a letter.[10] The hearings blossomed into a town meeting where debate ran deeper than in any recent election as conversations that began in the Senate were picked up in beauty parlors and living rooms from which Americans then reached out to legislators and drew them back into the discussion by writing and calling them.

I had no idea that I would be writing a book about television and democracy when I began, casually enough, to watch the Iran-Contra hearings in the summer of 1987. I was simply a curious, if partisan, viewer. I was angered to learn of covert actions by Reagan operatives in Nicaragua. I cheered Democrats' defenses of the Constitution and democracy. As May gave way to June, the hearings—and the fascinating testimony by a parade of spies, arms merchants, and military officers—grew into a summertime diversion from more important parts of my life and work.

The televised appearance of Oliver North, from July 7 to 14, changed all this. North's testimony set in motion a chain of events and discoveries that soon compelled me to write this book. North started events by eloquently claiming that the highest duty of public officials was to obey orders, however illegal or immoral, given them by superior officers. This sounded like a Nazi vision. A few leaders would tell the rest of us what to do, and we would "salute smartly," as North put it. The real shock came when journalists reported that most Americans were cheering Oliver North as a national hero. North's appearance, they reported, had galvanized individual viewers into a cheering mass that was bombarding congressmen with phone calls and letters that proclaimed North's heroism. "Olliemania" they called this popular frenzy.

Was this my country? I wondered. What were North's admirers thinking? I decided to ask the chairman of the House Select Committee conducting the Iran-Contra investigation, Lee Hamilton, whose Indiana district began a few miles from my house, whether he would let me see the letters he and the committee had received and that I imagined from press reports would be an outpouring from North's fans. Fine, he said. I rearranged my schedule so that I could spend several weeks that fall in Washington reading these letters and talking with aides who had answered mail and phone calls for other senators and congressmen.

So completely had I accepted the media's reports of Olliemania that nothing in my thirty years of practicing history prepared me for what I discovered as I read letter after letter, some five thousand that fall. First, I discovered that journalists were wrong about what these letters said. Most people did not write to praise North. Most did not write about North at all, and the majority of those who mentioned him were critical of him. This discovery sent me back to examine more closely the polls that headline writers had used to proclaim North a national hero. The actual polls revealed great popular skepticism, even fear, about North. Overwhelming majorities specifically rejected the label of "national hero" that Ronald Reagan had tried to pin on North.

The second discovery was that, far from having been reduced to a faceless mass of spectators, as journalists had depicted, Americans wrote congressmen across a spectacular range of topics and perspectives. I was amazed by the diversity and creativity of many letters. And yet, and this was a third discovery, liberal and conservative writers, supporters and critics of North alike, experienced politics in the same ways, disturbed by many of the new directions politics was taking.

My final discovery was that Americans were writing not to cheer television performances but to reclaim their voices from the opinion managing and interpreting industries that purported to know what Americans were thinking. They hoped by these letters and phone calls to create a more participatory democracy in which citizens and politicians talked among themselves without intervention and distortion by intermediaries. Writers demanded the right to be heard for themselves. To answer pundits' outrageous interpretations of what viewers were—or should be—thinking, Americans had spontaneously mobilized themselves into a reserve army of citizens, called forth by American folklore to save the republic in times of peril. American democracy, I learned, was incredibly healthy at the grass roots.

I was discovering the health of popular citizenship at the very time when both the theory and practice of American politics seemed dangerously, critically ill. As I stepped back, I came to see this rebellion by Americans against the fruits of opinion management as part of a worldwide revolt against the modern political systems that try to manage and claim to provide legitimacy for their rulers on the basis of the "voice of the people." In the United States, as in Italy, Nicaragua, Germany, or Russia, the great challenge from below was to invent new political theory and practice by which citizens could turn their grassroots conversations into popular policy and government.

The challenge of inventing democratic theory and practice has become harder with the passing of the twentieth century, however, as the habits of opinion management have become more firmly entrenched. Because the Iran-Contra hearings tapped the deepest concerns that voters and politicians have developed toward each other, they provide an extraordinary opportunity to examine the divergence between how experts in the modern crafts of politics—pollsters, journalists, advertisers, political scientists, candidates—think that voters experience political spaces and how voters actually do think and act in politics. This book explores how the theory and practice of democracy have become battlefields in a popular insurgency to reclaim the right to define the meaning and experience of citizenship. In these remarkable letters to congressmen in 1987, Americans displayed the everyday political folkways citizens have come to live by. They reveal how they have created their own sources and authorities for fact and viewpoint by which to evaluate what appears on television. So armed, television watchers have then interpreted and participated in politics on their own terms. In these letters Americans describe where they watched the hearings, the people they talked with, the experiences they drew on, and the everyday needs they met as they tried to make sense of and then influence the hearings.

In the course of talking about the hearings, Americans transformed themselves from television watchers into active citizens and patriots. By writing or calling a legislator, they defined citizenship in practice. While most writers expected politics and government to take place a long way from their daily lives, in remote self-contained worlds that required only their casual attention, they also felt a responsibility to reclaim government when politicians threatened bedrock principles upon which they founded their lives. These were the moments when they could only feel true to their private principles by taking an active part in the public arena. The core of democracy was the confidence that their interests, beliefs, and feelings were fully represented in public life. These were the times when they wanted to extend the feelings they held toward others in their intimate lives—feelings of pride, hope, fear, confidence, trust, responsibility—to a wider but invisible community that existed outside the range of their everyday conversations. Suddenly they were taking part with people and in spaces that they rarely encountered. By asserting their own values and talking of their own experiences, they lowered the barriers that had kept them hidden. Instead of talking the vacuous language of opinion management they spoke in the questioning, protesting, defending, quarreling, and asserting voices in which they ordinarily conversed with the people around them. They became citizens. In these letters they created citizenship in action.

As I tried to understand why these letters speak so powerfully about direct democracy, I realized that they were unique sources for answering the questions that have haunted me as a scholar and citizen for thirty years: How do we citizens talk with each other, find out what we share, enter and shape conversations that we and politicians carry on, and try to make representatives listen to us? In the 1960s and early 1970s I took part in some movements and studied others by which citizens made themselves visible and then explored responses to those movements by the institutions that mediated between citizens and politicians (such as legislatures, elections, media, political parties, and political cultures). By the 1970s I had concluded that there were many arenas other than politics where people tried to control their lives. So I explored popular expressions across a wide range of activities—leisure, workplaces, schools—but still I thought the important places for participation in life were large in scale: churches and religion, labor unions and social classes, pressure groups and political parties.

In these letters to Hamilton, by contrast, I could for the first time listen to individuals at the moment and with the sources by which they acted on their citizenship. I could listen as they tried to make sense of what they were watching on television and to imagine how they might add their own voices to public debate. I finally began to see that the vital and creative sources of interpretation and participation are the primary relationships where thinking and acting are inseparable from personal responsibility and everyday needs. Writers spoke out and tried to reclaim their voices from the media story of Olliemania, in order to demonstrate the vitality of their intimate relationships as sites for making sense of and taking part in politics.

But how to display that creativity and vitality? Believing that in focusing on primary relationships I was entering uncharted terrain for historians, I decided to use several approaches that together would illustrate the centrality of such relationships. I analyzed how journalists' accounts of the ways Americans made sense of the hearings inspired those Americans to reveal their usually invisible primary relationships as refutation. I gave an ethnographic reading of the letters sent to Hamilton in order to reconstruct how the writers wanted these letters to draw Hamilton into their personal relationships. I wrote a historical account of how primary relationships have become ever more important in shaping politics over the twentieth century. I concluded the book with some thoughts about how politics could more nearly resemble primary relationships. And throughout the book I quoted liberally from the letters in hopes of conveying the creativity and diversity of the places where they were composed.

When we begin to explore how watching television and writing letters are major activities in the making of citizens, we enter a world of "everyday life" where things are so obvious, or at least so near at hand, that they require prefatory comments to make them distant enough that we can see them clearly. The hardest part for me has been to find the voice in which I want to speak. I am an individual, a citizen, and a scholar and am eager to engage readers in all three ways. I want readers to judge whether the book resonates with their experiences, whether they share the vision of citizenship and community that I have heard in these letters and made my own, and whether the book presents a fresh perspective on these issues. The hardest part has been to decide how to describe my aims as a scholar. I understand the academic fashion of reviewing established scholarship and defining where and how an author's book makes an original contribution. As I tried my hand at several such introductions, however, I grew steadily more confident that this exercise was badly distorting my voices as a person and a citizen. Scholarship is as self-referential as the management of opinion that inspired the writers of these letters to rebel. It suffers from the same problem of asking its practitioners to privilege jargon and theory and originality ahead of experiences that emerge from everyday relationships with family, friends, colleagues, citizens, and students. Like the management of opinion, scholarship has become isolated from life where people experience it.

And yet I am a historian. I have drawn from writings on American social and political history, the sociology of primary groups, the economics of small scale, the ethnography of how readers and viewers decode texts, and the philosophy of pragmatism. I have been inspired by path-breaking ethnographic studies from many fields that explore how people think and act on their own terms. I have been inspired and instructed by rich American traditions of citizenship that have repeatedly generated movements for social and political change and by innovators in democratic theory and practice from Tom Paine to Jane Addams, from Fannie Lou Hamer to Ralph Nader. I have resolved my struggle to find a way to express my concerns as a scholar by deciding that rather than clutter the book with commentaries on scholarship, I will direct readers through notes to studies I found particularly resonant or insightful.

As I have continued to balance my critical training as a scholar with my feelings as a citizen, I have been deeply torn about how to frame one crucial issue in this book. Most of the writers, liberal as well as conservative, report not only that they are not heard but also that they feel manipulated by pollsters, journalists, politicians, campaign managers—the people I identify as "opinion managers." As I explored the tremendous chasms between the managers who imagined the political forum as an arena of opinion management and the writers of these letters, I understood why these writers felt manipulated and was tempted to present this book as the story of the revolt by the manipulated. And I still believe that this is part of the story. But in order to understand the problem from the perspective of the manipulators, I also interviewed two leading opinion managers of our day—David Gergen, inventor of spin for the Reagan administration and later pundit on public television, and James Carville, Bill Clinton's 1992 campaign manager and the most successful orchestrator of public opinion for the Democrats. As a result of these conversations I came to see that opinion management does indeed contain elements of manipulation but even more important that many of its expert practitioners feel as acutely as the writers of these letters that it is an artificial world, a world that traps and constrains them as individuals. And so I came to see opinion management as a self-referential arena that individuals enter and leave, a place where even its best practitioners feel uncomfortable as people.

From that conclusion I came to see that opinion management is a profession (or cluster of professions) like any other in that its members receive their identities from what sets them apart from what most people do most of the time. As professionals, they are committed to the techniques and technologies that their profession claims makes people become visible. But as individuals, they should know better than most that the tools of opinion management have severe limitations as means of talking and listening. The best managers, Carville and Gergen, challenge the conventions of opinion management from within—warning about the limitations of polling (as both did), urging professionals to gain wider experiences with life so they can recognize that polls do not fully reflect reality (as Gergen advocated).

If we acknowledge that opinion management is by nature a craft of manipulation but that it is also a self-enclosed arena of conversation that denies those who enter it—citizens, senators, campaign managers alike—the capacity to be seen and heard, we can begin both to recognize many apparent contradictions that occur at all levels and to use its tools to facilitate a wider public forum rather than to narrow it. Opinion polls can reveal which of options presented by a pollster at a particular moment is most attractive to a representative sampling of Americans, but they cannot reveal what people think about or how they change their minds. Americans of all stripes—citizens and pollsters—can condemn the media at one moment and yet approvingly quote a pundit a few moments later. Opinion management offers tools, not inherent evils.

I have grounded this book in letters from five thousand Americans to Congressman Lee Hamilton and the House Select Committee on the Iran-Contra investigation that he chaired. These letters are extraordinary sources, not so much because of the authors' conclusions, but because of what the authors try to make the letters do when they turn the relationships, authorities, and experiences of their intimate worlds into the means for making democracy resemble everyday life.

The decision to build my perspective on popular politics from these letters has prompted two reactions from friends. Some are astonished by the large number of these letters. After all, major original interpretations of how people experience culture and politics have emerged from books grounded in letters from forty-two viewers of "Dallas," conversations with fewer than twenty and questionnaires completed by fewer than one hundred suburban Kansas City housewives who read romance novels, or interviews with twenty-one newspaper readers in Evanston, Illinois.[11] At the other extreme friends have wondered whether these five thousand letters make up a large enough sample to reflect Americans as a whole.

I began by believing that the "representativeness" or "typicality" of these letters was a crucial issue and ended by concluding that it was unimportant. Early in the project I compared themes in the letters to Hamilton and the

House Select Committee with dozens of opinion polls and with mail and phone counts staffers assembled for five other congressmen, four senators, and the Senate Select Committee. The five thousand people who wrote Hamilton, taken as a whole, paralleled majorities in opinion polls and landed somewhere in the ideological middle between writers to liberals such as Louis Stokes (D-Ohio) and George Mitchell (D-Maine) and conservatives such as James Courter (R-N.J.) and William Broomfield (R-Mich.). Indeed, Americans who wrote Hamilton most closely resembled those who wrote moderate William Cohen (R-Maine). Throughout the book I cite opinion polls and mail counts to compare conclusions expressed by writers to Hamilton with those of other Americans.

Because my purpose was to understand how Americans were trying to reinvent politics by writing congressmen, not to define "typical" Americans, I lost much of my concern about the issue of representativeness when I found common patterns in letters from writers from all social backgrounds and political persuasions. They seemed to use letters in the same ways even though they reached different conclusions. Writers approached congressmen in the voice of intimate primary relationships and universal human qualities, qualities available to all Americans. I could not imagine how another sample of five hundred or five hundred thousand letters would differ from the sample I was using.

Because a majority of Americans did not write their congressmen, liberal or conservative, we might still wonder how Americans who wrote their congressmen differed from those who did not. It is certainly true that writers to Hamilton, like writers to congressmen in general over the past half-century, tended to be richer and better educated than Americans as a whole. The same thing is true of voters. Poor citizens have preferred to leverage the political system with strikes, mass assemblies, and riots, while richer and better-educated citizens have formed voluntary associations, written congressmen, and voted.[12] But to dismiss these letters because the aggregate profile of writers differs from that of Americans as a whole would be even more dangerous than to dismiss voting because voters do not resemble Americans as a whole. For one thing, writers to Hamilton came from all walks of life, ethnic backgrounds, geographical regions, and party affiliations. My conclusions grew as much from letters by poor writers as by rich ones, by Ph.D.'s as by high school dropouts, by blacks and whites, men and women, young people and old. For another thing, television has transformed politics and governing in ways that have made writing letters in response to televised congressional hearings an increasingly common activity, while changes introduced by television have made voting an increasingly uncommon avenue for popular participation. Because writing and calling legislators is one of the few forms of political participation that has increased over the past generation, it is a much better activity from which to imagine the future of political participation than is a declining activity such as voting or more episodic ones such as strikes, demonstrations, and riots.

In the end, however, the letter writers themselves gave the best answer to my initial concerns about the representativeness of their letters: We have become so accustomed to wondering how much individuals resemble an imaginary mass whole that we have lost the capacity to listen to real people. We have come to listen to people through polls, averages, markets, to "opinions" presented in the hopes of assembling individuals into aggregates, however low the denominators. We have come to expect political talk to take the form of sound bites, commercials, and press briefings that will offend the fewest people. The writers of these letters, by contrast, wanted to reconstruct political conversations so they would more closely resemble those of everyday life in which individuals really listen to people they know, in which they try to meet those people's needs, in which they talk until they reach conclusions, in which they say what they mean and mean what they say. Most writers wanted to recapture political conversations for themselves and their fellow citizens. We talk and listen to each other in ways that are both unique and universal, not in ways that are "average" or "typical."

One

❖ ❖ ❖ ❖ ❖ ❖ ❖ ❖ ❖ ❖ ❖

The Participatory Moment

At 10:01 on the morning of Tuesday, May 5, 1987, Senator Daniel Inouye gaveled murmuring legislators and spectators to silence in the Senate Caucus Room. At last Americans would meet the shadowy figures who had defied public opinion, the laws of Congress, and perhaps the wishes of President Ronald Reagan by selling American missiles to the Iranians and using the profits to support rebel guerrillas in Nicaragua. Four television cameras were planted around the ornate hearing room to beam the sounds and images across the land. Network anchorpersons came down from New York to Washington so they could introduce viewers live to what *Broadcasting* promised would be a "mega-media event."[1]

The suspense was real. Events had been building to this moment for a long time. Seven months earlier to the day, on October 5, 1986, a young Sandinista infantryman on a routine patrol through a Nicaraguan jungle had spotted a C–123K flying low, directly toward him. He had taken aim with his SA–7 and pulled the trigger, and the plane exploded. The next day searchers found a survivor, Eugene Hasenfus. With the crash of this plane and the investigations that followed, officials from the State Department, Central Intelligence Agency (CIA), and National Security Council (NSC) knew that they could no longer get away with the lie—as they had for a year—that they were not aiding the Nicaraguan contras in violation of congressional mandate. Four weeks after the crash in Nicaragua—on November 3, 1986—a Lebanese newspaper, *Al Shiraa*, reported that the United States had sold weapons to Iran. On November 25, Attorney General Edwin Meese III stunned journalists and citizens alike by tying the two events together. Americans, he stated during a press conference, had sold weapons to Iran and used the profits to resupply the Nicaraguan contras.

The news that national security officials were defying the government's stated policies—and breaking the law to do it—sent Reagan's approval rating crashing by the largest one-week drop in polling history. It opened demands for investigations into both the activities and the lies that shielded them: How could such things have happened? How had they gone undetected? Reagan immediately removed National Security Adviser John Poindexter and one of the NSC's operatives, Lt. Col. Oliver North. He appointed a special prosecutor to identify the crimes committed and to prosecute the lawbreakers. He set up a three-person presidential commission, headed by Senator John Tower, to investigate and report policy recommendations. In early January the House of Representatives and the Senate established special committees to hold joint hearings and issue reports. While legislators and their staffs were constructing the story they wanted to present to viewers, the presidential commission made its report on February 26, 1987. A small band within the government, the commission declared, had run its own foreign policy out of sight of a president uninformed and unengaged in the everyday governing of the country. This news only heightened curiosity—and deepened concern—about who, in fact, made policy. Behind those issues were graver questions about whether policymakers were accountable to the public, the Congress, or even the president.[2]

When Inouye opened the hearings by announcing that their purpose was to "clear the air and let the facts of this unfortunate and sad affair emerge," people knew that pursuing this seemingly bland course would produce explosive results because of what the Tower Commission had termed "the obsession with secrecy" that had pervaded the Iran and contra deals at every stage. The sales of weapons to the Iranian government and the Nicaraguan contras were, first and foremost, "covert operations," actions designed never to see light behind cover-ups intended to deceive Congress, the press, and the people. Cloaking their deeds in secrecy, the perpetrators had presented to outsiders all kinds of faces—sales pitches, lies, distortion, silence—that would permit them to continue to do what they pleased without hindrance. They drew a line that divided those who knew what was really happening from the bulk of people in and out of office who knew only what the dealmakers wanted them to know. On that opening morning Senator Orrin Hatch announced that he hoped to learn whether and when the president of the United States had known the truth of what had happened. From the opening gavel onward, the lied-to—congressmen, citizens, journalists, and maybe even the president—would together assert their rights at last to know what the dealmakers had really done.[3]

With the start of the hearings, Americans soon learned that the answers to their questions would emerge through the personalities and concerns of individual legislators. The stern rectitude of the cochairmen, Senator Daniel Inouye (D-Hawaii) and Representative Lee Hamilton (D-Ind.), created an aura of earnest inquiry. Within this context viewers, over the next several weeks, developed strong feelings toward committee members, expecting individual legislators to infuriate or enhearten them with the questions they would ask and the opinions they would express. The wide variety of legislators offered a wide range of perspectives through which individual viewers could take part in the hearings.

Some viewers told Representative Henry Hyde (R-Ill.) that they liked his irrepressible needling of Democrats. Others applauded the outspoken bluntness of Representative Jack Brooks (D-Tex.) and Senator Warren Rudman (R-N.H.). Those with more ideological agendas chose points of access on the spectrum from conservative Senator Orrin Hatch (R-Utah) and Representative Jim Courter (R-N.J.) to liberal Representative Edward Boland (D-Mass.). Some wrote Senator Paul Sarbanes (D-Md.), Senator Sam Nunn (D-Ga.), and Representative Ed Jenkins (D-Ga.) that they admired their tough questioning of witnesses, their insistence on getting answers instead of speeches. Others were moved the eloquence of Senator George Mitchell (D-Maine) and Representative Louis Stokes (D-Ohio). Yet others preferred the judiciousness of Senators William Cohen (R-Maine) and Howell Heflin (D-Ala.).

Before they adjourned on August 3, the committees heard 250 hours of testimony from 28 public witnesses. Although all the witnesses were architects, operatives, or beneficiaries of the Iran-Contra deals—and all were thus supporters of those transactions—they varied tremendously in the candor and contrition that they projected as they answered questions. The hearings began with a spirited defense of private munitions sales to unpopular foreign buyers by Air Force general turned arms merchant Richard Secord and tearful contrition from his Iranian-born partner, Albert Hakim. They moved through a shaky and apologetic account from the manager of the deals between 1983 and 1985, National Security Adviser Robert McFarlane, to a defiant defense of his actions, including his lies to Congress, by the ideological architect of the war on the Sandinistas, Assistant Secretary of State Elliott Abrams. Many of the minor players—ambassadors, legal advisers, couriers, contra leaders, spies—told gripping stories. And the final witness before the recess on June 10, Oliver North's loyal secretary, Fawn Hall, was at once defiant and compliant as she fenced with legislators about her boss's activities. Following the recess, on July 7, Marine lieutenant colonel and NSC operative Oliver North began six days of testimony. All three commercial networks returned to live coverage for the first time since the opening day. The tremendous popular interest in North shaped and overshadowed viewers' reactions to the witnesses who followed North, including his boss, Admiral John Poindexter, national security adviser since 1985, and the top Reagan administration officials whose testimony concluded the hearings.

■■ From the opening gavel on May 5 to the closing one on August 3, millions of Americans drew large parts of the hearings into their lives that summer. When General Secord testified on the first afternoon, 37 percent of Americans told pollsters that they watched the hearings, and the three commercial networks reported that 11.7 million television sets were switched to the hearings. By the second day the Cable News Network (CNN) reported a 70 percent increase in its audiences over those for the programs the hearings replaced. Within weeks CNN announced that the hearings attracted audiences that were three times larger than those for its regular programs. By the climax of the hearings, when the three commercial networks returned to televise Oliver North's July testimony, the audience reached 55 million viewers, roughly five times that for the most popular daytime television program, "General Hospital." More than seven of every ten Americans watched and told pollsters that they were "somewhat" or "very" interested in the hearings.[4]

For many viewers the hearings became an important part of their daily lives. A Fort Worth homemaker, Lucile Blakeman, reported that she watched "every minute" of the televised hearings even though daytime television was not an ordinary part of her routine. In one community on the California coast an 87-year-old woman who was legally blind had to sit almost on top of her color set in order to make things out, but she did not miss a day of the hearings. A New Yorker wrote Lee Hamilton that "friends of mine who've *never* shown too much interest in government are glued to the hearings." At Leisure World, in Orange County, California, two dozen retired friends got up early each morning to catch live coverage from the East Coast and called each other during the commercial breaks to discuss the day's revelations. Many whose jobs prevented them from watching live coverage, such as Baltimore bank vice-president Steve Schoeneman, "stayed up later than I normally would and gave up some of my usual shows" to watch three-hour highlights telecast at night. In airports and bowling alleys, country clubs and shopping malls, offices and bars, Americans watched the hearings. The hearings "spawned a subculture of TV junkies," in the words of a *USA Today* reporter as people became addicted. On the last day a woman from California confessed to Hamilton that she was "going to miss the Iran-Contra Hearings! They have provided me with countless hours of fascination, dismay, pride and education."[5]

By the time North left the stand on July 14, viewers had transformed the hearings into a national popular debate on the meaning of patriotism and heroism. Viewers reached for phones, for paper, for cards, to encourage, to chastise, to advise legislators. The volume of calls, letters, and telegrams from citizens to legislators exploded in July. One Democratic senator received 4,000 calls over a three-day period at his Washington and constituency offices, and his Capitol Hill receptionist described the volume as the "worst in my seven years here." Receptionists for Jim Courter answered over 200 calls on a single day of North's appearance, and those for Jack Brooks counted 392 calls on a single day. On one day, July 10, staff answering Senate Select Committee telephones logged 1,409 calls before they staggered home for the night. Over the course of the hearings the number of incoming letters and telegrams ranged from the 3,000 delivered to reticent Congressman William Broomfield (R-Mich.) to the 16,000 to outspoken Jack Brooks. Among senators, 8,200 pieces of mail were delivered to William Cohen, 10,000 to David Boren (D-Okla.), and 11,000 to Paul Sarbanes. By July 27, about a week before adjournment of the hearings, George Mitchell had received 7,207 letters and telegrams and 2,623 phone calls related to the hearings. By the time of its adjournment in early August the Senate Select Committee had received—in addition to letters to individual legislators—49,500 letters, 28,000 telegrams, and enough telephone calls to bring the combined total to well over 100,000 communications. The House Select Committee received at least the same volume.[6]

The half-million letters, telegrams, and phone calls that Americans sent to the committeemen over three months in the summer of 1987 together represented perhaps the largest spontaneous popular response to a congressional activity in American legislative history. Among them, Jack Brooks, Lee Hamilton, and Louis Stokes had represented the Texas Gulf Coast, the hilly countryside of southeastern Indiana, and the heart of Cleveland for three-quarters of a century. They had risen to positions of great prestige and visibility within the House of Representatives. And they all agreed with Stokes that the letters and phone calls they received on the Iran-Contra hearings constituted "the greatest public outpouring" they had seen in their careers. The same popular response overwhelmed Republican legislators; an aide to Jim Courter called the magnitude "unprecedented."[7]

By late summer voters used telephone and telegraph lines and the mail service to add their voices to what Courter called "a giant town meeting." And the meeting was empowering to those who attended. "Democracy in action is wonderful to see," a woman wrote Hamilton from Cairo, Georgia, and a woman from San Antonio concluded from the experience that "activated Americans are the greatest force for freedom and democracy in this world." Amid all this participation citizens and legislators also reached deeper than usual, probing for their fundamental convictions about patriotism. Iran, Nicaragua, and Oliver North were touchstones in an exploration of their fears, hopes, and beliefs about their own and their country's future.

Congressmen to citizens, citizens to congressmen, in living rooms and in the Senate Caucus Room, back and forth the messages went in a massive struggle over the meaning of patriotism and who had the power to define it. On July 14 Louis Stokes was scheduled to add his voice to the town meeting. As the only black member on the investigating panel, he wanted to contribute a special perspective on patriotism. The rule of law had unique meaning for blacks, he said, because they had "had to abide by the slow and arduous process of abiding by law until we could change the law" and win "full privileges of justice and equality." Fixing North in his gaze, Stokes concluded: "And while I admire your love for America, I just hope you will never forget that others, too, love America just as much as you. And while they disagree with you and our Government on aid to the Contras, they will die for America just as quickly as you will." The committee's chairman reached for a pad in front of him, scrawled a note, and passed it to Stokes: "Louis— Your closing statement was the most profound and powerful one heard during this hearing. With admiration, Dan Inouye." Ed Jenkins wrote, "Lou: I have heard many speeches during my years of political service; however, I do not believe that I have ever experienced a more meaningful, a more eloquent, or a more important statement than you have just delivered." Word traveled quickly on Capitol Hill. That afternoon, the chairman of the Congressional Black Caucus, Californian Mervyn Dymally, wrote Stokes that his speech had "brought a new benchmark to the legacy of the Black caucus" by articulating "our view of patriotism in the truest sense of 'We the People.'" Around the country viewers joined the legislators in the room in applauding Stokes. In the six working days following the speech he received more than 1,300 phone calls and 2,100 letters, 82 percent of which cheered his position. To Stokes, this remarkable popular response to the televised hearings proved that "people are concerned about government and watching it more than ever."[8]

█ █ █ The congressional investigating committee—and live television coverage of its deliberations—has become a major twentieth-century forum for citizens and politicians to explore the concentration and abuse of power. As power became increasingly centralized in fewer hands and local communities lost the capacity to restrain it by the traditional means of religious sanction, neighborhood gossip, marketplace discipline, or criminal prosecution, legislators assembled the investigative resources of government—and the publicity to accompany their use—to identify concentrations that menaced traditional liberties and to propose remedies.

From the 1910s through the 1930s congressional committees focused on threats from concentrated economic power. The Pujo Committee of 1912–13 exposed how large private bankers formed the most dangerous of all monopolies, a "money trust." In the 1920s congressional committees revealed how large oil companies had seized public mineral resources, and in the 1930s how large employers used huge arsenals of weapons to keep workers from forming unions. In the early 1930s the Senate Banking Committee traced the stock market crash of 1929 to concentrated power on Wall Street. The Nye Committee of the mid–1930s blamed American participation in World War I on the power of private investment bankers over government foreign policy. In 1938–40 the Temporary National Economic Committee held the most extensive congressional hearings ever into the concentration of private wealth.

The Cold War turned congressional investigations—now entering the age of television—toward abuses of concentrated political power. Beginning with Martin Dies's House Committee on Un-American Activities (HUAC) in 1938, extending through HUAC's high (or low) point in the late 1940s with Richard Nixon, and including the Senate investigations chaired by Joseph McCarthy in the early 1950s, congressional committees probed Americans who seemed to be aiding powerful foreign enemies and ideologies such as nazism and communism. But beginning with the Army-McCarthy hearings of 1954 and running through the Senate Watergate committee of 1973 to the Iran-Contra committee in 1987, legislators were more troubled by officials who used anticommunism as an excuse to deprive Americans of liberties. These three investigations, as well as those into Vietnam policy in the late 1960s and the CIA in the mid–1970s, probed how officials curtailed the liberties of citizens at home as they advanced American power abroad. The concept of national security that accompanied the pursuit of empire, heightened by military stalemates and failures abroad—Korea in 1953, Vietnam in 1973, and Iran and Nicaragua in 1979—provided an excuse for officials to brush aside traditional restraints on the exercise of power. The most earthshaking of these investigations each centered directly on charges that the leading anticommunists of the time—Joseph McCarthy, Richard Nixon, and Ronald Reagan and Oliver North—had threatened democratic processes in a zealous crusade against communism. Through these investigations ran complex themes of privilege and resentment, loyalty and treason, subversion and surveillance, mobilized majorities and persecuted minorities, to deepen and reshape older struggles between the president and Congress, Republicans and Democrats. As a result of the first two hearings, McCarthy was condemned by the Senate and Nixon resigned the presidency. By the time the Iran-Contra investigation began its televised probe from the Senate Caucus Room—the same place as the Army-McCarthy and Watergate hearings originated—North had already been fired and Reagan had muted his anticommunism. But for Americans the issue remained: Was the loss of democracy at home an acceptable price for the expansion of American prestige abroad?

Televised hearings gave Americans an opportunity to observe government at first hand. The electronic media brought closer the voices of government, radio in the 1920s and 1930s, and television by the early 1950s.

The first congressional hearing to attract millions to live coverage was the Senate Crime Investigating Committee's probe, chaired by Estes Kefauver, into links between racketeers and politicians in 1951. On Monday morning, March 19, 1951, 26.2 percent of television sets were switched on for the Kefauver hearings, twenty times the number of sets that ordinarily played during those hours. Bars and restaurants lured people in to see the excitement on the novelty of their television sets, while grocers, bakers, and Red Cross blood drive operators complained that people were watching television instead of shopping or donating blood. Viewers turned the hearings into what *New York Times* critic Jack Gould called "a social phenomenon virtually without parallel." As 89 percent of viewers in one sample reported that they talked with others about what they saw, the hearings became an even more lively topic of conversation than baseball had been at World Series time. Television, observed the *Times*, "enables a viewer to be a participant in the same sense as one personally present at a public meeting" has the chance to "see with his own eyes, to hear with his own ears, and to form his own opinion at first-hand." "The event has revived in some measure the ancient, original form of Athenian democracy, in which all citizens of Athens participated directly in public affairs," exclaimed one critic: "The excitement of sitting in intimate judgment on the officially exalted and the glamorously corrupt and the thrill of having powerful figures, customarily remote or mysterious, make personal account to the viewers, each has been exhilarating."[9]

The same thing happened three years later when the Army-McCarthy hearings burst onto American television screens for 187 hours of live coverage. By the twenty-fifth day of the hearings some 45 million adults had watched some portion on television. "It seemed that little else was talked about," noted one observer. *Newsweek* reported:

> From coast to coast—in homes, bars, clubs, offices, even in GI day rooms—men and women clustered around television sets to watch the developing battle between Sen. Joseph R. McCarthy and the Army officials. . . . And while they looked, they argued among themselves. Who was lying? Who was telling the truth? America was making up its mind in the new American way, studying the witnesses as they flashed on the TV screens.[10]

As congressional hearings and mass communications brought government into people's homes, the people wanted legislators to hear their views. The right of citizens to petition Congress was proclaimed in the Bill of Rights and had been tried by fire when Southerners attempted to block petitions from abolitionists during the slavery crisis. But it has only been with the rise of mass communications that Americans have increasingly turned letters and phone calls to public officials into a major form of political participation. Over the decade following World War I, as radio blanketed the nation and citizens could for the first time hear government at first hand, the number of communications received by a typical member of the House of Representatives skyrocketed over thirty-five times, from fifteen letters a week in 1917, to six hundred a week by the late 1920s. Desperate circumstances in the Great Depression encouraged many more people to overcome their reluctance to ask for help. Franklin Roosevelt asked people to write to him, and in his first seven days as president, he received 450,000 communications from Americans. As government moved into new areas of regulation, welfare, and warfare that touched more people in more ways, as television extended the immediacy of radio, even more citizens wrote to public officials. Between 1934 and 1981 the number of communications to Congress rose from an estimated 6 to 9 million pieces in the first Roosevelt Congress to an estimated 92.5 million pieces in the first Reagan Congress. Congress received, on average, a communication from 5 percent of all Americans in 1934 and from 25 percent of Americans in 1981.

This rise in direct response to televised hearings has coincided with a decline in voting in response to election campaigns. Between 1964 and 1976, for example, the proportion of people writing letters to public officials rose from 17 to 28 percent while the proportion of eligible voters who cast ballots fell from 63 to 56 percent.[11] These trends reflect major changes in the places where Americans form and express political opinions. In the nineteenth-century most Americans identified their individual interests with the interests of the particular culture of which they were a part. Voting was a means by which such groups as Southern whites or Irish Catholics could defend or advance their distinctive cultures, and political parties spoke to and mobilized Americans, not as individuals, but as contesting cultures. With the erosion of those cultures and parties, citizens have shaped their political identities with family and friends. They have encountered political opinions, not in the party press and partisan street rallies, but on television sets in their own homes. By appearing through the intimacy of radio and television, politicians now seem almost present in the rooms they enter. "TV has made what was once public and mythic accessible and intimate. It has thrust strangers from the worlds of show biz and politics into our homes, making them our seeming familiars," observed Paul Zimmermann at the peak of the Iran-Contra town meeting.[12] The most natural way to approach people with whom one feels familiar is to call or write to them.

The participatory moment of the 1987 Iran-Contra investigation repeated the pattern established during the first televised hearings, the Kefauver crime probe of 1951. One of every twelve viewers of the Kefauver hearings had written a letter or telegram to let public officials know how they were reacting to what they were seeing.[13] By continuing to write letters and make phone calls as they watched congressional hearings, Americans developed a pattern of political participation in the age of television by which they hoped to shape public discussion and policy.

Televised congressional hearings have often exploded into a singular type of participatory forum to which people have brought different, even contradictory, needs. Since its success as a place of conversation depended on the capacity of people to see and hear what each person contributed, to study the forum sparked by the Iran-Contra hearings we begin by probing how different participants approached the forum and what they brought to it. In contrast to elections, which as forums begin and end with a voter's choice between two or three people for a single job, televised congressional hearings operate in many places and on many levels, offering a variety of appeals and appearances. To some they are places that offer spectacles of combat and intrigue. To others they are scenes whose performers' faces blur with those of other celebrities of the moment on magazine covers. To others they are places for finding the truth about the past. To still others they are places to define, debate, and resolve policy differences.

Although many viewers experienced the hearings as citizenship in action, they disagreed on where the experience of citizenship ultimately resided. The hearings invited all viewers to explore different places to connect with their nation and its citizens and government. For some Washington was the place to make the connection because they envisioned the forum as a place to debate and settle policy issues such as how Congress should respond to revolution in a distant land, how tax dollars should be spent, where military force should be deployed. For others the forum existed in connections citizens hoped to establish with a representative through a letter or a phone call. For still others the forum centered in their own homes; it revolved around the basic values they wanted to live by—whether to tell the truth at all times, when to follow one's conscience, when to obey orders.

Live television coverage inspired different expectations about how viewers would experience the hearings. For some the millions of viewers appeared to be a uniform mass that could by skillful appeals to low common denominators be compressed or galvanized to support a single policy or political party. To others the millions of viewers appeared to be scattered and unique individuals who watched the hearings in millions of different settings for different reasons and reached different conclusions. Viewers watched some legislators grandstand and sell to the faceless mass that they imagined to be the audience in televisionland, but they watched other legislators ask questions and raise doubts in an attempt to figure out what had happened much the way that individual viewers investigated mysteries in their own lives. To some the hearings were a chance to hear evidence and gain perspective from which they formed tentative conclusions they wanted to discuss with others, while to others they were simply a place to push an established agenda. Some people entered the forum as fierce partisans, perhaps mobilized by activists for a cause in which they deeply believed. The hearings offered opportunities to make that cause visible either to citizens through television or to a congressman by a phone call. Many were veterans of earlier struggles, the core constituents of the issues at stake in the hearings. But for many others this was their first entry into a political forum, their first letter or phone call to a congressman.

Participants disagreed about the content of the hearings. To some they were about heroism and values. To others they were about the government's Nicaraguan policy or more generally about democracy, revolution, and communism in the Cold War. To still others they were a partisan battle between Democrats and Republicans or a constitutional struggle between the president and Congress.

Because participants imagined the forum in different ways, it was simultaneously a place of hope and of suspicion, a place of empowerment and of bewilderment and dismissal. Through the different perspectives that people brought to this participatory moment, the different layers on which they experienced it, one conflict overlapped all the others. This was a conflict about how the American people would be entitled to speak and be heard. It pitted the construction of the public as a faceless and abstract mass against the reality that the public was composed of real and unique individuals. By taking part in the forum, Americans made visible the intimate worlds in which they made sense of life as they met primary needs in relationships with people who mattered to them. From these worlds they brought their experiences to the forum, hoping to create a politics that resembled the way they talked and listened to others in their everyday lives. What they found in that forum instead was a managed debate that defined and limited what Americans were and should be thinking. Before we can explore how and why citizens sought to reshape the forum along the lines of their primary relationships, we need to see how the expression of opinion itself became the fundamental line of battle that revealed the forum's contradictions. The participatory moment in the summer of 1987 took shape and direction when Americans insisted that they had the right and capacity to speak for themselves and to shape the public forum unmediated. To reclaim their government, citizens had first to contest the ways the mass media had constructed the public forum.

Two

"Reagan's Magic" and Olliemania"

HOW JOURNALISTS INVENTED

THE AMERICAN PEOPLE

While individual journalists brought different media, audiences, and ideologies to the task of making the forum where citizens and politicians found each other in the summer of the Iran-Contra hearings, they were drawn to the same two stories to define that forum, using the common theme of the stories to frame their reporting of politics in the late 1980s. Individual reporters might emphasize different parts of the stories, but the overall agreement across media and ideologies about how and what Americans were thinking about the hearings was remarkable.

Although the two stories journalists told about the relationship between citizens and newsmakers came from different genres and featured different characters, they both returned to journalists' basic political understanding of the 1980s. The first story, "Reagan's magic," was familiar long before Meese's disclosure of the Iran-Contra deals. It was a slow-paced, good-natured mystery. All but conservatives wondered how a president of ordinary talents and unpopular policies could so completely control the political course of the 1980s. The second story was more epic. "Olliemania" spread like wildfire following its naming by *USA Today* reporter Stephen Stern on July 10, 1987, during Oliver North's testimony. It was the account of the people's sudden discovery and elevation of a folk hero. The theme of the epic was the solution to the mystery: the judgment of the American people was deeply flawed. That they preferred expert acting performances to integrity and substance—as Reagan's magic and Olliemania made obvious—was proof. While this flaw left them passive and dumb when isolated as individuals, it made them volatile and dangerous when fused into in a mass. And it was precisely the experience of watching Reagan's beloved television that seemed to many journalists to fuse individuals into this terrible mass. So deeply did journalists believe in the theme of a flawed public that no amount of evidence to the contrary could convince them to change the stories they told about it.

▌ The mystery at the core of Reagan's magic was how Reagan could have dominated the political agenda more fully than any president in half a century. How had he managed to overcome both journalists' doubts about his intellectual and administrative competence and a solid Democratic majority in the House of Representatives (and after 1986 the Senate), on the one hand, and the public's opposition to his policies, on the other? To understand the answer that journalists arrived at, we need to trace how some journalists and politicians came first to invent and then to fear the American citizenry as a faceless mass and how they came to see the manipulation of that mass as the basic responsibility of governing.

The magic began, according to commentators, with an actor's spell over his audience. People loved Reagan because he was "a superb political actor who has conveyed exactly what the American psyche needs in the role of President, reassurance." "He was the good-looking, easy-talking type out of Hollywood every mother warned her daughter to avoid—irresponsible but irresistible," pronounced James Reston: "We didn't really elect him but fell in love with him. . . . Nothing broke the spell."[1] Presidential leadership was an acting performance, and at an acting performance all members of the audience are supposed to see the performance in the same way. Individuals become identical members of an audience that derives its very definition— as well as its capacity for thought and feeling—solely from the actor's initiative.

Reagan's ability as the "Great Communicator" to speak lines and act emotions with unprecedented skill was only part of what *Newsweek* called "state-of-the-art White House media manipulation." His speeches were pieces of a larger managerial strategy through which administration leaders applied advertising, polling, and marketing techniques to sell him and his policies. "In the White House," observed columnist Sidney Blumenthal, "the main standard of judgment on most matters was Reagan's favorability rating in the polls, which became an end in itself." "No government in history can have been more sensitive to the media, or more driven by the printed word and the television image, than the Reagan Administration," declared its chief of staff, Donald Regan, who took pride in his ability to manage news. Reagan's managers exploited "the news business's frailties, especially television's, first to turn news into publicity and then to turn publicity into news," observed Russell Baker: "Now we have news reporting how publicity experts use 'photo opportunities' and 'spin control' to reduce the news to publicity."[2]

For this administration, with its unprecedented skill at monitoring and manipulating measurements of mass response, the challenge to Reagan's magic came suddenly. Edwin Meese triggered it with his November 25, 1986, revelation of the Iran-Contra deals. "Poll Rating Dives," read the page-one headline of the *New York Times*. Overnight the percentage of Americans who approved of Reagan's performance fell from 67 to 46, "the sharpest one-month drop ever recorded by a public opinion poll in measuring approval of a Presidential job performance" since such polls began in 1936. Soon other polls reported "a sharp drop in the President's popularity." The *Times* proclaimed that "the Reagan White House was in its worst crisis."[3]

This fall in his approval rating inspired commentators to turn "Reagan's magic" into "Reagan's failure." Fixing on a decline from 67 to 46 percent, commentators reported a change in the mass. The change was significant, in their view, because it was "the sharpest one-month drop ever recorded." That four-fifths of the people did not change their opinions of Reagan's performance was considered unimportant when a number that measured an abstract mass had changed more than it ever had before. That was "news." The unprecedented drop meant that Reagan had lost the ability to manage the mass and thus to govern the nation. "The Reagan Magic has come undone," editorialized the *New Republic:* "The country should never fall under the spell again."[4]

The magic evaporated when the bond between actor and audience snapped. "In October the columnists say that the Reagan era will last forever; in December they wonder if the Reagan era can last through the end of the month. Who else but an actor, himself as light as a waterfly, could preside over the kingdom of dream and counter-dream?" asked Lewis Lapham in *Harper's*. The basis of an actor's appeal was his believability. When polls revealed that many people no longer believed Reagan, Nancy Reagan and others blamed the change in mass perception on Donald Regan's poor management of the news. Reagan had fallen, as Lapham observed, to the position of "an aging matinee idol." The way back was the way he had come. He could reassert his appeal by giving better performances and benefiting from better news management. "There is this latent desire that Ronald Reagan be the Gipper again," *Newsweek* quoted one of Reagan's advisers: "People want to see him come off the deck; it's like Rocky 50."[5]

While journalists speculated on how Reagan could recover his audience, the mobilizers of conservative opinion tried to demonstrate that Reagan's ideology was more popular than his acting. Part of the story of Reagan's magic had been his ability to inspire unprecedented numbers of calls, letters, donations, and opiniongrams to support conservative causes and candidates. Conservatives portrayed themselves as the voice of the mass, claiming through television ads, buttons, and bumper stickers that the mass was both conservative and aroused. When the Iran-Contra scandal broke, conservatives feared that journalists and Democrats might see an opportunity to try to erode what they insisted was the conservative orientation of the American people. Less than two weeks after Meese's announcement, conservative organizations mobilized a $2 million campaign to repair the public images of their beleaguered heroes Oliver North and Ronald Reagan. On December 12, Citizens for America launched a 60-second television commercial that compared Reagan to Abraham Lincoln over a background of patriotic music. With this ad they hoped to manufacture better numbers for pollsters to measure and pundits to discuss. "I think it will impact on the polling," explained Chairman Gerald Carmen. By filling the public airwaves with their messages, conservatives hoped to deter liberals from making public statements that would either "deceive" viewers or, worse, lead journalists to question the myths at the core of 1980s politics: that there was a mass and that it was conservative. "These people want to undo the election results," warned conservative activist Richard Viguerie: "They want to institute Walter Mondale's vision for America and not Ronald Reagan's."[6]

Many journalists accepted the myths. They believed in the mass and that it was ignorant and conservative because that faith reinforced their feelings of superiority over their fellow citizens. Americans fell under Reagan's "spell," according to the dean of commentators, James Reston, because "they're like him: well-meaning, optimistic, credulous, stubborn and a little bit dumb." The American people had caused the Iran-Contra scandal, Reston argued, because they had elected Reagan. "The public" was incapable of seeing "great moral wrong" in Reagan's activities because he was "the very embodiment of folk morality," explained sociologist Jeffrey Alexander. Reagan merely did what was in the public's ignorant, emotional, amoral heart. By April 1987, reported the *New Republic*, Reagan once again "envelop[ed] himself in the proffered goodwill of a public tired of thinking about the scandal." Convinced that the audience was ignorant and lazy, many commentators believed from the start that acting and public relations would entrance a electorate that was susceptible to slick political salesmanship and at heart conservative.[7]

An ignorant mass needed to be managed to keep it from becoming dangerous. Skilled insiders would have to frame acceptable alternatives, and pollsters would have to identify the options that attracted the largest following. *New York Times* reporters pored over polls to advise that "Mr. Reagan could gain in popularity by focusing on economics" or "Mr. Reagan may have to make further gestures of contrition."[8]

Managing the mass required exquisite sensitivity to timing. In a business whose pace and rhythms for collecting and interpreting information were shaped by television, journalists conveyed advice with an urgency that warned politicians against attempting to learn from the past or plan for the future. Often imagining their viewers as fans at an athletic spectacle, journalists described the forces ruling political debate as those of momentum at a ballgame. "Reagan's window of opportunity is closing," darkly warned *Newsweek*'s White House correspondent, Thomas DeFrank.[9] An undifferentiated mass, in any case, was only capable of responding viscerally, commentators assumed.

Unable to see citizens except as faceless outsiders, commentators defined what was acceptable by the standards of the very visible insiders who ordinarily managed government. Journalists placed an importance on the names, titles, opinions, influences, interests, and privileges of individual insiders that they never gave even to the idea that individual members of the audience might have such characteristics. Journalists therefore shaped their interpretations around the perceptions and perspectives of insiders.

Insiders believed from the start that North and his associates had done unusual and unacceptable things. "How Reagan's 'Cowboys' Got Out of Control," *Newsweek* headlined its first cover after the news broke. Professional policymakers such as Secretary of State George Shultz knew that insiders in the media and Congress would support him in his fight "to win control of U.S. policy from a set of 'cowboys' in the CIA." "Some part of the Government had to preserve credibility," pronounced the *New York Times*, without explaining why. Shultz, declared the *Times*, was that part. *Newsweek* reported that undisciplined outsiders had temporarily possessed the government: Oliver North and a "tough-talking group of ideologues" engaged in "harebrained adventuring" as they "ran amok" and ran "wild through the NSC's corridors," inventing "a crazy quilt of covert activities" that "made James Bond look wimpish." "Too much derring-do had led to disaster," concluded *Newsweek*. In late February all three networks interrupted their evening programs to report the Tower Commission's condemnation of Reagan's managerial failure to hold North and the cowboys within familiar limits. The indictment was not the democratic one that the policy had defied the wishes of most Americans (for they were outsiders, by definition unqualified to judge), nor was it the constitutional one that the policy had defied Congress. Rather, the indictment was the insider's lament that North and the cowboys had ignored insiders like Shultz. To insiders nothing could be worse than the "picture of confusion and amateurishness" that the Tower Commission painted.[10]

To recover legitimacy, managers needed to tighten control over employees and announce that unusual policy initiatives had been managerial mistakes that would not be repeated. Reagan won immediate "bipartisan support" when he fired North, replaced John Poindexter with Frank Carlucci to head the NSC, and named three respected insiders—John Tower, Edmund Muskie, and Brent Scowcroft—to investigate what had gone wrong. Carlucci immediately wiped out North's NSC unit. When the Tower Commission criticized amateurs for poor management, Reagan replaced his friend Don Regan with the ultimate Republican insider Howard Baker as White House chief of staff. The result was "something approaching euphoria in the capital," according to the *New York Times*. On Baker's first day he reassured insiders that the CIA would no longer be the uncontrolled foreign policy operation that Reagan's friend William Casey had tried to design. Baker withdrew Reagan's nomination of Casey's friend Robert Gates to head the CIA and replaced him the next day with FBI head William Webster, who brought "experience in fixing a troubled agency," praised the *Washington Post*. *Newsweek* depicted Baker, Webster, and Carlucci as insiders who launched Reagan on the "comeback trail."[11]

With their fondness for prescribing what needed to happen next, television and newspaper commentators primed Americans on March 4, 1987, for Reagan's televised response to the Tower Commission's report. The *Washington Post* explained that it would be a "crucial speech" in Reagan's bid to recover his ability to govern. "At stake: Reagan's credibility," proclaimed *USA Today*.[12]

Professional interpreters reported with awe how the actor combined words with delivery to give a superb performance. Claiming to be "angry" and "disappointed" with the actions of people like North and Poindexter, Reagan embraced the insider doctrine that a few cowboys had irresponsibly exceeded their authority. Carlucci, however, had now put an end to "freelancing by individuals" and imposed "proper management discipline," Reagan explained, and Reagan himself prohibited the NSC "from undertaking covert operations—no if's, and's or but's." For the first time since November he acknowledged that the deals had exchanged arms for hostages, that it had been a "mistake," and that he was responsible even if he had not known all the details.[13]

"The president did what he had to do," the *Washington Post* beamed: "He has acknowledged enormous error and chosen the right people to help him avoid any repeat of it." "The president said what he needed to say," proclaimed former Democratic National Chairman Robert S. Strauss. "Reagan told the American people what they needed to hear," concluded Senate Republican leader Robert Dole. The speech "won as much ground as any speech could," declared *Newsweek*. Canvassing insiders to find out whether "Mr. Reagan met the test," R. W. Apple, Jr., reported in the *Times* that "many people gave him high marks." After four months of poor acting and managerial drift, the mass finally got what it wanted and needed.[14]

Amid all the euphoria about the restoration of sound management a few observers questioned whether the insiders knew what Americans really wanted. Reagan's speech "guaranteed his presidency while destroying his ideology," observed Hodding Carter, Jimmy Carter's State Department spokesperson. For conservatives, Reagan's embrace of Washington insiders was more alarming than reassuring. Reagan's 1984 campaign chairman, James Lake, agreed that Reagan's speech sacrificed his principles to guarantee his political survival with centrist elites. The appointment of Howard Baker kindled fear in many conservatives, who assumed that Baker would use his new power to subvert the dreams that had lured them into politics. "Howard Baker's specialty in life is blurring issues, pale pastels, compromise, conciliation," grumbled one conservative about Reagan's choice for new White House chief.[15]

In order to claim that Reagan's speech had restored his popularity, journalists had to ignore their favorite measures of the mass, public opinion polls. Some pundits pointed eagerly to rises of between 6 and 10 percentage points in Reagan's approval rating in three polls taken after the speech, but those same numbers meant that between 90 and 94 percent of people did not modify their judgments. More precise polls revealed even less popular enthusiasm. In response to *Newsweek*'s question "Did President Reagan's speech make you feel more or less confidence in him as a leader?" half the respondents replied that it made no difference, one-quarter reported less confidence as a result of the speech, and one-quarter reported more confidence. And those proportions were almost identical to popular responses to the State of the Union speech a month earlier that journalists had proclaimed an example of Reagan's failure as a manager. Following that speech, 22 percent had reported more confidence in him, 29 percent had reported less, and 48 percent had reported no change in their confidence. The confidence of real people in their president, as measured in such polls, was irrelevant to what journalists thought citizens needed, wanted, or actually experienced, when they listened to his speeches.[16]

Relieved that the mass was back under control, satisfied with the help they had provided, journalists muzzled any questions they might have harbored either about Reagan as president or his particular handling of the Iran-Contra scandals. But the imagination and single-mindedness they showed when they invented and then "solved" the mystery of Reagan's magic paled by comparison with the effort they put into the even more remarkable tale, Olliemania, by which they imposed the same vision on events in the summer of 1987.

■■ Journalists prepared Americans to expect the same theme of actor and audience to shape coverage of the congressional hearings that would begin in May. The presence of television, and through it of a huge audience, insured that the hearings would become entertainment, not news, journalists believed. *Newsweek* introduced readers to the hearings with "A TV Viewer's Guide: Who will star? Will the series outdraw the soaps?" The story began, "If it all works out, the show will be a hit spinoff" from the earlier Watergate hearings.[17]

From the start many journalists assumed that viewers could comprehend the story only as entertainment and would need to be reminded of the difference between reality and fiction. "This is not a television show," Dan Rather lectured the first day's audience: "This is the real thing." This did not keep journalists from playing to what they expected to be the public's conflation of the two, however. They titled their accounts "The Real Daytime Drama" (*Washington Post*) and "Iran-Contra Drama: A Cast Change" (*New York Times*). Looking for evidence of this popular response, journalists eagerly accepted Reagan's attempt to divert attention from his misdeeds: "When you get a mile and a half away from the Potomac River, there are an awful lot of people that have gone back to their favorite television shows." Because the proceedings were "so difficult to convey to a general audience," NBC News President Lawrence Grossman justified his network's decision to abandon live coverage with the assertion that viewers would be bored. Bryant Gumbel of "Today" complained that the hearings seemed to be "droning on." They were "often tedious" to the *New Republic* and "sometimes soporific" to the *New York Times*'s Maureen Dowd. The most significant criterion these critics could apply to this show was the entertainment yardstick that measured whether it was interesting or boring.[18]

Journalists found viewers where they looked for them. "What seems so gripping in Washington seems to those farther away convoluted, contradictory, episodic and endless," wrote R. W. Apple, Jr., about popular reaction in Columbus ("no place is more Middle American"), Ohio, in a story that sounded as though Reagan had ghosted it. Accompanying Lee Hamilton back to his rural Indiana congressional district, Kenneth Noble reported in the *Times* that Hamilton's "Middle American" constituents "appeared emotionally removed, even oblivious, to the political maelstrom on Capitol Hill." Here, then, were the faces of the television audience: too geographically remote to engage, too stupid to understand, too self-absorbed to care, too escapist to concentrate, too "middle" for any political beliefs.[19]

By framing the hearings from the opening gavel as entertainment, many commentators constructed the outlines of the new story that would emerge when the hearings reconvened on July 7 to hear the testimony of Oliver North. Investigators and Reagan critics had proceeded cautiously as they prepared the foundation for North's testimony because many thought that the Iran-Contra deals raised basically managerial issues that insiders could best answer and because they did not want to awaken an audience they assumed to be bored now but dangerously conservative when aroused. North was the star witness who could reveal the extent of Reagan's involvement—as well as the full range of other covert operations he had managed. It was a perfect situation, as so often arose during the Reagan years, for skilled conservative activists to mobilize a show of support that would frighten critics of their heroes North and Reagan with evidence of a mass in motion. North himself was the perfect focus for such efforts, costumed and scripted for patriotic theater. Some 25,000 people answered appeals from the patriotic Right to contribute to North's legal defense. "God Bless America and Oliver North" bumper stickers sprouted on the eve of his testimony. Organizers urged North's admirers to bury the table at which he sat under telegrams. And North's attorney, Brendan Sullivan, continually tried to equate these telegrams of support with the voice of "the American people." To Capitol Hill veterans such as the people who had long answered phones for Jack Brooks, the campaign that accompanied North's testimony was instantly recognizable as a conservative creation. The press, however, reported it uncritically.[20]

"'Olliemania' sweeps USA," *USA Today* headlined. The story began with the staggering size of the audience that tuned in to watch North. "Ollie's TV hit: Bigger than the soaps," shouted another *USA Today* headline that equated the success of a show with the size of its audience. Any program that lured three-quarters of all Americans was "a hit."[21]

After initially measuring popularity by the entertainment standard of size, commentators soon found other evidence of popular enthusiasm for North. North contributed by stacking on the witness table a pile of telegrams that he claimed applauded his performance. As the pile rose higher, North, his attorney, legislators, and journalists referred increasingly to the telegrams as though they proved his popularity. Vendors emerged to sell buttons, t-shirts, songs, billboards, books, and posters. "Olliemania was breaking out all over," observed *Time.*[22]

Few reporters scrutinized the sources of this "mania"—how and by whom it was organized. Instead, most reporters focused on the relationship of entertainer to audience that they saw at work. Whether reporting for electronic or print media, for liberal or conservative audiences, for the *National Enquirer* or the *New York Times,* journalists told the same story. North was "a natural actor and a conjurer of illusion," in *Time*'s words. "For pure entertainment, you couldn't beat the guy," began columnist Ellen Goodman. "Move over, Vanna," warned Russell Baker: North was a "TV smasheroo." Reporters thought mainly of actors as they described North's testimony. "He's Jimmy Stewart in *Mr. Smith Goes to Washington;* Clint Eastwood in *The Good, the Bad, and the Ugly;* John Wayne—the Duke himself—in *The Sands of Iwo Jima,*" concluded *USA Today:* "He's Lt. Col. Oliver North in *The Iran-Contra Affair.*" "America has just had a profound movie experience," concluded David Denby in the *New Republic:* "The face that was gazed at, studied, and apparently loved, day after day—Oliver North's face—possessed the power and guile of an actor's instrument." "As pure theater, it was hard to beat," judged *U.S. News and World Report.*[23]

To some reporters North's stardom was more that of an athlete than an actor. In this variation the hearing was a sports event, not a movie. "Colonel

North has hit a grand slam," gushed NBC's Tom Brokaw, who broke free from baseball imagery on another occasion to declare that North had driven "a hole in one." When House counsel John W. Nields, Jr., yielded the questioning of North to Senate counsel Arthur Liman, CBS's Dan Rather explained to viewers that "the committee is changing pitchers, so to speak. Arthur Liman is expected to throw hardballs." "Score: 'It's Ollie 4, Congress zip,'" read a *USA Today* headline. Fairly did Carl Bernstein complain that "mostly what we have been given in the way of interpretation has been atmospherics and a running commentary better suited to a sports event than the Presidency."[24]

Whether they preferred to cast him as a movie star or a slugger, commentators agreed with Art Buchwald that North had become "a designated national hero." Ronald Reagan, as so often before, pointed reporters in the direction they later followed when he characterized North as "a national hero," but it was not a presidential proclamation that led commentators to seize so suddenly and unanimously on the idea of North's heroism. Rather, what impressed them most deeply about North was that he seemed to "capture the imagination of America," in *Time*'s words. North, wrote *Christian Century*, "is touching deep emotional chords in the American public." His heroism, in short, welled up from below. He was a "folk hero," *Newsweek* blazed across its cover.[25]

Folk heroes are made by folks, and journalists from the start turned the story of North into the story of the American people. They quickly titled the story "Olliemania" because that phrase fitted their assumptions about the audience. Since the hearings were entertainment and North was a hero, most commentators thought of the viewers as movie or sports fans. "You can almost hear his supporters around the country chanting, 'Ol-lie,' 'Ollie,'" explained NBC's Tom Brokaw: "We were the audience; he was the virtuoso performer. That's entertainment." He "electrified TV viewers," wrote *MacLean's*. He was "an overnight hero of the media age," summarized *U.S. News and World Report*.[26]

Audiences were assumed to be judging North's performance by the standard of how believably he acted his part. "What an actor does in his role becomes less important to audiences than their conviction that he is real when he is doing it," wrote David Denby in the *New Republic*: "Oliver North achieved that kind of belief." To Duke University political scientist James David Barber, "what concerns me is the readiness of the public and the media and Congress to simply conclude he's telling the truth based on his performance as a witness."[27]

From the assumption that audiences judged North as an entertainer, many commentators concluded that the standards by which Americans evaluated North's testimony came from movies they had seen. Americans were "more comfortable judging performance than substance," grumbled

Ellen Goodman. North's emergence as "a TV star" raised "serious questions" for *U.S. News and World Report* "about television's blinding power to elevate style over substance." Journalists were reminded by North of movies and so, they assumed, were viewers. North "played brilliantly upon" Americans' "memories of a thousand movies," explained *Time,* and *Newsweek* declared that "Ollie Enters Folklore" because "Americans . . . carry old movies around in their heads."[28]

Convinced that Americans were responding to the hearings as if they were watching a movie or sporting contest, many journalists found similarities among the audiences for the three kinds of events. The defining feature, for them, was that such audiences form a single mass. Members had no individual faces or voices. Each person was an interchangeable piece of a whole that commentators variously labeled "the imagination of America," "the public," "Middle America," "the public mood," "America," or "Americans." Americans all watched the same actions on the screen or playing field. As all fans were expected to follow the flight of the ball when a batter hit a home run and to cheer if he belonged to the home team, as all members of an audience were expected to feel sorrow at the same sad moment in a movie, all viewers of the hearings were expected to focus on the same things and to react in the same ways.

The greatest advantage to defining the audience as a mass was that its inventors could now give it its voice. They would interrogate it and decide what topics it should discuss. *Time* deserved an award of some kind for seriously asking people whether Oliver North was "someone I would want to marry my daughter." Although the thought probably occurred to very few viewers, *Time* by means of a poll claimed that 26 percent of viewers believed that North would make a good son-in-law. Even when the wide variety of opinions held by individual viewers managed to percolate through to poll results—and in no case did a majority consider North a hero or indeed anything more favorable than a victim—journalists declared in headlines that the polls showed "Why America Loves Ollie."[29] Journalists overlooked the actual diversity of poll results to conclude—most bizarrely with *People*—that "daily polls profiled a nation that supported him 5 and 6 to 1."[30]

Commentators clung to their vision of mass adulation for North because it reinforced their prejudices about the ignorance and naïveté of outsiders and fitted the stock story of the lone hero. Olliemania was finally, in their eyes, a true "mania," a "massive, spontaneous outpouring of emotion" that acted with "waves of mass enthusiasm," in *People's* phrases. The audience moved elementally—like a "tide of emotion"—for Lewis Lapham. The uncontrollable "public spasm of adulation" revealed an audience that was drinking, not thinking, Curt Suplee explained in a *Washington Post* essay that sought to "understand the nature of our intoxication . . . before the nation sobers up from its Olliebender." In another image of how Olliemania eroded traditional impulse control, Lee Eisenberg wrote in *Esquire* that "the citizens . . . are going wild." Charles Colson referred to "the country's emotional orgy over Ollie," while *U.S. News and World Report* observed that "the image of Oliver North . . . is fixed fast in the national psyche." "Alone," believed *New York Times* reporter Wayne King, "Colonel North appears to have transmuted the psychic tenor of the nation from cynicism and suspicion to patriotism and belief." To most commentators North transformed television viewers into a monolithic and visceral mass.[31]

The elemental force that set this mass into motion, most commentators said, was a profound popular yearning for amusement and escape. This yearning led people to flip the dials on their television sets in search of escapist laughter, tears, consolation, inspiration. North's testimony replaced soap operas on the networks, and commentators assumed that the same needs drove people to watch both. North's popularity "testified to the ignorance of a credulous American public increasingly in thrall to the fairy tales told by the mass media, " complained Lewis Lapham: "The longing of the moment" was the driving force. "Television values have superseded more traditional American values, or become those very values themselves," pronounced *Newsweek*.[32]

Having endowed the audience with impulsive and escapist appetites, commentators then blamed it for lacking the critical capacity for reason and independent action. Arguing in the *New York Times* that television "is in the main shaped by its audience," George Fasel accused audiences of "the abdication of the responsibilities of democratic citizenship in favor of the easy pleasures of entertainment." But the desire for "easy pleasures" led beyond mesmerized passivity to a loss of moral standards. North "conveyed an aesthetic impression of rectitude that was assigned moral significance by an audience too lazy to work out the difference," wrote David Denby: "We no longer have a culture and a set of standards that we can draw on in times of trouble—a way, short of the law, of judging anything. There's no center, no core, just endless media images that are believed or not believed, and anyone who tries to see something for what it is risks sounding priggish, dull, and out of it."[33]

An audience that only wanted amusement was an audience that had no interest in history or politics and no capacity for objective or critical thought. Having stripped from viewers the capacity to think or speak except when spoken to, journalists then complained that "audiences lose the habit of memory and let slip their hold on the ladders of history and geography," in Lewis Lapham's words. "Americans haven't a clue about what's in the Constitution," huffed Steve Barnett, chairman of Research & Forecasts, Inc., to explain popular enthusiasm for North. "Americans seem to have fallen for North," explained Richard Cohen in the *Washington Post*, because "they like his stunning simplicity. Ambiguity, the plight of the thinking person, seems never to have plagued North." Further, journalists attempted to demonstrate the collective shortcomings of the mass: A *New York Times*-CBS News poll tested whether viewers could correctly locate Nicaragua on a map. An ABC News/*Washington Post* poll tested whether viewers understood "very well," "fairly well," or "not well at all" "what had happened," a particularly strange question because it asked viewers whether they knew in advance precisely what congressional investigators were holding hearings to find out.[34]

Convinced of the ignorance and passivity of their audiences, commentators drew a line that defined whose opinion was worth listening to and whose was not. On one side were the professionals with the training and insider credentials that entitled them to interpret events. On the other side was everyone else, everyone who viewed "the news" as amusement. Viewers might watch the hearings, wrote John Corry of the *New York Times,* but the real meaning of those events would "emerge more clearly when the evening news broadcasts and other television programs determine which ones were important." An ignorant audience needed professional commentators to explain the world.[35]

■■■ The most remarkable fact about "Reagan's magic" and "Olliemania" was that the storytellers overlooked overwhelming evidence that neither story was true. Although Ronald Reagan won the election of 1980 with less than 51 percent of the vote and 26 percent of the electorate, many journalists began soon after his inauguration to overlook such evidence and to repeat the White House line that Americans admired Reagan's job performance and his policies. By March 1981 James Reston reported in the *New York Times* that Reagan had "public opinion on his side," and by August the same paper's Hedrick Smith reported that Reagan's "warm popularity" explained his ability to propel his programs to the top of the political agenda. In fact, as Michael Schudson has shown, Reagan during his first two years in office had the lowest average job approval rating of any postwar president. After his first month, Reagan's 55 percent in a Gallup poll compared with 61 percent for Nixon, 58 percent for Eisenhower, and 71 percent for Carter after the first month of their terms. After his first two years, Reagan's 35 percent approval rating lagged behind Carter's 43 percent, Nixon's 56 percent, Eisenhower's 69 percent, and Kennedy's 76 percent. What polls did show was that during Reagan's first years in office, many Americans liked him as a person but—in sharp contrast to the pundits' interpretations—did not respect his presidential performance or admire his policies. In two polls by the Gallup organization in 1982, when asked to distinguish what they thought of Reagan as a person from what they thought of him as a president, Americans gave him 25 to 30 percent higher approval as a person than as a president.[36]

Not only did many Americans distinguish the person they liked from the president they did not respect, but throughout Reagan's presidency they carefully distinguished their convictions on issues from their conclusions about Reagan both as a person and as a president. Well before the Iran-Contra disclosure, Reagan received negative majorities in polls for his positions on most major issues. By 64–32 percent, Americans rejected his position on defense spending, 54–40 his position on a constitutional amendment to ban abortion, 58–36 his handling of affirmative action, 64–27 his handling of South Africa, 49–41 his Supreme Court appointments, 60–37 his handling of unemployment, 68–27 his handling of farm problems, and 62–34 his handling of the federal deficit. Asked to grade Reagan's performance in eleven areas in 1985, when his personal popularity was high, more than half the public gave him a grade of C or lower in nine of the eleven areas, ranging from his handling of the Soviet Union to his approaches to poverty and crime. Perhaps the most dramatic gap between Reagan and the majority of Americans was related to the Iran-Contra deals. The percentage of Americans who approved of Reagan's handling of Nicaragua ranged between 20 and 35 percent in all nine Gallup polls between 1983 and 1988. In ten *New York Times*/CBS News polls between 1984 and 1988 the percentage favoring aid to the contras ranged between 24 and 40 percent, never coming close to a majority even though Reagan requested and Congress appropriated aid to the contras for most of this period.[37]

The inventors of Olliemania had to ignore even more obvious evidence in order to keep retelling that story. It was certainly true that many Americans watched North's testimony, but they neither admired his performance nor agreed with his views. In public opinion polls, for example, majorities considered North a scapegoat, some thought well-meaning and patriotic; they would not elect him to public office, however. And by overwhelming majorities, respondents made clear that they did not regard North as a hero of any kind. In an ABC News/*Washington Post* poll three times more people considered North a "victim" than a "hero." The basic fact, as Jefferson Morley observed, was that "the folk themselves seem to view North more ambivalently than . . . the media. . . . North is honored by his supposed enemies in the press, pitied by his supposed admirers in the public."[38]

Journalists had more direct evidence than polls that the story of Olliemania was an inaccurate picture of popular attitudes. That evidence arrived in their own offices. Among readers who sent letters to the *Washington Post*, for example, 39 were favorable to North and 91 were unfavorable. Puzzled by the inconsistency between the media proclamation of Olliemania and the content of actual letters received at the *Post*, Kathryn Stearns checked with other newspapers to discover—and report—that North was more often criticized than applauded in letters received at the *Chicago Tribune*, the *Los Angeles Times*, and the *New York Times*. Most letters to most editors were critical of North. The *Louisville Courier-Journal, Sacramento Bee,* and *Cleveland Plain Dealer* reported more anti-North than pro-North letters. In Bloomington, Indiana, the conservative *Herald-Telephone* asked readers to indicate whether North had acted "appropriately" or "inappropriately." A week later the paper reported that 229 readers had considered North's activities "inappropriate" and 155 had labeled them "appropriate."[39]

Businessmen soon learned a painful lesson about the inaccuracy of the Olliemania story. Believing stories that North was a popular hero, a San Francisco entrepreneur, John Lee Hudson, marketed a twelve-inch Oliver North doll for which he projected sales of 450,000 dolls. A few weeks later, with a total of only 200 orders, Hudson glumly admitted, "I guess we sort of miscalculated the people's support for Ollie." MPI Home Video made the same discovery when it marketed 102,000 videocasettes that portrayed a heroic "Oliver North: Memo to History." Finally concluding that the company would be lucky to sell half the cassettes it made, Jaffer Ali, vice-president for sales, echoed Hudson: "We thought there was this tremendous outpouring of support for Ollie. But if there was, they haven't been showing that support by buying our tapes in droves." The only entrepreneur to do much better than he had anticipated—and he sold ten times more copies than he had projected—was the publisher of a satirical coloring book that deflated North's claims to heroism.[40]

IV We now turn to the real mystery of how these stories could outlive evidence that refuted them. How did the real individuals who responded to polls, purchased political souvenirs, and wrote letters—most of whom rejected Reagan's policies and North's performance—escape the view of journalists and politicians? Why did the public forum of the hearings threaten for many journalists to become a place where a single mass emotion replaced conversation among real individuals?

The construction of viewers as voiceless pieces of a faceless mass grew out of the partisan political environment of the 1980s. Olliemania unfolded at a time when Reagan's handlers and conservative activists had perfected the skills needed to turn what they knew was a minority of Americans into what appeared to many observers to be a majority determined to have its way. Trying to seize the initiative from the mainstream media and Democratic politicians who had for decades set the political agenda, conservatives and Republicans used their new methods of identifying, measuring, funding, mobilizing, and presenting mass opinion so that they could shape debate. Their enthusiasm was so great and their techniques so new that many believed that the apparent majority the activists created was in fact a real one. "Reagan handles the media better than anybody since Franklin Roosevelt, even including Jack Kennedy," declared House Speaker Tip O'Neill. Television journalists likewise "seemed lost in admiration for [Oliver North's] mastery of their own medium," editorialized the *Columbia Journalism Review*.[41]

Mark Crispin Miller, a Johns Hopkins expert on mass media, believed that conservative orchestrations intimidated journalists as well: "The majoritarian impulse has been manipulated by the right—a well-run phalanx able to flood a switchboard or fire off a million threatening letters at a moment's notice. Thus supervised, those choleric partisans can easily seem to be 'the people'—the buying entity that TV advertisers fear profoundly." Convinced that the mass was ignorant, conservative, and dangerous, liberal reporters "bent over backwards not to seem at all critical of Republicans. Eager to evince his 'objectivity,' the edgy liberal reporter ends up just as useful to the right as any ultra-rightist hack," Miller continued. "Editors and reporters are clearly more sensitive than in the past to the potential for a backlash against the media," ran *Newsweek*'s explanation of journalists' reluctance to investigate the Iran-Contra story in more depth. Only a few of Reagan's critics saw that behind these mobilizations lay, not a mass at all, but an organized minority: "The spasm of reactionary passions at the beginning of July was a combination of the hype industry and the Republican telegram network," wrote Christopher Hitchens of Olliemania.[42]

Neither the timidity of journalists nor the skill of conservatives would have been enough to fill the public forum with Olliemania had liberals and Democrats chosen to contest that story, to mobilize their supporters behind popular alternatives to the programs of Reagan and North. Indeed, the failure of Democrats to defend positions that could have won them votes created a void that helped to shape Olliemania as the forum in which political elites expected conversation to take place. Barry Sussman, former director of opinion polling for the *Washington Post*, explained: "When people judged Reagan according to what they wanted in a president, he got mediocre grades, even at a time when political leaders and most of the news media were lauding him as extremely popular. It was only when the public compared Reagan to his Democratic opposition that he did magnificently." Americans told pollsters that they did not approve Reagan's policies, but Democrats were unwilling to present alternatives with any conviction. The same failure to offer real alternatives—to appeal to majority sentiment or to mobilize their traditional constituents—during the Iran-Contra debate added up, in the *Nation*'s words, to "a Democratic surrender on the political issues generated by the hearings."[43]

Leaders in the Democratic party were unwilling to appeal to majorities in part because they shared with Republican elites a common vision: because the essence of governing was management of the mass, the purpose of the Iran-Contra investigation was to restore the ability of government to manage that mass, not to pursue truth or weigh alternative policies or derail Reagan's presidency. Since "our system of government is effective only if it enjoys respect and trust," House Committee Chair Lee Hamilton proclaimed on the first day of hearings, the most important task of the committee was that of "rebuilding that respect and trust." Determined to avoid the eight months of "paralysis" that had accompanied the Senate Watergate hearings—an investigation on which he had served—Senate Committee Chair Daniel Inouye promised that the public phase of the Iran-Contra hearings "should take about one-third as long." Each time North began to describe a covert American operation, Inouye cut off the discussion of the topic in public session so that the committees could stay focused in public on the misdeeds of a few individuals and on the president's failure to manage a tighter ship. "We do not seek radical change," declared Hamilton on the first day.[44]

Democrats inherited other traditions that may have inhibited enthusiasm for appealing to majorities. Champions of minorities, defenders of the rights of individuals to determine how to live their lives and manage their bodies, Democrats harbored a deep suspicion of majority rule. Creators of the administrative state and generally the voice of the culturally privileged, Democrats feared that a mobilized majority might threaten their prerogatives. With deep roots in a fading New Deal past, Democrats lacked the zeal to remake politics that Republicans brought from their years of exile in the 1970s. The huge deficits that the federal government began to run by 1981 deprived Democrats of their traditional policy alternative of spending money for new initiatives. "Moderates" within the party pointed to Richard Nixon's defeat of George McGovern in 1972 and Ronald Reagan's of Walter Mondale in 1984 to suggest that voters would reject Democrats with liberal agendas. For all these reasons perhaps, Democrats were unsure of how to respond to Republican initiatives.

Whatever inhibited Democrats, the result in 1987 was clear. Confusing the rhetoric and activities of conservative activists for the voice of the people, and knowing no other way to listen to the people, Democrats repeatedly decided against trying to mobilize voters to challenge Republican initiatives. Democrats believed, according to the *New York Times,* that "the worst thing for the country and the [Democratic] party" would be to criticize Reagan or his policies because he was "personally very popular" and the public would take vengeance on anyone who criticized him. Conservatives would persuade the mass that Democrats were "weakening the country."[45]

The most telling example of the Democrats' unwillingness to appeal to popular opposition to Reagan's policies came over the very issue at the core of the Iran-Contra deals, American aid to the contras. Ever since the Sandinistas had overthrown the brutal Somoza regime in Nicaragua in 1979, large majorities of Americans had opposed armed intervention in that country's domestic affairs. For many conservatives, however, the Sandinistas were a growing obsession, and they repeatedly pushed a sympathetic Reagan administration ("I am a contra," Reagan declared) into schemes to overthrow the Sandinistas. Whenever Democrats opposed contra aid out of either conviction or a desire for votes, Republican hard-liners such as Patrick Buchanan tried to intimidate them with fears of a mass in motion: "With the vote on Contra aid, the Democratic Party will reveal whether it stands with Ronald Reagan and the resistance or Daniel Ortega and the communists." The Democrats' timid response to such charges created Reagan's magic.

Instead of voting against contra aid because an overwhelming majority of Americans actually opposed it, Democrats fretted that Buchanan and the conservatives would somehow inspire the mass to punish them. Instead of defending the right of the Sandinistas to hold power that they had won by popular revolution in 1979 and consolidated in a landslide electoral victory in 1984, Democrats worried about how the Republican Right might manage the issue to lose them votes. And so, throughout the 1980s, the Democrats maneuvered within an agenda largely set by conservative activists within the Republican party. Unwilling to follow their inclination to stop aiding the contras, Democrats approved $100 million in aid in June 1986 at a time when public opinion polls opposed that aid by 30–60 and 33–62 margins.[46]

Although the silence of Democrats was puzzling because they could have harvested votes by speaking out, Republicans were as intimidated as Democrats by the story of Olliemania that they had contributed so much to creating. During the televised hearings, it was a Republican congressman's fear of Olliemania that drew the most comment from reporters. On June 25, 1987, two weeks before North was scheduled to testify, Republican Representative Bill McCollum of Florida declared that North had probably committed a crime and was in any case guilty of "one of the highest acts of insubordination and one of the most treacherous things that has ever occurred to a President it seems to me in our history." Three weeks later, after watching Olliemania emerge from North's week-long performance, McCollum concluded his "questioning" of North by telling the Marine that he may well have been a hero and that, in any case, "you've served your country admirably. . . . For that, I personally, and I know the country is grateful, and will remember forever."[47]

Even the chair of the Senate's investigating committee, Democrat Daniel Inouye, as he took his turn as the final legislator to confront North, illustrated the same fear of the mass that had animated Republican McCollum only a few hours earlier. Referring to North's pledge to obey any order he received from a superior officer as evidence of his failure to understand democratic government, Inouye began to remind North of the principle Americans had proclaimed during the Nuremburg trials after World War II: military officers were required to disobey "unlawful orders." North's attorney, Brendan Sullivan, suddenly interrupted. He challenged Inouye in the name of the pile of orchestrated telegrams: "Why don't you listen to the American people and what they've said as a result of the last week. There are 20,000 telegrams in our room outside the corridor here that came in this morning. The American people have spoken." Rather than ignoring Sullivan's irrelevant interruption or pointing to plentiful evidence that "the American people" were not enthralled by North, a rattled Inouye forgot about Nuremburg, declared that he opposed communism, apologized for his vote against contra aid, declared that the telegrams showed "the strength of this democracy," complimented Mrs. North, and adjourned the hearings.[48]

By following the rules of opinion management and compressing real individuals into a uniform mass, journalists and politicians invented a new form of "blame the victim"; they excused their own timidity by describing a flawed and dangerous public. Some critics within the media—for example, the *Nation* and *In These Times*—challenged the tendency to blame the public for the failures of political leaders, but most journalists and Democrats seemed to mute their doubts about North and Reagan because they feared that at any moment a dangerous mass might burst the restraints that insiders and commentators had constructed to limit conversation to what was thinkable and manageable.

Because Democratic and Republican officeholders alike imagined the forum as a place where leaders assumed responsibility for managing the mass—precisely the vision underlying the stories of Reagan's magic and Olliemania—the real challenges to these two inventions came, not from insiders with access to money, training, and microphones, but from the people themselves, who insisted on being heard as real individuals. Knowing that they were not pieces of a faceless mass, citizens spoke out for themselves. They tried to remake political conversations so that citizens and politicians might once again be able to see and hear each other. And in this attempt they remade the forum into a place where conflicts among partisans over policy were swallowed up in a much angrier and more basic conflict: Would conversation in the forum be shaped by the distortions and silences of opinion management or by the experiences and relationships of everyday life? They moved the forum from the columns of editorial writers and the sound bites of politicians to the phone calls and letters in which Americans explained how they thought political conversation should be conducted.

Three

❖ ❖ ❖ ❖ ❖ ❖ ❖ ❖ ❖ ❖ ❖

The Living Traditions
of Citizenship

FROM MONITORING TO MOBILIZING IN THE

SUMMER OF 1987

"We are not mindless and faceless individuals but still strong independent Americans," an angry woman from Wichita wrote
Congressman Lee Hamilton. She deeply resented hearing her voice reduced by journalists to the visceral emotions of a mindless mass. She wanted
to refute the story of Olliemania by adding her own voice to the town meeting that Hamilton was chairing. In letters like this, unprecedented numbers
of television viewers reached out to communicate with legislators in ways
that they hoped would reshape the public forum that was opening around
Oliver North's testimony. With their letters they tried to make that forum
into a place where they could be seen and heard as individuals with minds
and faces of their own.

The "town meeting" in the summer of 1987 was remarkable because it
took place in and tried to connect two very different kinds of places. It
opened from the central, visible public arena of televised hearings, nightly
news, and newspaper columns with their accustomed inhabitants into vast
numbers of intimate conversations around family dinner tables, at office wa-
tercoolers, across seats on an airplane or pews in a church, places that were
invisible to most of the forum's participants but also places where life mattered most to the participants. In so doing it brought out in the open the
conflicts, doubts, and interests between citizens and elites that are immediately recognizable but usually lie hidden from sight.

Viewers realized that within their everyday conversation with people
around them was the kind of political conversation that should shape the
public forum. Looking for a familiar way to draw others into these conversa-

tions, they turned to two means by which they reached individuals who mattered in their lives—writing letters and making phone calls. By adapting these intimate forms of communication to the task of connecting citizens and their representatives, many viewers revealed how they experienced citizenship and democracy in practice.

Individuals reported very different personal inspirations for writing—sorrow, anger, confusion, pride—but they gave very similar reasons for why this event made them feel that they had the right, even the responsibility, to write to legislators, why they had "standing" to enter forums from which they ordinarily felt excluded. Their letters allow us to see how the personal uneasiness citizens felt as they watched television and read newspapers prompted them to take the unusual step of writing to congressmen. We can watch them cast about among larger and more recognizable frameworks of ideas and institutions for ways of giving greater clarity, authority, and legitimacy to their personal concerns. We can see their crusade to change the structure, spirit, and content of political conversation among citizens, between citizens and leaders, and even among leaders.

The analysis of how writers turned these letters into an extraordinary form of political participation will unfold in layers across the next five chapters. Here we begin by exploring the critical moment that inspired so many citizens to write to their congressmen. We probe one of the oldest mysteries in representative government: What motivates widespread political participation? Why have citizens taken part in politics on some occasions while ignoring even elections—by tradition their primary civic responsibility—on others?

Faced with the ubiquitous and corrosive story of Olliemania in the summer of 1987, viewers wanted legislators first to understand the powerful defenses they had carefully built over the years, with their friends and families, to resist attempts by pitchmen and pundits and pollsters to erode their capacity for governing themselves and then to see how Olliemania breached those defenses, threatening the bonds that connected them with others. The letters described how things they could ordinarily dismiss had become menaces that compelled them to act, to move from the dismissive role of monitor to the activist role of citizen-soldier, charged to sound the alarm when danger approached.

From the event that inspired the popular outpouring, we move on in chapter 4 to examine the act of writing itself. Where in their everyday experience did writers imagine that they would find legislators? What could they say and do to build relationships with those legislators? Why letters at all? Why not instead mobilize street demonstrations or join political parties? We explore how writers turned a medium of intimate communication into a means for drawing legislators into their worlds of family and friends and, in so doing, for reshaping the public forum into a place that resembled their primary relationships with those around them.

In chapter 5 we turn from the challenge of building a relationship to that of choosing a voice. How did writers try to be recognized? How could they reconcile a desire to speak in an individual voice, on the one hand, with a desire to be recognized and counted, on the other?

We then ask in chapter 6 what the letters tell us about how writers used their primary relationships to shape what they wanted to say. How did they turn what they valued and experienced in personal relationships into values for shaping politics? How did their political thinking emerge from meeting needs in their primary relationships? We will see, above all, that writers found in their primary relationships standards for authenticity and authority, so that those relationships became powerful sites from which to challenge the constructions of the mass media.

What, finally, did writers want legislators to hear? Reporting the conclusions writers sent legislators about the issues at stake in the hearings, we explore in chapter 7 how citizens approached issues differently from congressmen. While legislators tried to narrow issues into limited debates about means and details, citizens wanted both to widen the debate and to move from the details of this case to identify underlying principles, ranging from rule of law to the proper role of the United States in the world. They wanted to address basic conflicts over what constituted heroism and patriotism and treason. And as they reached back to bring to the forum their basic ideologies and values, writers explained how these values were shaped by their primary relationships, how in those relationships they learned lessons about trusting and feeling responsibility toward others.

∎ The experience of watching the hearings firsthand confirmed viewers' convictions that politics as it ordinarily appeared on television belonged to a different world than everyday life. "My husband and I have been listening to the Hearings on Television," a 65-year-old woman from Amherst, New Hampshire, began her letter to Hamilton: "It was so much better to hear exactly what [witnesses] said, instead of hearing a few excerpts on the evening news. . . . The American people finally had a chance to hear all the facts and not just a few." The chance to observe the give-and-take for themselves meant, in the words of an engineer from Gaithersburg, Maryland, that "we can form opinions without relying on media reporting." By watching the conversations between legislators and witnesses firsthand, viewers concluded anew that stories on the nightly news both distorted the realities they depicted and encouraged politicians and reporters to talk and act differently than ordinary people did.

Television was a place where pitchmen tried to sell something—a product, a policy—and where success was measured in sales or votes or ratings. Many citizens deeply resented and feared the industries that had emerged to market political opinion as though it were a commercial product. "Colonel North might merit an A in Marketing and Public Relations (his own PR, but not that of the U.S.), but I would certainly give him an F in Democracy and Ethics," wrote a man from Houston. Although most writers trusted the people around them to recognize and dismiss a sales pitch, they still resented the new political merchandisers for trying to trick people into buying unwanted products, policies, ideas, even "facts."

Viewers had constructed particularly powerful defenses against the marketing ploys of politicians. The promises of politicians seemed to bear little relation either to their real purposes or to what they would actually do after an election. Because politicians seemed interested mainly in advancing their careers or their parties ("too tied into their own agendas," complained a woman from New Jersey), their values were alien. From Memphis a woman wrote that she had quit even reading about politics "years ago" because "no politician in the city or Federal government has *any* integrity." "Everyone knows the words 'politician' and 'crook' are synonymous," declared a New Yorker. For these reasons politicians were "dirty" (Fresno), "sleazy" (Chicago), and "disgusting" (Columbus).

Driven by a desire "to influence the [A]merican people to conform to whatever agenda it is that you are pursuing," wrote a man from Fairfax, Virginia, politicians craved access to the mass media in order to sell their projects by "deception and miss-representation [*sic*] to the public." "Give you a microphone and T.V. camera and you go bananas," complained a man from Anaheim, California, to which a woman from neighboring Glendale added: "How you prima-donnas love the limelight!" Legislators made speeches about "law and democracy," wrote a viewer in Alexandria, Indiana, but such speeches were actually "only a case of 'Hey look, Maw, I'm on TV.'" Television cameras encouraged politicians to appeal to low common denominators behind which they hid their real agendas. "Underneath the movie cliches about American values," observed a woman from Worthington, Massachusetts, "this administration has delivered philosophies and policies which demonstrate an ignorance of and contempt for the great mass of Americans and for the democratic process."

Writers noted that entertainment and marketing had become intertwined on television. Some witnesses and congressmen seemed more concerned with their acting performances than with a search for truth. North's testimony reflected "the theatrical training he received before performing at these hearings," in which he was "led by the more experienced actor, our President," wrote a woman from Burlington, Vermont. Reagan might have a reputation as "the great communicator," observed a woman from Clarksburg, West Virginia, but he should more correctly be called "the great manipulator": "I grant he's the best quipper and jokester and smiler—oh! he can smile and wave. When it comes to having enough intelligence to be President—that he lacks." Reagan, complained a woman from Victoria, Texas, "should stop using Bob Hope's old stale jokes, stop acting like Vanna White turning over letters, acting like C. Eastwood saying make my day." A couple from Eureka, California, tendered Oliver North "best actor of the year" award. "If he has earned an award," corrected a woman from Omaha, "let it be an Emmy for his television performance before your committee or a medal for 'keeping the body and soul' of the American Junta together."

Acting performances infuriated viewers because they were designed to distract citizens and investigators alike from the truth. "This is not Hollywood," wrote a doctor from Oakland, California, "and this is a real world." "Ignore the Rambo Wayne James Bond Image," a naval officer and his wife wired from Long Beach: "Continue your interrogations to get facts." North was "a consummate actor" who "finds it difficult to separate reality from fantasy" and neither "understands nor comprehends what democracy is all about," warned a San Franciscan. "Has it all become just 'cinema'?" wondered a woman from Philadelphia. "America," worried an angry woman from Plainview, Texas, "has been devastated by all these theatrics."

Many journalists had blamed the audience for turning the hearings into an entertainment spectacle, but most viewers believed that it was the politicians and journalists who confused acting and politics. The point of perceiving that North was an actor was not to blame the audience, citizens explained, but to hold North responsible for trying to fool others with a performance instead of telling the truth. "Since when is outright DECEPTION of the American people a part of our democratic tradition?" demanded a woman from Scarsdale, New York. "The idea of having private people giving money to conduct a war without the knowledge of the Congress and the people" was "absolutely right-down sinister, outrageously, betrayerly, to the American people," declared a woman from the Bronx. "The thing both sides take for granted is the necessity to deceive and manipulate the American people. Isn't that the issue here?" demanded a woman from Cerritos, California.

The chance to watch the proceedings armed viewers with the ability to judge for themselves what they saw by standards they had developed for evaluating stories they heard in their daily lives. North tried to pull "the biggest 'snow-job' in the history of this country," wrote a man from Ridgeway, Missouri, while Congress ran the hearings like "The Super Bowl of Bullshit," to a man from Pasadena, California. Writers responded to the performances of witnesses with the combination of jokes and folk wisdom that they had long used to dismiss distortions by salesmen and actors:

Folks in covert activity see the truth not quite the same as the truth [was] taught to me in Sunday School and Church. ("A sad, sad American," Washington, D.C. postmark)

After listening to North, believe he is like a three dollar bill. Congratulations for not being fooled. (Husband and wife. Chestertown, Md.)

Believe Poindexter? No way, Jose. One must be bereft of common sense and logic to buy his nonsense. If you believe Poindexter—I have some swamp land to sell you. (Man, Largo, Fla.)

In the words of my dear, departed grandfather when he doubted another man's story: "Anyone who would believe that mess should poke out his left ear [drum]." (Woman, Des Moines)

Mr. Poindexter is lying. It came across very clearly to us. (Woman, Cherryville, N.C.)

If you believe this you will indeed believe in the tooth fairy. (Man, Iowa Falls, Iowa)

In President Reagan's last televised speech he strongly criticized the press and anyone else who happened to disagree with his peculiar brand of Democracy. He began it with a poem about bullfighting. How telling. If anyone knows about throwing the bull it's the president and his staff. (Woman, Brooklyn, N.Y.)

If there is a place in Hell that is especially hot, I hope that the people who have lied to you find a place reserved for them there. (Man, Englewood Cliffs, N.J.)

And, unfortunately, I think [Poindexter] is still withholding vital facts. You might try checking in his pipe. (Ha!) (Man, postmarked Hawthorne, Calif.)

Viewers voiced such dismissals with an ease that spoke of their tested value as defenses.

Many writers distrusted news reporting more than acting or selling because journalists professed independence and accuracy as their creeds. The experience of watching the hearings "unfiltered and unfettered by the media" confirmed for a woman in Birmingham, Michigan, "the belief of many that the media in this country can and often does distort important issues."

Writers complained in particular that the reporters and interpreters of opinion distorted conversations between citizens and politicians in two ways that made it much harder for citizens to find places to enter those conversations. The first was simply that their biases prevented reporters from seeing or reporting reality as viewers saw it. "I watched and listened with total absorption," reported a woman from Bolton, Massachusetts, "and I declare to you that I understood Messrs. North and Poindexter more accurately and more fully than did Messrs. Rather, Jennings, and Brokaw," who "misquoted, misconstrued, [and] misunderstood" the witnesses. "The majority of our 'free' press (most media) are incapable of understanding and reporting truth," a woman wrote from Plano, Texas.

Many believed that the commercial, ideological, ethnic, or political commitments of the media's owners led them to select topics and tell stories in particular ways. A Chicagoan blamed control by wealthy owners for the failure to represent "the working people like me." A man in Appleton, Minnesota, believed that "Jewish control" of the media excluded his voice. Still others thought that "pro-communist" (Glen Burnie, Md.) or at least "very liberal" (Santee, Calif.) influences forced journalists into "slanting the news to favor those left of center" (Hollywood, Fla.). To a woman in Houston, on the other hand, "the past six years have been deeply disturbing ones for me" because "the press gave Mr. Reagan good reviews." Writers from all ideological perspectives agreed that "the media gives a distortion of what's going on by what it continually accents and spotlights, by what it repeats over and over, and by what it ignores," as a woman from Topeka put it. In other words, declared a woman from Sun City West, Arizona, "it is frightening how the news media manipulates, deletes, and omits the truth."

Through distorted reports, journalists narrowed what citizens and politicians could talk about and thereby excluded voices, experiences, and ideas that individual citizens or politicians wanted to contribute and hear taken seriously. "When we are bombarded with news that does not present the *true* conditions," a man from McAllen, Texas, explained to Hamilton, "you and we draw incorrect conclusions." Citizens worried that "months and months of *brainwashing*" (Milwaukee) by journalists would "seduce the public" (New York) or have the effect of "politically poisoning the minds of the American public." Because congressmen seemed to assume that other people believed journalists' stories, "the media" had the ability to shape which issues would be taken seriously and which would be dismissed. "Unelected men of the media have more power than the President and the Congress combined because the media molds public opinion and free governments are guided by public opinion," concluded a man from San Francisco. "You people there in government may think you are running the country," wrote a man from Gladstone, Missouri, but "you don't. The news media runs this country. All of you in both branches of government are afraid of the news media and you all know it." "Congress has been bamboozled again by a wild and erroneous press," grumbled a woman from Evanston, Illinois.

But reporters and interpreters of opinion distorted conversations between citizens and politicians in a second, more dangerous way by listening to citizens through what by the late 1980s had become a $2.5 billion a year "opinion industry."[1] Rather than asking people what they were thinking about, pollsters selected topics and choices for citizens to respond to. "All results of political polls are colored by precisely how each question is framed," observed a couple from Fort Collins, Colorado. "Polls generally reflect the wishes of the pollsters," complained a man from Richmond, Kentucky. In real life an opinions were neither formed nor expressed as either-

or, on-off choices among equal alternatives presented by a stranger, but out of conversations among people who knew each other, as they tried to distinguish intensity and conviction from significance to reach a conclusion. For all these reasons, "it is not 'the will of the people' that is measured," concluded a man from Oldwick, New Jersey. "We're all aware that a poll is baloney," were blunter words from Birmingham, Alabama.

Writers complained about the desire to identify common denominators, however weakly held, instead of listening to individual voices. "We the American people cannot be lumped together as one big blob or glob," protested a woman from Jacksonville, Florida: "We do have a voice [as individuals]." "The diversity of American opinion" was more impressive to a woman from Rolling Hills Estates, California, than common denominators constructed across individual perspectives.

By talking and listening to people in ways that kept real individuals from being heard and conversing with each other, pollsters and other interpreters of opinion created political conversation that badly distorted communication between citizens and politicians. As they watched the hearings, many viewers concluded that many congressmen spoke not from conviction, but from expectations about how the "blob or glob" would react. When Warren Rudman declared that Congress rejected contra aid because polls revealed large majorities of Americans opposed to it, several viewers agreed with one who wrote Hamilton that "What makes Col. North look so good and your committee so bad is his reliance on his beliefs and convictions for his opinions and your willingness to change your stance to satisfy the latest opinion poll." "After living 77 + years," a man from Cohoes, New York, urged Hamilton to pay attention to "what is right or wrong" and not "sway with the wind" of a "majority" invented by pollsters. And a woman in Carmel, Indiana, believed that congressmen "might be surprised at the additional support they would receive if they took a stand and did not vacillate with popular opinion polls."

Viewers wrote to legislators in protest when they saw committee members suddenly retreat out of obvious fear of offending the Olliemania that journalists proclaimed to be animating the mass. "The manner in which some senators and representatives pandered to North made us ill! They assumed he had been proclaimed a 'hero' by the American people!" "I'm going to nominate you for the chicken-shit of the year award," fumed a man from West St. Paul, Minnesota, to Hamilton: "We're sick enough already of your doormatism. . . . When are you, if ever, going to show courage and put those creeps where they belong!" Watching legislators buckle before Olliemania, a man from Brooklyn observed that "Congress panicked and treated him with deference, throwing cottonball questions at him and failing to follow up on his lying answers."

To many viewers this fear of audience reaction came most vividly into view when the committee voted, at the peak of Olliemania, to deny Oliver North the opportunity to show the slides that he had used to persuade wealthy conservatives to support the contra cause. "Don't you think out of fairness the Ollie North tapes should be shown to the American people with Ollie North narrating?" asked a woman from Flint, Michigan: "All of you seem to be afraid to show them." "Why the fear of airing, in its entirety, an opposing opinion?" wondered a man from Charleston, South Carolina.

Viewing lively controversy as a natural part of everyday life and believing that Americans spoke as individuals, citizens conceived fairness in political controversy very differently from journalists who envisioned America as a faceless mass. Citizens did indeed hear and protest bias. "The blame-America-first media" presented an anticontra perspective on Nicaragua, complained a man in Rosenberg, Texas, while a writer from Albany blasted the hearings as "a telethon for contra aid." Complaints from conservatives that a presentation was too liberal and from liberals that it was too conservative delighted journalists because that meant that their target, the middle of the mass, would find a story "objective" and fair.

But the citizens who wrote to Hamilton sought neither neutrality nor absence of controversy. What they meant by "fairness" was the chance for their own views to be heard. This kind of fairness would translate into more facts and greater diversity of opinion than investigators had been willing to probe, politicians to discuss, and journalists to seek and report. They wanted more than the two competing viewpoints on the limited topics that insiders were willing to permit; they wanted politicians and journalists to widen the discussion to include facts and opinions that were known only to a few. "Only half the news in this country is printed," a woman from San Diego complained to Hamilton. "What can be done to get all viewpoints presented on television?" a woman from Topeka asked Inouye: "How can the American people start getting all sides of all issues?" A couple from Gillett, Wisconsin, demanded the "freedom to know—ALL the facts." Journalists' definition of objectivity as neutrality and their preference for knowledgeable insiders as sources reinforced the tendency of opinion polling to concentrate debate around conventional views and insider concerns rather than represent the diverse voices in which individual Americans actually wrote Hamilton.

Instead of pursuing the frightening leads or deeper issues that briefly surfaced during the hearings, journalists preferred topics that cautious insiders wanted to be discussed. When Mary McGrory published a typical insider column that held up Secretary of State George Shultz as a model, a preacher from Liverpool, New York, complained to her: "I am perplexed by your praise of Secretary Schultz. Perhaps in a kingdom of pygmies even a short man could be regarded as a giant." Citizens demanded, by contrast, that outsiders be heard as well as insiders, that diversity, not neutrality, be the standard of fairness. The ideal range of debate would be as wide as the range of opinion in the audience. "I am so frustrated!" wrote a woman from Lavallette, New Jersey, who "wanted to reach so many people," but "I have no newspaper or T.V. station to be heard." A viewer in Fremont, California, spoke in the name of "the millions of Americans who do not have access to TV and radio to plead OUR cause."

Citizens wrote to Hamilton to demand that the hearings be widened to include viewpoints and facts that journalists and politicians had ruled beyond the range of acceptable discussion. Angered that the committees ignored whole areas of inquiry, a viewer asked Hamilton to "please continue the hearings until all possible truth is revealed." "The Committee does not want to be too hard on the President, but history will reveal the truths the Committee does not want to get into," wrote a man from Largo, Florida. "The President himself should be called to the floor to answer for the actions of his men," said a man from Hartford. To a woman from Florida the prime focus should have been how Reagan was "the secret leader of this whole mess." Other viewers urged Congress to widen the investigation to probe "the leftist affiliations and associations of some of your colleagues whose actions are far worse than Messrs. North or Poindexter" (Waxahachie, Tex.) and to uncover the "queers, drunks, dope [users]" among congressmen and those with "'girl friends' on the side" (Kilgore, Tex.). Since he believed that violation of a military officer's oath to defend the Constitution was "a criminal and military offense," a man from Dallas wondered why North and Poindexter had not been court-martialed.

Many citizens complained when the committees refused to explore in open session other covert activities, especially a plan to create a secret force that would be responsible only to the president. From San Francisco through Granite City, Illinois, to Radford, Virginia, viewers called this "the most crucial issue," "the most important question," and "the fundamental question." "Your denying Congressman Brooks the privilege of questioning Lt. Col. North about the plans to rescind the Constitution and establish a military dictatorship is but another example of why the Congress, in my opinion, no longer deserves the trust of the nation," a man from Huntsville, Alabama, wrote Inouye. "The primary cover-up," wrote a man from New Haven, Connecticut, was "the way in which the U.S. Congress has yet to publicly examine its failures over the past two years to provide militant overseership of the operations of our foreign policy after the Boland Amendments mandated it to do so," a failure caused by fears of losing "the public's support when it blows the whistle on a popular president and his unilateral militarism."

Viewers demanded that Congress widen the investigation to include other perspectives on Central America. "The narrow focus of the questioning," complained a woman from Great Barrington, Massachusetts, left the "documented atrocities" of the contras out of public view. The committees paid too little attention to the World Court's ruling in favor of Nicaragua against the United States (Culver City, Calif.), death squads in El Salvador (Minneapolis), Israel's role (Zig Zag, Oreg.), and "the reality of Soviet expansionism" (Chicago). Citizens proposed solutions that ranged from a moratorium on building nuclear weapons (Julian, N.C.) and more civilian teachers in military schools (Glendale, Ariz.) to more federal aid to education (Elkins Park, Pa.), from rewriting the National Security Act (Oakland, Calif.) to curbing the influence of campaign contributors over politics (Half Moon Bay, Calif.).

Experienced with salesmen, actors, politicians, and journalists, letter writers described defenses that usually enabled them to dismiss the political performances they encountered in the media. They saw themselves not as the passive (or cheering) spectators imagined by the retailers of Olliemania, but as guardians ready when necessary to defend values and people that mattered to them. Because politicians and journalists imagined that citizens thought in low common denominators, they usually advanced their agendas with appeals to vague values—"education" or "freedom" or "the family" or "the environment"—that left individuals feeling vaguely included but, more important, willing to let politicians and journalists go about their business. What happened on television usually did not matter much. It neither engaged nor threatened them, neither included nor excluded them. What they saw was usually reassuringly predictable, vaguely acceptable, and mostly irrelevant to what mattered in everyday life.

Viewers simply dismissed what they found irrelevant or pandering or unbelievable or biased. "Many people . . . do not watch the news anymore," wrote a woman, "because it is so obviously slanted." Others monitored politicians and journalists and then decided, in the words of a Kentuckian, "if they get too far left, I will tune them out and return to my library." The most common response was indeed to tune out banal or offensive messages: "Some of us just don't bother to read and listen to much of the news any more," reported a woman from Orlando Beach, Florida. After watching for a while, a man from Fresno announced: "I am not wasting any more of my time listening to any more of bull." Viewers needed to keep an eye on journalists and politicians, of course, but they rarely expected to see anything that did not deserve to be dismissed.

■■ As they monitored politics in the summer of 1987, many Americans began to see politicians, journalists, and even citizens acting in strange ways, ways they could neither ignore nor dismiss. In place of the usual, if minimal, connections they expected to feel with fellow citizens and with politicians, they now saw things that swamped their defenses and overwhelmed them with both unusual civic hope and unusual civic fear. The hearings had broadened to offer some viewers hope that their deepest values might at last be expressed and some viewers fear that they might discover they shared nothing with their fellow citizens. Whether driven by confidence or vulnerability, Americans experienced the democratic awakening in the summer of 1987 as a time to step over their crumbling defenses to reclaim a government that seemed to have come adrift from its traditions, its laws, and the wishes of its citizens. "When something important must be done," wrote a woman from Brea, California, "it [is] up to the American people" to do it. With bizarre stories about Olliemania presented as a picture of how they were thinking, many citizens felt compelled to shape a very different forum, to mobilize to reclaim their government.

From the start, the Iran-Contra hearings differed from the ordinary television performances that Americans instinctively dismissed. Television's intimacy highlighted the contrast between moments that seemed real and those that appeared to be staged, between the voices of firsthand experience and those of rehearsed texts, inviting viewers to participate as well as to dismiss. Viewers listened to witnesses reveal nightmares in which citizens could no longer take for granted basic assumptions about government and citizenship. They listened as legislators sought to identify the underlying issues and clarify how things had reached this point. In the earnest spirit of the inquiry, in the diversity of perspectives it elicited from among legislators, and in the growing sense that the American people were the real subject as well as the real authority for resolving the debate, the hearings frequently resembled the ways individuals talked and listened to the people around them. Each of these unexpected resemblances to everyday life breached defenses that had kept the two worlds apart.

As the hearings lurched between the genuine inquiry and conversation so familiar in everyday life and staged spectacle, Americans felt a full range of emotions. To a man from Burke, Virginia, the hearings were "a mixed bag of entertainment, enlightenment, stupidity, disappointment and anger." "I have been made angry, resentful, irritated, sad, excited, and very proud at various times," wrote a woman from Lehi, Utah.

From the opening testimony of General Secord the hearings replaced television's familiar hucksterism with the spirit of the everyday and the real. By starting with Secord's detailed account of precisely how he had arranged the Iran-Contra deals, the hearings cut through the official posturing and press speculation that had shrouded the events ever since Meese had revealed their existence six months earlier. When Secord's testimony triggered a sharp debate among legislators over whether he had been justified, the hearings established from the start that some legislators were determined to figure out not only what happened but what was at stake, not only whether a crime had been committed but what it all meant. What Americans saw on their screens was an unusual range of opinion and style, an unusual frankness of give-and-take, an unusual earnestness of purpose, an unusual depth of topic. Legislators debated values in the context of specific actions with the details that gave depth to what might otherwise have been windy generalities. Participants cared about each other and about the outcome. Committee members treated the hearings as a genuine inquiry in which each revelation, each story, each reaction, each controversy seemed spontaneous. The unrehearsed atmosphere encouraged individual viewers to identify with the particular congressman whose spontaneous reaction in the hearing room seemed to coincide with the viewer's at home. The exchanges among lawyers, witnesses, and committee members helped viewers to resolve similar confusions and contradictions they had been observing as they watched at home.

The hearings provided viewers an extraordinary opportunity to find people on television with whom they could engage. "Each character had his individual objectives . . . to project," observed one writer. Among the twenty-six committee members, individual viewers found at least one representative on whom they could project their deepest hopes and values, who could "represent" them, as the personalities and issues unfolded. "We feel after these many weeks that we have come to know the committee personally," wrote a husband and wife who found the committee "remarkable" because its members were so "varied, competent, and sincere." For once, viewers could find someone on television who spoke and acted as people did around them.

Arguments between committee members over the meaning of democratic values seemed more urgent and inviting because they took place in the spirit of everyday conversations. "The lesson, for me, of these past few weeks," summarized a woman from Port Huron, Michigan, "has been to watch a few who can disagree, articulate their differences, respect each other—and command our respect, because they operated from a common basis of concern for truth and our democratic process." As witnesses and legislators debated the meaning of democratic values, a woman from Sunnyvale, California, "liked seeing the process, the dialogue, the congressmen, the senators, the system of democracy, in other words, actually working."

The intensity of their pride as citizens depended on how the strangers they watched reinterpreted common traditions or proclaimed new ones. Some traditions were so basic to each citizen's definition of national identity—and they differed dramatically from one citizen to the next—that each had assumed all Americans, and certainly all policymakers, supported them. Many viewers were astonished to discover that some policymakers and citizens did not view these basic securities in the same way they did. "Who would have ever thought that on the Bicentennial of the Constitution we would have a hearing to investigate attempts to subvert that document?" asked a man from Framingham, Massachusetts.

Because the hearings were about how public officials had applied these traditions in their names as American citizens, viewers felt personally responsible and implicated. The feeling of personal responsibility was hard to escape because live television coverage made the hearings a topic of everyday talk. The hearings became one of those rare televised events—like other congressional investigations, state visits, or assassinations—that have attracted huge audiences as they have become occasions for talk wherever people went about their lives.[2]

"I feel deeply implicated by our actions abroad," wrote a woman from New York. "If Oliver North *is* a hero, an American patriot," declared a woman from Oakland, California, "then I am, for the first time since Vietnam, truly ashamed to call myself an American." A husband and wife from Kirkland, Washington, explained their feeling of responsibility through a vivid metaphor: "In the same way the driver of an escape car is guilty of the crime, we, the American people, are responsible for the crimes of the Contras if we support them. I do not want my, or anyone's, senators or representatives making me responsible for the atrocities committed by the Contras." "I do love America and freedom," wrote a woman from Eugene, Oregon: "I hate to give it all up to something as preventable as a bunch of boys without ideals and no regard for the rules." A woman from Massachusetts grieved that the defenses of witnesses violated her patriotic values until she felt too sad to continue. "I can't write much more without getting sick," she lamented: "Something has died in this country." A lifelong Republican from Marietta, Georgia, felt "betrayed" and "truly depressed" by Republican politicians who supported the "lying and deceit of the principals involved in the Iran-Contra debacle" while bearing the name of her party.

At the same time that the unusual similarities between the hearings and everyday life invited citizens to participate, journalists and politicians said things that shook deeply many viewers' confidence in democracy. The crisis began when key witnesses, participants, and storytellers insisted that they knew what was best for citizens who were, in any case, stupid, irrational, and untrustworthy.

For many viewers, Oliver North and John Poindexter sparked an overwhelming need to try to speak out and reshape the public forum when they testified that citizens lacked the right or competence to participate in shaping their government's policies. While many viewers expected to feel manipulated when they watched television, few expected to hear their autonomy and competence challenged directly. They were appalled when North and Poindexter claimed that disclosure of their covert actions would have made it harder to fight communism or free hostages around the world. "Instead of coming to the end of Poindexter's testimony with our heads held high," wrote a couple from Louisville, "we felt that we had been reduced from the status of informed, voting citizens to mere subordinates in a quasi-military order." A woman from Richmond wondered "what good is it to vote" if neither she nor her elected representatives could be trusted with the information that determined policy.

Even more disturbing than the charge that they were untrustworthy was the message that citizens were too stupid or irrational to understand, too conformist to think for themselves, and too escapist to care what was happening. Over and over citizens heard officials proclaim that they knew what was best for voters. "Right-wing Birchite" policymakers conveyed to a man in South Pasadena, California, the vision that they "know what's good for us, and if the rest of us aren't convinced, tough, they'll go ahead and do it anyway." Another viewer concluded that officials were "full of 'ELITISM' and 'MILITARISM,'" that is, "the clear sense that *they* are smarter than President, the people, legal counsel, laws, etc." "I am deeply offended" and "deeply frightened," a viewer from Elysburg, Pennsylvania, wrote to Oliver North, "by the arrogance with which everyone of you on the NSC has assumed that you know best for the rest of us."

John Poindexter infuriated many viewers when he claimed that most Americans trusted their leaders to do what was in their best interests and did not even want to know what leaders were doing. "It appalls me," exclaimed a woman from San Jose: "Unlike Poindexter, I believe the American people understand the democratic process, and value our institutions highly." "Admiral Poindexter's remark about the American people not wanting to know what the government was doing in their name," wrote a man from Astoria, New York,

> was the most arrogant and contemptuous statement made by anyone I've heard testify. The cat was finally out of the bag. The American people are too stupid to make a considered judgment about the activities of their government and leaders. It should all be left up to those who know better, i.e., whoever is running the show at that moment. If that's the case then why bother having any elections?

North's supporters felt equally offended by what they heard as patronizing elitism from investigators. "I'm tired of the Congress and Senate telling me what's good for me," groaned a woman from Pittsburgh. A man from Sharon, Pennsylvania, complained to Inouye that the senator did "a tremendous disservice to the democratic process and the intelligence of the American people when you lecture to us about democracy" in such a way as to suggest that "those who support Colonel North's actions are naive, emotional and superficial."

By telling citizens that they were too incompetent to think and too untrustworthy to act, public officials ignited a revolt by people who insisted that they could indeed think and, more important, that they were the best judges of what was best for them. In the midst of a national town meeting on the meaning of democracy they could imagine few more offensive ways of attacking democracy at its core than for officials to claim to know what was best for them. Only by reclaiming their capacity to speak for themselves could they begin to restore their democratic competence and confidence:

> I am sick of these people making judgments for me and the American people. We all are not stupid. (Woman, Cincinnati)

> I have never believed that you all were so much smarter than I or that you knew so much better what was and is best for me. I never gave you that right. (Woman, El Monte, Calif.)

> I realize the voter is only intelligent at election time—after that, we must be led like children, but you would be amazed how many people have a few brain cells clicking together. (Woman, Mendham, N.J.)

> Please stop telling us what people want, and let it all "hang out" so that we can respond with our opinions based on honest information. . . . I feel cheated, because I do want to know, and it is very hard to find the truth about what is going on by reading or listening to managed press releases that are written to keep me from knowing. . . . I am not stupid, and I don't like being spoonfed pap and being subjected to diatribe, and I most certainly do not like being told it is what I want. (Woman, Moorpark, Calif.)

> The American people is not a tribe of fools. (Man, Memphis)

> It could be that we, the people, that live out here in the sticks are so dumb that we can't read the Constitution or know who we are voting for. If this is what you or any one else in Congress thinks we might as well stop voting. (Man, Wisconsin Dells, Wisc.)

Many citizens were furious when commentators framed the hearings as entertainment and then announced that the audience was mesmerized. "Come on!" protested Deborah E. Saunders of Metaire, Louisiana, to *Newsweek:* "[You can] disagree with me about Ollie North, but can't condescend to me or accuse me of viewing only for entertainment."[3]

Democratic government was becoming a hollow shell, many citizens feared, because journalists and politicians no longer cared what citizens thought, or worse, claimed to know what they were thinking. They felt individually excluded and politically unrepresented when pundits claimed to know what the American people wanted:

> We're really mad! We resent pollsters and political commentators saying that they know what we think. No one has asked *us*. (Husband and wife, Gates Mills, Ohio)

> Please stop talking as if you know what the American people want. (Man, Toledo, Ohio)

> Who is [Poindexter] that he is all knowing and able to speak for people he does not even know exist? If you were to ask him who I was, I'm sure he wouldn't know. Yet how on earth is he able to know my mind and speak for

me??!?? Please inform Mr. Poindexter that the next time he wants to speak on behalf of me, or any other American for that matter, . . . to give me a call, or write me first, and then maybe I'll give him an answer if he seeks my approval for his illegitimate, treasonous activities!! (Man, Great Mars, Pa.)

Another resentment so many have . . . is the members speaking each sentence, asking each question, making each statement "for the American people." Each person should speak for themselves and not wrap their utterances in "the American people want this and want that." (Man, Birmingham, Ala.)

But the deepest source of the crisis of democratic confidence came not when journalists claimed to know what citizens thought, for individuals knew what they thought, but when they invented Olliemania to describe what others thought. The story of Olliemania threatened the faith of individuals in their fellow citizens, the starting place for feelings of citizenship and patriotism. North's supporters felt merely alienated from journalists who accused them of mindless emotion, a familiar—if infuriating—condescension, but they felt included when the story concluded that most Americans admired North. For North's foes, however, the story of Olliemania suggested that they were alone.

Opponents of Oliver North invented many ways to keep the claims of Olliemania from corroding their connections with other citizens. Some asserted that Olliemania was just another familiar sales gimmick or acting performance that people would be able to dismiss in the same way they dismissed other marketing and entertainment ploys. These citizens described Olliemania as "the contrived onslaught of pseudo patriots" (Broadview Heights, Ohio), "a special movement to generate masses of letters" (Racine, Wisc.), a "well-organized and vocal" campaign (Concord, Calif.), or a "tremendous propaganda campaign" (Santa Barbara) by "a certain lunatic fringe who call him a hero" (Kennewick, Wash.). Other viewers minimized Olliemania's impact by observing that "Colonel North's 40,000 congratulatory telegrams hardly represent 260 million people" (Queens, N.Y.) or "hardly . . . constitute a marvelous outpouring" (New York). Some had a simpler retort. A man from Templeton, California, answered the report of an avalanche of pro-North telegrams: "I say bull shit." Others fell back on faith: "I cannot believe it represents the views of a majority of Americans," wrote a man from San Diego.

At a time when many viewers felt their own defenses falling away, however, many of North's enemies wrote Hamilton that they feared that other Americans, those they did not know personally, might be applauding North's acting performance. The tragedy was that the story of Olliemania saturated the media at the precise moment when many citizens wanted to enter the unfamiliar public forum to seek support for their deepest values among strangers. The story was disturbing because viewers were unable to test its accuracy for themselves, and many assumed that strangers were being swayed by the propaganda that they themselves dismissed.[4] And they could see the tens of thousands of telegrams that defense attorneys piled up in front of North to create the impression of overwhelming popular support for their client. So troubling were these yellow reminders that on July 10, 1987, thirty-one people called the Senate Select Committee office to protest the telegrams and insist they be removed, and another fifty called for the same purpose on the following day of the hearing.[5] From their sudden fears about being isolated from their fellow citizens grew the crisis of democratic confidence:

> It disturbed us very much to see Oliver North become an instant hero to the public when he had done so many illegal things. (Husband and wife, Sarasota, Fla.)
>
> Shocked by Ollie's popularity. Now understand Hitler's takeover. (Woman, New York)
>
> I find it appalling that so much support and adulation has been bestowed on Lt. Col. North. (Man, Los Angeles)
>
> I awoke the other morning with a sense of dread. Oliver North has captivated, it seems, a very large part of this country with his patriotism, bravery and willingness to sacrifice for his principles. He is giving a whole new credibility to machismo. (Woman, Philadelphia)
>
> Obvious how Hitler gained power. A few Ollie Norths would suffice. (Woman, Birmingham, Ala.)
>
> I am sick that my fellow citizens think he is a hero. (Woman, Pasadena, Calif.)
>
> It is frightening that so many of our citizens feel "sincerity" is the highest virtue. Many of those tried at Nuremburg were very "sincere." (Man, Plainfield, Conn.)
>
> Hearing Oliver North described as hero and super-patriot, reading reports of a massive groundswell of public support, it has become chilling. (Man, Seattle)
>
> To have the nightly news tell me each night that the American public admires North and thinks he is a hero angers me. (Woman, Yucalpa, Calif.)

North's "popularity" made many viewers fear that entertainment and marketing values had undermined principles instilled by civics lessons and nurtured by parents, teachers, and clergymen, leaving nothing to protect democracy. "I am appalled that we have not taught the lessons of a democratic government well enough," wrote a woman: "The public has been taken in by an image on the television screen." Olliemania was "a terrible shock" to a woman in Muskegon, Michigan, who consoled herself with the thought that North's admirers were "those who are not clear about the normal correct processes of government."

Denied a voice by journalists and politicians and fearing isolation from fellow citizens, many viewers felt that the survival of democracy required them to claim their right to be heard as individuals and as citizens. "All of us are at fault, including the American public," wrote a woman, "because of its apathy." North's testimony "opened the eyes of a sleeping . . . America" (Westland, Mich.) and "single-handedly awakened the dozing patriots" (Coral Springs, Fla.). "The recent televised hearings have reawakened in me" a commitment first born in Vietnam to prevent American military interventions abroad, wrote a man from Albany, California. "Save us from apathy," added a woman from Oklahoma. "I sat quietly and watched Viet Nam develop into a disaster in the 1960s," wrote a man from Fort Worth: "I don't intend to do that again." "I have stood aside from politics," confessed a man from Stigler, Oklahoma, who concluded that "too many of us have stood aside, hopefully not too long." "This old lady" will "get a little more active in looking after the welfare of my country," promised another writer. Concluding from the hearings that "the government IS the citizenry," a Milwaukeean pledged that "I personally have realized my responsibility of citizen participation." A woman in Chicago concluded that she could no longer leave political participation to politicians: "I am now fully aware that one must always fight for freedom."

"Never before have I felt so compelled to express myself—and so forcefully—to a congressman," wrote a woman from Riviera Beach, Florida, to Hamilton. Americans reached for telephones and paper. "After watching proceedings on T.V. for the past 2 weeks, I feel compelled to tell you my view of your actions," a woman wrote Hamilton from Murray, Kentucky. When interpreters and politicians professed to know what they were thinking without asking them, Americans claimed the right to speak for themselves. "Because no one has asked me my opinion I am volunteering it," proclaimed a woman from San Francisco. "Please help me with this identity crisis I feel today as an American," a couple from Wellston, Ohio, signed a letter to Hamilton: "I need to know my voice can be heard." Citizens needed to be heard.

They felt the crisis with rare urgency as they asserted their authority as democracy's reserve army:

> In the twenty-nine years that I have been a registered voter, I have never written to my elected officials. We elect you and depend on your wisdom to direct your actions when you go to Washington. If you do not hear from us, you certainly cannot know what our desires are. . . . I refuse to remain silent any longer. (Man, Chickasha, Okla.)

> I never write letters (political), but if people like me don't let you know that we recognize right from wrong, then we deserve what's happening. (Man, Fort Lee, N.J.)

This letter is unique for most of us. We are ordinarily content to rely upon the collective judgment of Congress to see, and do, what is best for our country. We rise to speak now. (Man, Seattle)

As one of the usually silent majority, I want to . . . (Man, Stafford, Va.)

Many of us have been the "silent ones," too busy trying to leave this a better world, to let our leaders know how we feel. . . . I have felt too much in awe of the "learned VIP's" in our country to express myself. (Woman, Epsom, N.H.)

They wanted legislators to know that they, as individual American citizens, resented both the arrogance and the inaccuracy of the story of Olliemania as a description of what Americans thought. They formulated their conclusions about Olliemania:

So much fuss has been made about our new American hero, Oliver North, that I wish to put in an opposite view. Far from being a hero, I think he is a farcical patriot, vainglorious and dangerous! (Woman, Grapeview, Wash.)

This is no yellow telegram, but it is a way of saying that not all the people out here in the boon-docks are stark-raving stupid. (Woman)

I cannot arrange a flood of messages, but I can lift my voice to endorse the democratic process, and my prayer that it shall return to the government of the people. (Methodist preacher, Chicago)

Please consider this postcard to be a "poor person's telegram." I would like to let you know that I do *not* support Lt. Col. Oliver North. (Man, Galveston, Tex.)

Many in this country see Oliver North as a Hero—a lying hero, yet a real hero. I want to let it be known that many of us see him as a killer of innocent men, women, and children. (Man, Los Angeles)

I don't send telegrams but I feel just as strongly against Oliver North as the people who wired. (Woman, Pacific Palisades, Calif.)

To write Hamilton was to claim one's responsibilities as a citizen, one's participation in the community, and one's ownership of government in a democracy. And writers developed their conception of citizenship out of the trust they felt toward people around them, trust they generalized into bonds to connect themselves to strangers they knew only as fellow citizens. To be a citizen was to defend these bonds of trust against threats like Olliemania that corroded trust at its core.

A panoramic view of the historic Senate Caucus Room, site of the Iran-Contra hearings as well as earlier nationally televised congressional hearings, including the Army–McCarthy hearings of 1954, the Senate Watergate Committee hearings in 1973–74, and the Clarence Thomas confirmation hearings of 1991. All four hearings sparked national popular debates. (Courtesy: Senate Historical Office)

Oliver North testifying. (Courtesy: Senate Historical Office)

During a break in the hearings Co-Chairs Senator Daniel Inouye (D-Hawaii) and Representative Lee Hamilton (D-Ind.) confer with Senator George Mitchell (D-Maine) and Representative Peter Rodino (D-N.J.) and with chief attorneys, Arthur Limon for the Senate committee and John W. Nields for the House committee. Staff members surround them. (Courtesy: Senate Historical Office)

Lt. Col. Oliver North testifies before the joint congressional Iran-Contra investigating committees with the ever-present media between him and the legislators. (Courtesy: Senate Historical Office)

Two views of Representative Lee Hamilton (D-Ind.). (Top): Being briefed on an issue by two aides (with backs to camera); (bottom): posed listening to a constituent, with the Capitol in the background. The photographs appeared in the 15 March 1986 edition of the *Dubois County Herald* (Jasper, Ind.), accompanying a feature article on the congressman who represented its readers. (Photographs by Steve Mellon, reprinted by permission of the Herald)

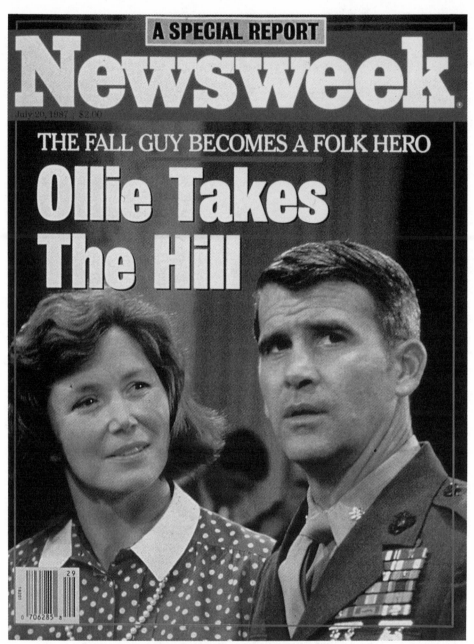

A SPECIAL REPORT

Newsweek

July 20, 1987 / $2.00

THE FALL GUY BECOMES A FOLK HERO

Ollie Takes The Hill

The basic theme of "Olliemania"—"The Fall Guy Becomes a Folk Hero"—was emblazoned on Newsweek's cover of 20 July 1987. The illustration depicts two props of the story: his Marine medals and his wife Betsy. (Photograph © 1987, Newsweek, Inc. All rights reserved. Reprinted by Permission)

Chicago Tribune cartoonist Dick Locher depicts "Olliemania" at its peak as an irresistible attraction to journalists, Democrats, and others in "Magnetic North" (11 July 1987). Two months later, Jeff Mac-Nelly depicted "Olliemania" in "Garbage Barge II" (15 September 1987). The reference is to a barge, the *Mobro*, loaded with garbage that was denied permission to land and off-load its increasingly rancid cargo by six states and three countries. The barge became a national symbol of unwanted garbage. (Both: Reprinted by permission of Tribune Media Services)

A vivid and controversial illustration of "popular" enthusiasm for North was a stack of orchestrated telegrams that North and his lawyers displayed to reporters to make their case that North was a folk "hero" to most Americans. (UPI/Bettmann)

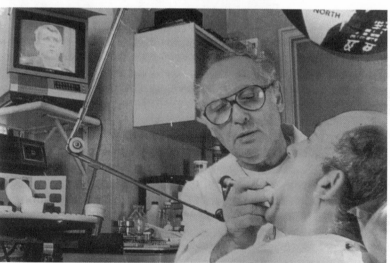

The New York Times and *Time* magazine hired different photographers to take a picture showing a patient watching Oliver North's testimony while a dentist works on his teeth.

Journalists copied each other in telling the "Olliemania" story. In these front-page illustrations two different newspapers depicted the omnipresence of Oliver North in nearly identical images. Other variations appeared in the *New Orleans Times-Picayne* and *The New York Times*. (Top: Photograph by Bill Greene, reproduced with permission of the Boston Globe; bottom: reproduced with permission of *The Courier-Journal*)

"I LIKE THAT OLLIE NORTH CROWD— THEY CARE ENOUGH ABOUT DEMOCRACY IN NICARAGUA THAT THEY'RE WILLING TO KICK THE HELL OUT OF IT IN THE U.S."

—from *Herblock At Large* (Pantheon Books, 1987)

Four

✸ ✸ ✸ ✸ ✸ ✸ ✸ ✸ ✸ ✸ ✸

Turning the Intimate into the Public

THE PARTICIPATORY ACT OF

WRITING A CONGRESSMAN

On the afternoon of July 14, 1987, seventeen people gathered around a television set in a living room in Hulbert, Oklahoma, watching Indiana Congressman Lee Hamilton explain to Lt. Col. Oliver North that a free government could not survive on lies and lawbreaking by public officials. When Hamilton concluded, all seventeen spontaneously rose to their feet and applauded. "We were so proud of you . . . a true American," one of them wrote Hamilton, reporting that the people in her living room spoke "many, many other words for you of love and respect. Our prayers will continue for the Good Lord to give you Courage and Health." At the same moment about a thousand miles away, at Madeira Beach, Florida, a man reported to Hamilton that "I had just walked into the room when you were confronting Lt. Col. North. Your attitude needed correcting, but I was not there, and consequently you were not chastised, as you should have been." He fired off his rebuke by mail.

The act of participation began with an impulse to reach out to a particular congressman. Writers began with what they wanted letters to be and do, not with what they wanted to say. Because writers wanted the letters to draw congressmen into their intimate worlds, we need to explore how they imagined that drawing a legislator into a face-to-face relationship would help them fulfill their duties as citizens of the nation.

Viewers most often wanted to join conversations when they heard people say things they believed or things that invited them to volunteer their own experience (see table 1). Because they often waited until they heard themselves represented, Americans with different points of view entered the hearings at different times. For example, a major shift in viewpoints that accom-

Table 1 Major Appeal of Hearings to Letter Writers

Appeal	Hamilton Supporters (%)	Hamilton Critics (%)
Opportunity to hear new information and viewpoints	25	20
Opportunity to hear own viewpoint represented	68	63
Opportunity to volunteer own information and opinion	67	70
N	60	60

Note: Some writers referred to more than one appeal.

Table 2 Log of Phone Calls to Senate Select Committee

Position	7/7	7/8	7/9	7/10	7/13	7/14	7/15	7/16	7/17	7/20
Pro-North	687	705	765	700	288	518	234	102	120	53
Anti-North	196	238	299	664	564	472	305	176	196	114

Note: I am indebted to Laura Ison for making available the telephone, telegram, and correspondence logs of the Senate Select Committee.

panied North's testimony was matched by a major shift in the perspectives of the people writing to the Senate Select Committee. From the beginning of North's testimony on July 7 until the afternoon of July 10, North answered attorneys' questions and gave speeches defending his activities. His admirers responded. On Friday afternoon, July 10, legislators began to question his story. On Monday, July 13, viewers heard particularly eloquent responses from George Mitchell, Paul Sarbanes, and Jack Brooks, and on July 14 from Louis Stokes, Lee Hamilton, and Daniel Inouye. Many critics of North did not participate until they heard voices they agreed with. The log of telephone calls to the Senate Select Committee illustrates how the ebb and flow of the hearings provided different occasions for different Americans to participate (see table 2).

George Mitchell received an "immediate and overwhelming[ly]" positive outpouring when he upbraided Oliver North. Jack Brooks received an equally positive response when he aggressively questioned Elliott Abrams about the State Department official's arrogance and lies to Congress.[1] The shift the committee saw was not in the opinion of "America," but in the times when particular people found a point of access, a chance to feel that they were represented and included in the conversation.

Finding a time to participate was usually intertwined with finding a person toward whom they developed the intense feelings they had about the people that mattered to them. Viewers wrote, not to the cautious legislators who seemed reluctant to say what they thought, but to those who took strong positions at the farthest ends of the ideological spectrum. The most

Table 3 Major Themes in Letters to Hamilton

Theme	Number	Percentage of Total
Oliver North		12.4
Pro–Oliver North	109	5.5
Anti–Oliver North	137	6.9
Hearings/Investigation		25.3
Stop/limit investigation	294	14.8
Like investigation as is	106	5.5
Expand investigation	98	5.0
Lee Hamilton		51.5
Pro–Lee Hamilton	685	34.6
Anti–Lee Hamilton	334	16.9
Other	216	10.9
N	1,979	

Note: The letters were randomly selected from the twenty-three boxes in which House Select Committee staffers stored incoming correspondence (after removing most letters from Indiana). Since staffers placed the letters in thirteen "procommittee" and ten "anticommittee" boxes I selected the thirteen boxes to examine for this sample in the same proportion as "pro" and "anti" sentiments were represented in the total volume of incoming correspondence. See the Note on Sources and Method.

outspoken member of the committees, Jack Brooks, received more mail than any other individual member. In fact, he received five times as many communications as the reserved and moderate William Broomfield. Brooks was sent 15,876 letters and telegrams, while Broomfield was sent fewer than 3,000.[2]

Viewers participated in the hearings, as in real life, not so much *in* a topic as *with* a person. In much the same way that citizens were more likely to vote in elections when a candidate stirred their feelings and embodied their dreams, viewers wrote letters more as personal communications to individuals whom they wanted to engage in conversation than as commentary on the details or issues or on the acting performances. The most frequent kind of message in the letters to Hamilton was a comment on Hamilton, not on the investigation or on Oliver North (see table 3).

The basic theme in the 7,747 letters to Republican Senator William Cohen of Maine followed a strikingly similar pattern.[3] By far the most frequent single message was to encourage the legislator to whom citizens addressed their letters. Praise for the legislator was the major theme of 36.1 percent of the letters to Cohen and 34.6 percent of those to Hamilton. Both legislators received five times more letters whose basic theme was to support them than letters that supported North. (Pro-North letters accounted for 6.9 percent of letters to Cohen, 5.5 percent of those to Hamilton.) Americans wrote twice as often to tell a legislator how they reacted to something he had said than to comment on the hearings in general.

Participation and membership in the community exist, after all, not as geographical or legal facts but as a composite of relationships with others. In everyday life people look to others to be lovers, mentors, friends, rivals, champions, and they try to deepen their relationships to meet these needs. They develop feelings about their larger community from the trust and pride, shame and guilt, hope and fear, they feel in their personal relationships with particular individuals. It is thorough these relationships that people experience and interpret the things that matter to them. And as in everyday life, during the hearings, in a time when they felt most alone, viewers looked for someone with whom they could discuss their needs and with whom they could reaffirm their deepest values: they looked for someone they could trust. When they miraculously found such people on the other side of the television screen, they embraced them as friends. Their feelings toward community emerged through their bond with a representative. "Our faith in our government is in direct proportion to our faith in you," a woman wrote Hamilton.

Writers explained that their feelings toward the nation depended on the personal bond they were communicating to the legislator. They had chosen to write to this particular person because he had said or done something that had deepened or awakened the writer's sense of feeling part of the nation's future. By their diagnoses of issues, for example, legislators helped viewers to clarify the larger issues and contexts that had left them feeling uneasy. At stake in the letters, most writers explained, were powerful feelings toward the wider whole that they hoped to strengthen by expressing them to the most accessible or sympathetic participant at the hearings. "I have had many sleepless nights" and am "very disturbed and distressed by the situation," a woman from Springfield, Missouri, explained to Hamilton as she told him that he was "holding the key" that would enable "the American people . . . to be proud of their leaders again. Please open the door." They felt compelled to write Hamilton because they felt deep threats to "my great faith and trust and enthusiasm for our system of government" (woman, San Leandro, Calif.) and "my confidence in U.S. Government" (man, McLean, Va.)

With their letters —by writing to the individual they saw within the congressman—they drew legislators into their intimate worlds. They introduced themselves as they would to someone they had met in real life: "It was a wonderful experience for me to meet you on the TV," a woman wrote Hamilton from Westfield, New Jersey. "It has been good to come to know you on C-SPAN," echoed a man from Portland, Oregon. A retired naval officer hoped to engage Hamilton in a conversation about military strategy: "So, Lee, you be up front with me all the way. . . . Now, what do you say? Dare you tell the *full* truth to just one American?" Soon after the hearings ended a woman from Ramsey, New Jersey, wrote Congressman Jack Brooks that "I watched every minute of the hearings, and must tell you, I miss my time with you each day." From Vienna, Virginia, a man extended his hand to Hamilton as though to an old friend: "Anyway, thanks for being such a nice guy and I'm glad you're there."

As they reached to establish a relationship with Hamilton, many citizens looked for some personal connection or experience. "My mother was a Hamilton," explained a woman from South Jersey, New Jersey. "The name Hamilton is something else!" exclaimed a woman from Sanford, Florida: "Beautiful it is and I married it." A man from Bolton, Massachusetts, drew closer to Hamilton by remembering a common bond: "I must exclaim my delight at discovering you are a son of Frank Hamilton, who was my father's most cherished personal friend. My father was a very reserved, strong man; I have never forgotten that he shed tears on learning of your father's death." Two Methodist women found in Hamilton's religious affiliation a basis for mutual trust. Still others found common ground in links to Indiana, Hamilton's home state. "We are connected," a family from Milwaukee telegraphed Hamilton, because "our sons attended Earlham College in Richmond, Indiana." A woman from Carmel, Indiana, acknowledged a more direct link "as someone who has voted for you in the past." Similarly, a Marine veteran from Longview, Texas, recalled to Oliver North a personal experience that he hoped would deepen their bond: "My wife has also bought leotards at Parklane for our daughter." Writers remembered a rich variety of associations that they hoped would draw them closer to the legislators and witnesses to whom they addressed their concerns.

By the ways they closed their letters, writers expressed the range of ways they wanted to engage Hamilton:

> With love, congratulations, and best wishes. (Family, Astoria, N.Y.)
>
> Best wishes to you and your family. I honor your parents for the honesty they must have modeled. (Woman, San Francisco)
>
> Thank you for hearing my voice, and I will continue to be in touch as the scandal continues to unfold. (Clergyman, Philadelphia)
>
> You made my vacation. (Woman, Long Beach)
>
> Good night and thank you for listening. (Man, Midland, Mich.)
>
> Your new friends. (Husband and wife, Madison, Wisc.)
>
> Hey, need any more help just call me. (Man, Sebastian, Fla.)
>
> God bless you. (Woman, Los Angeles)
>
> Thanks for your quiet and intellectual heroism. You're a *real* man. (Man, Palos Verdes Estates, Calif.)
>
> I hope this finds you in good health and spirits and your family also. (Man, New York)
>
> I'm as sincere as I know how to be. (Woman)

When you are passing out shame reserve some for yourself. (Man, Orlando, Fla.)

May this word of appreciation and encouragement solidify the best that is in you, and inspire you to continue on bravely. (Man, Geneva, N.Y.)

We thank you with all our hearts. (Husband and wife, Blooming Grove, N.Y.)

"Many of us are seeking re-assurance, sir, that it is not all a fix," concluded a man who was "humbly requesting something a little more specific than a form reply letter." Fearful that the hearings might at any point dissolve into one of the familiar staged "fixes" of politicians and salesmen, writers also began to hope that their new relationship with a legislator would become a place for real conversation. They wrote congressmen as though they were new friends from whom they needed advice. "I would . . . like to ask you what one can do to prevent something like this from happening again. To make things better," wrote a woman from Philadelphia, who quickly added that she wanted more from Hamilton than the stock answer: "Don't tell me to vote, I always do." "May I hear from you concerning my question?" asked a man from Kimball, Nebraska. "Please be gentleman enough to completely answer my questions," began a man from Abilene, Texas. By daring to request a personal reply, writers tried to make the conversation one between citizens, shaped by the terms of everyday life. Because the right to demand an answer is perhaps, as Milan Kundera observed, the most peremptory and far-reaching source of power in societies grounded in mass media,[4] these writers were imagining a forum where citizens and representatives were equal participants.

By letters and phone calls Americans offered everything from encouragement to criticism, from help to threats, from advice about personal appearance to advice about constitutional law. "I only wish I could be on your panel and ask questions," volunteered a woman from Kirkland, Washington. They recommended things to read. Others, like a retired intelligence officer from South Carolina, offered to meet with Hamilton and Inouye "on Monday afternoon, July 29th. I suggest you also invite Dick Helms." A lawyer from San Antonio suggested a question that he was confident would compel North and Poindexter to reveal the truth. A man from Ridgecrest, California, outlined techniques of detective work that began with checking with White House "cooks, cleaners and the like" who "may have overheard conversations" and ended: "Digging in the garbage may seem farfetched, but it springs to mind when thinking of this crowd." A man from New York believed that the truth would only come out if Hamilton would "call the President to testify. Even let him bring Nancy to whisper in his ear." To one woman the only hope for Hamilton was to "get down on your knees and pray, asking the Lord to come in and take over your life."

Because relationships with real people shaped feelings toward the nation, writers believed that the most important things they could communicate were their needs and feelings. The quality of the legislator's response—and therefore of the relationship—depended on the writer's ability to express precisely the needs that prompted the letter. With the shape and intensity of their participation as citizens and patriots at stake, writers conveyed their feelings toward congressmen with at least as much urgency as they would in relationships with the people around them. "I need to express my feelings to you," began a woman from Decatur, Georgia, to Hamilton. "You listen now Mr. Hamilton!" demanded a man from Chattanooga. A woman from Glendale, California, apologized to Hamilton for calling him "utterly disgraceful," "but I had to express my feeling." The compulsion was overwhelming. "I'm sure these thoughts will not 'shake you up,'" wrote a woman from Adamsville, Alabama, "but I feel better that I have this off my chest." In East Dundee, Illinois, a woman hoped that the passage of time would temper compulsion with clarity: "I have waited 24 hours before writing this letter to allow myself time to get my feelings under control."

Because their relationship with the recipient could only be as fulfilling as the needs that person could hear, writers conveyed their feelings with the intensity they ordinarily reserved for their most intimate relationships. Trust and candor between people was, after all, both the central issue of the hearings and the personal need viewers wanted most to convey in the letters. The intimacy with which they expressed their feelings toward legislators shaped the intensity of their confidence in their fellow citizens and government alike. Writers sent messages of love as well as anger. "Bless you and all whom you love. A heartful of love from me," was the entire letter sent by a woman from Tucson. "You are magnificent and a joy to behold!" exclaimed a woman from San Francisco. Writers expressed anger with equal candor. "I must say you make me sick," a man from Hattiesburg, Mississippi, told Hamilton. "We are ready to explode in anger," began a couple from Lancaster, California. "The Lord rebuke you!" was the sole message from a woman in Eugene, Oregon. A viewer from Hampton, Virginia, was "so angry I can't write or spell. You are one devil and a true S.O.B." "If I could only meet you and some of the others on the panel I'd rip you up one side and down the other and give you a good dressing down," threatened a woman from Sun City, Arizona. Sometimes they surprised even themselves with the intensity of their feelings. "I am so mad as I write this. Why do I have to write this or feel compelled to do so?" seethed a correspondent from California. The need for Hamilton to know the feeling behind a letter was so great that a writer in Sacramento scrawled "G-r-r-r" on the outside of the envelope in case the congressman got no further.

Many writers explained that the letter was the culmination of a longer relationship in which the legislator had already affected the citizen's feelings toward the nation. A "housewife" confided to Hamilton that it "took me quite a while to get over my depression" from hearing one of his speeches early in the hearings. "I got over my 'depression' and am not in awe of your speeches anymore," she said, after she watched a newsclip that showed Hamilton riding through a small Indiana town, "waving an American flag back and forth and smiling broadly to a crowd that just wasn't there" while, in the foreground, a woman and her little girl were "looking back in amazement with bewildered looks on their faces." Several others had even more actively shaped an earlier relationship with Hamilton. "I am praying you out of office along with Inouye," reported a woman from Downey, California. A viewer in Texas reported that "I have sentenced you to be shredded in effigy. The sentence was carried out on 8–6–87."

Writers conveyed the same range of feelings to congressmen that they expressed in their intimate worlds. In a random sample of eight hundred letters to the House Select Committee, they described fifty-seven different feelings. To construct patterns among those feelings is to miss much of the originality, precision, and urgency that each writer used to convey each feeling, but a simple list conveys the range of needs writers hoped to meet in writing congressmen (see table 4).

By their letters writers insisted that the active relationships of everyday life provided the surest guides to interpreting and participating in the public forum. Instead of accepting the usual experience of having their needs ignored, reduced to vacuity by journalists, condescended to by experts, diverted by entertainers, manipulated by salesmen, they believed that this was a time to explain those needs fully. Viewing the relationship as the means to deepen democratic confidence, writers monitored it closely. "It is important for me to understand why you in your final speech berated and tried to condemn Col. North. . . . I would like very much to hear" the reasons, wrote a woman from Rogue River, Oregon.

Because with those around them they breathed life into precepts with details and personalities, many writers reacted to controversies—between Hamilton and North, for example—not as contests over ideologies but as human relationships that should be guided by the ways people wanted to be treated in their own lives. Enclosing a picture of North, a woman from Montebello, California, urged Hamilton: "Please listen and help him instead of tearing him apart limb by limb. This could be your son or grandson. Please look at the picture!" "Do you think you are above the rule of decency and being a responsible person?" demanded a woman from Heber Springs, Arkansas, who thought Hamilton should "hang your head and apologize and ask the Lord to forgive you." The conviction that one should be treated as one treated others led many writers to empathize with principals in the hearings. A man from Berryville, Virginia, "'sweated' every question right along with Col North for all of us have fibbed." "As YOU judged Col. North, do remember that YOU will be JUDGED by myself and others,"

Table 4 Feelings Expressed in Letters to Hamilton

Feeling	Number of Letters
Gratitude and appreciation	**217**
Thanks	151
Appreciation	39
Gratitude	27
Admiration	**112**
Commend	30
Congratulation	23
Support	21
Admiration	14
Applause	13
Inspiration	6
Compliment	5
Regret, shock, and disgust	**110**
Appalled	23
Sickened	19
Disgust	17
Disturbed	14
Concern	8
Shock	7
Frustrated	6
Distress	5
Dismay	4
Alarm	3
Troubled	1
Deplore	1
Perturbed	1
Repulsion	1
Anger	**59**
Outrage	19
Anger	18
Resentment	9
Insult	3
Offense	2
Contempt	2
Irritation	2
Displeasure	2
Incensed	1
Disapproval	1
Confidence and hope	**36**
Hope	21
Confidence	5
Faith	3
Reassurance	2
Relief	2
Comfort	1
Encouragement	1
Heartened	1

(continued)

73

Table 4 *continued*

Feeling	Number of Letters
Shame	**35**
Shame	19
Disgrace	13
Embarrassment	3
Fear	**26**
Fear	21
Terror	3
Scared	2
Sadness	**23**
Sadness	11
Disappointment	9
Grief	2
Disheartened	1
N (letters)	800

wrote a woman from Seattle, who added: "I KNOW your closet is not pure."

Writers encouraged legislators to talk as real people did rather than posture for faceless audiences. Infuriated by grandstanding aimed to compress individuals into a mass, many viewers wanted legislators to talk and listen with the same directness that people did in everyday life. They wanted legislators to take risks in saying what they believed and responsibility for moving the investigation beyond partisan point-making and toward solutions in which individuals would be accountable for their deeds. When they saw politicians pull punches out of fear of Olliemania, they were appalled. They cheered Hamilton for speaking with candor. Many even equated such candor with courage. "You displayed true courage in your refusal to kow-tow to misplaced hero worship," thought a man in Fort Worth. "Thank you for not being intimidated by the silky rhetoric—and the support it engendered on the part of the American public," a couple praised Hamilton from San Mateo, California. Because feelings about democracy depended on relationships with letter recipients, some found Hamilton's speech to North "so refreshing after listening to others sink below tide of public opinion," in the words of a couple. In one woman's ideal community people would tend their relationships with each other, instead of staging performances aimed at moving common denominators to win an election: "I feel the United States should be like a family," she wrote. And a woman in High Point, North Carolina, provided an example of how she wanted participants to relate to each other:

> So, let me get this thing started. I apologize to Mr. Liman for having felt the way I did. I *deeply* apologize for the squirt gun remarks. I sincerely apologize

Table 5 Qualitites That Writers Noted in Hamilton

Quality	Hamilton Supporters (%)	Hamilton Critics (%)
Whether Hamilton's views agreed with the writers	70	63
Hamilton's qualities of personality and character	25	32
Hamilton's appeal to faceless audience of "Americans" or "public"	8	12
N	60	60

Note: Some writers referred to more than one quality.

for having thought most Democrats were unreasonable. I honestly *mean* all this. OK. Now it's your turn.

The issue at the core of popular participation was whether the trust that people sought in their personal relationships could become the kind of bond they felt with citizens they did not know and, through them, with their nation and government. To help them turn personal trust into public trust and public trust into democratic hope, citizens needed someone they could trust to carry their vision into government. During the hearings, Americans were thrilled to find representatives who spoke for their distinctive worlds instead of to common denominators. They needed these people to think as they did, to have access to government, and to fight courageously for their views. By their letters they tried to draw these people into their personal worlds. They offered their newfound champions encouragement, advice, and information just as they did to people around them. While a few citizens wrote to criticize, most wrote to praise a legislator for defending values they cherished. Over two-thirds of the communications to conservative Republicans Jim Courter and William Broomfield came from viewers who agreed with them. Over four-fifths of the mail received by liberal Democrats George Mitchell and Louis Stokes came from their supporters.[5] Because they saw legislators as their champions, citizens wrote Hamilton first to comment on whether he reflected their views, secondarily to comment on his personality or character, and only marginally to comment on his mass appeal (see table 5).

Citizens looked to their champions to protect them from dangers that originated in military threats from abroad or from lawbreaking public officials at home because individual citizens could not protect themselves against these threats. Citizens strengthened their bonds with representatives by providing information, encouragement, and advice that the representative needed to champion their shared values in public. "We hold YOU responsible" to prevent the outbreak of war, a couple wrote Hamilton from Santa Cruz, California. Other writers explained to Hamilton that "we count on you to continue the work of trying to restore the Constitution to some semblance of health" (Mashpee, Mass.) and were "counting on you to . . . protect the integrity of our constitutional system" (San Francisco). A woman from Newton Center, Massachusetts, explained why Americans needed champions like Hamilton:

> Some of us still remember having been taught that "eternal vigilance is the price of freedom." But, regretfully, most of us who believe this have neither the skill nor the energy actively to defend our freedom against those who threaten it. We are particularly helpless against the charismatic Norths, the well-spoken Poindexters, and the manipulative Caseys, those totalitarian patriots who would destroy our democracy in order to save it. I therefore must express my deepest thanks to you [for conducting the hearings].

To other writers it was Hamilton's "job to see that the American people are protected" against communism (La Grange, Ill.), to "protect us and protect our borders" (Sierra Madre, Calif.), and "to defend me and my family" from foreign attack. Their responsibility to defend basic values compelled citizens to express democratic confidence by strengthening relationships with representatives.

By encouraging representatives to uphold basic values, citizens believed they were fulfilling their duty to create strong participatory bonds in which legislators used their access to government to champion the things that mattered most to a writer. Citizens found many ways to encourage representatives to expose, punish, and prevent threats to cherished values. Representatives needed to be told by individual citizens that they were doing something authentically important, defending important positions in a crucial public debate, not just something that would sell or amuse faceless audiences. Viewers combined praise for congressmen with faith in the relationship that connected citizen with representative as the means to connect private with public and to advance their shared values.

> Keep up the good work. The Constitution is worth the effort. (Woman, Bayhead, N.J.)
>
> Thank you for defending my rights and our Constitution. (Husband and wife, Atlantic Beach, Fla.)
>
> You are doing an excellent job. Stick with it and we might still have a Constitution in the next 100 years. (Man, Jacksonville, Fla.)
>
> Thank you for keeping our country safe. (Woman)
>
> [Your work] gives me a great sense of security that the Democratic process will continue to function and thrive, despite the bureaucrats. (Woman, New York)

By defending their values at the hearings their champion encouraged citizens to feel connected once again to each other and to government. "I was beginning to feel very much alone until your brilliant summation," a man from Los Angeles wired Hamilton. Instead of looking for and appealing to low common denominators, a champion represented—literally represented—citizens' deepest convictions about citizenship and democracy. Once again they felt democratic pride and hope as they heard their values affirmed in public.

> You said so eloquently what has been in my heart. (Woman, Pasadena)
>
> You spoke for us today. (Husband and wife, Los Angeles)
>
> You told [North] what I have been yelling at him throughout the testimony. He could not hear me. He did hear you. I only hope he listened. (Woman)
>
> Even now, as I remember your words, tears come to my eyes. I had felt so alone in my thoughts on this grave affair, and then you, in such a remarkable and reasonable and courageous way, gave voice to my thoughts. (Woman, Oklahoma City)
>
> Your eloquent words precisely expressed our feelings. (Husband and wife, New York)
>
> There were [many] statements which I applauded. (I often inter-act with TV shows.) I am very glad you were there and very happy to hear in public what I have been saying in the privacy of my home. (Woman, Citrus Heights, Calif.)
>
> Your eloquent concluding remarks reflect our feelings. (Husband and wife, Bonner Springs, Ark.)
>
> Your speech as well as Senator Inouye's today were marvelous! I would have got up and waved a flag but I was taking oxygen and I don't have a flag. (Woman, Chickasha, Okla.)

By expressing what the writers thought, their champion reconnected them with the traditions that mattered most to them. The thrill at hearing their thoughts come through the voice of a defender they had brought into their intimate worlds—the voice of a fellow citizen—was the thrill of renewed confidence in the community. "My soul was aching (I suppose it was at the seeming demise of America) and your words healed the hurt," a woman from Eugene, Oregon, thanked Hamilton. Participation in personal relationships became the essence of participation in politics. With newfound feelings of pride in their community, pride expressed as gratitude for what a member of their community did at just the moment they feared they shared nothing with others, writers conveyed a sense of democratic hope that went much deeper than the minimal bonds they usually felt with politicians. The thrill of hearing his values proclaimed in public by George Mitchell transformed one viewer so fully that he decided, for the first time in the twenty-three years since he had left Canada to settle in the United States, he would become an American citizen. The act of private encouragement to their champion, an act that emerged naturally from everyday life, became the means by which they expressed the pride of participation, the trust in democracy. "When I hear Lt. Col. North referred to as a hero, I fear for the future of our great nation," a woman wrote Hamilton. She overcame this fear and felt renewed hope by calling his office, praising his speech, and asking for and rereading the text. The strengthened bond between citizens and legislators transformed viewers into active participants:

> Your closing statement today made me more proud of being an American than I've ever been in my life. (Santa Barbara)

> Your closing remarks re-instilled in me a great and proud feeling of patriotism that I have not felt in a long time. (Man, Prescott, Ariz.)

> I stand straighter as an American after listening to you. (Woman, Portland, Oreg.)

> Today you made me and my family proud to be Americans living under the rule of law in the United States of America. (Man, Riverdale, N.Y.)

> Thanks for raising our morale as we watch you and hang on your every word. (Woman, Williamstown, Mass.)

> Your closing statements today . . . brought tears to my eyes and pride in being an American. (Woman, El Cerrito, Calif.)

> You made me proud to be an American, something I've had trouble with in recent months. (Man, New York)

> The comments that you made yesterday gave me back my faith in my country and gave me some hope for the future of the United States. (Woman, Albany, Calif.)

> Your closing remarks at the end of Col. North's testimony made me cry and very proud to be An American. (Man, San Francisco)

> It is difficult for me to exaggerate the relief and exhilaration I experienced listening to your two summations. [You] re-establish[ed] the American people's faith in our form of government. (Woman, Kensington, Calif.)

> What a wonderful thing you have done for our country. . . . [You] gave us confidence in our Government again. (Woman, Fresno, Calif.)

Their champion's power to restore confidence in democracy lay in his identity as a fellow participant in that democracy, and citizens proudly drew the representative into their lives. They told—and in some cases showed—their families and friends how their champion was protecting their worlds. "Everyone who walks into my house is treated to" a videotape showing of Hamilton's remarks to North, reported a woman who taped them. A woman in Chatham, New Jersey, told Hamilton that she had "quoted your statement on at least five occasions" to friends. "I have sent copies of your remarks . . . to friends and teachers alike, and especially young people," a man from Erie, Pennsylvania, wrote Hamilton. And in Sherman Oaks, California, a man taped Hamilton's remarks and "saved them for my children to watch." In another household a family read and reread Hamilton's major speeches during the hearings. "Unforgettable," wrote a correspondent: "My son says they make history."

Once writers had imagined letters as bonds between them and their representatives, as means for making a legislator part of their everyday relationships, they faced the more formidable task of getting legislators to see them as individuals and hear their particular messages: the relationship would now have to evolve from one of encouragement given and accepted to one of genuine conversation. In order that legislators might actually hear their experiences and respond to their needs, writers experimented with ways to be seen and heard as individuals by the people who read their letters. As they sought to reconcile the desire to be heard as individuals with the need to be recognized, writers illustrated the tremendously diverse faces and voices of citizens as they watched the same story unfold on television.

Five

. . . .

Choosing a Voice and
Making It Count

The challenge of writing a congressman was to figure out where to be seen and how to be heard. In order to be seen and heard many writers believed that they had to make themselves familiar enough to be recognized. They imagined that their letters would have to overcome two barriers if they were to be heard by legislators and their staffs. First, the letter would arrive in the congressman's office with thousands of others and would receive only cursory attention. Second, the reader of the letter would be a stranger whom the writer had only met through television. The reader would want to know whether the writer was an isolated individual or a representative of many others and perhaps whether the writer brought credentials or experiences that entitled the views expressed in the letter to special consideration. Many writers expected that recipients would solve both problems by reducing what they had written to things they could recognize and count. And yet writers wanted to strike up a serious conversation, to offer so much— encouragement, advice, questions, experience—that they tried many ways to be heard and recognized.

Citizens experimented in their letters with different ways of claiming an individual voice in which to express their unique feelings and experiences, on the one hand, while being recognized and counted as part of something larger, on the other. They struggled to adapt a vehicle of intimate communication between individuals to an arena that existed to count and aggregate opinions. Seeking to be heard in a forum where marketing managers and scholars alike assumed that collective experiences shaped the views of individuals—as yuppies or evangelical Christians or women—and thus provided the places where they could be found and appealed to, writers tried to explain that they wanted to be recognized as individuals whose views could not be predicted on the basis of larger aggregates because those views grew from their unique needs and experiences and personal relationships.

To explore how writers sought to resolve the tension between the need to report personal experience and the desire to be recognized and counted, this chapter will contrast how writers resolved that tension in two very different kinds of letters that they sent congressmen. The basic issue as they sought recognition from strangers was whether to speak as an individual or as part of an orchestrated campaign. At the one extreme they wrote unmistakably individual letters and faced the challenge of finding some larger identity by which they could be recognized. At the other extreme they submerged their individual letters in a collective effort that would impress legislators primarily with its size while abandoning the authentic voice and experience of a real person. Although they covered a continuum between writing individual communications on their own initiative and writing at the invitation of an organized group to join hundreds of others who endorsed identical words, all writers yearned to be heard as clearly as possible.

Whether this political conversation and public forum would be shaped by personal letters or by orchestrated ones was as real an issue to congressmen and their staff members who read the letters as it was to the writers. With traditions that valued "the mail" as a good place to listen to popular concerns, congressmen were as eager to hear their constituents as writers were to talk to them. Because many letters came from strangers, it was hard to tell whether a letter's sentiments were widely shared. Both congressmen and citizens knew that letter-writing campaigns were often professionally orchestrated around particular opinions so that those opinions would be recognized and counted. Congressmen valued spontaneous and original letters more highly than communications mobilized by pressure groups because an original letter was more likely to carry an authentic voice and to be representative of others who did not write.

For congressional aides who read these letters and answered the phones in the summer of 1987 the difference between wanting to be heard and wanting to be counted was very clear. They were particularly sensitive that summer to the ways pressure groups used expressions of individual opinion because the Iran-Contra hearings coincided with the largest campaign ever to mobilize public opinion toward a judicial nomination. On July 1, 1987, a week before Oliver North began his testimony, Ronald Reagan announced that he would nominate Robert Bork to the Supreme Court. By the next morning labor unions, civil rights organizations, women's groups, and other liberal lobbies had launched an all-out campaign to defeat Bork's confirmation in the Senate. Organizers insisted that individuals and groups stifle their particular concerns and only express conclusions that pollsters could identify as broad common denominators.[1] The resulting letters and phone calls

to senators' offices, aides reported, bore the classic pressure group im-
print—a brief statement that could easily be counted toward an impending
vote in the Senate.

In the case of the Iran-Contra debate, by contrast, legislators and their
aides were struck by the huge gap between the majority of communications,
which bore the diverse voices of individuals, and the minority of communications, which were the unmistakable products of pressure groups. Most
writers and callers wanted to carry on long conversations—they raised
questions, volunteered advice, shared experiences, suggested lines of investigation, and in general wrote in ways that were very hard to tabulate.

The terrible choice between expressing an opinion and making it count
was a choice between the everyday conversations of real people and the
formulas of opinion management in which pressure groups and pollsters
aggregated individuals behind a single thought. In everyday life citizens did
not express fully formed conclusions ready to be counted. Rather, they
formed and reformed ideas as they weighed different experiences as an active, sometimes incidental, accompaniment to meeting different needs with
different people. Interrupting and freezing everyday talk and asking participants to choose among alternatives that seemed pertinent only to the opinion industries simplified the terms of the debate and silenced the ways
people talked among themselves. By defining goals, expecting all members
to support those goals, providing resources that attracted politicians, pressure groups particularly narrowed and concentrated popular discussion. By
forcing the focus onto a particular moment, pollsters ignored the experience
that many people were much more eager to contribute to the discussion
than their tentative conclusions. The imperatives of aggregation interrupted, narrowed, and silenced citizens as they tried to find ways to report
their individual feelings, experiences, and perspectives, as they sought to be
heard. The price of being counted was having their voices distorted. The
price of speaking freely, individually, was not being heard.

■ The first step in seeking recognition was to identify an experience or association that was both important to the writer and recognizable to others.
Politics, of course, had long consisted in naming the identities in which
people wanted to be heard. A man from Hattiesburg, Mississippi, thought
he could best avoid being dismissed by Hamilton as "just some nut writing
you" by embedding his voice in experiences and roles he shared with others:
"I served in the Korean War. I'm a college graduate and run a successful
small business. I am a Christian (Baptist) and teach Sunday school." To describe oneself as a secretary or African American or Republican or Chicagoan or parent was to project political claims more clearly and effectively
than citizens could if they spoke only as individuals. By the identities they

acknowledged, individuals became immediately recognizable (and perhaps countable) to others and established their authority to draw conclusions.

The starting place for selecting a voice and experiences was each individual's unique sense of who they were, a basic self-image through which that person brought integrity, coherence, and authenticity to the challenge of making sense of a new experience. The hardest part of constructing a voice was to figure out the group to identify and stand with on this occasion. Each possible group identity brought with it different answers to questions at issue in the hearings: What do we believe? Who are our friends and enemies? Where did we come from? And the difficulty of turning experiences into a collective identity was compounded because the content of a group's identity was not fixed. Members neither brought identical experiences to the group nor valued its traditions identically. The reality of attending Mass or voting Republican or raising adolescent boys or enjoying murder mysteries meant different things to different people and, in fact, different things to the same person at different times and in different places. Even so, viewers were so eager to be recognized, to have their voices count and their authority respected, that they persisted in trying to find an identity larger than their own in which to express themselves. A few writers answered the challenge by explaining themselves in several voices:

> Your candid and eloquent statements made me proud—to be a Democrat, an American, a former Hoosier, a politically active woman, and a human being. (Woman, Wellfleet, Mass.)

> As a high school English and history teacher, I pride myself on trying to be objective. . . . I am a registered Democrat; I try to study issues and personalities and vote for the person I believe will be best for the job. . . . As a Christian, I believe it is better to "love thy neighbor"; perhaps it is because that as an English teacher (a communicator), I believe that communication is very important; or perhaps it is because I have two sons (aged 23 and 21), and the thought of them going off to fight a war that we cannot possibly win, over a cause which cannot even be defined, seems ludicrous. Whatever the reason, I believe that it is important for respected individuals to present the case for the "peacemaker." Therefore, I was very pleased and emotionally moved at the speech you made on Monday. (Woman, Aztec, N.Mex., to Hamilton)

By the experiences in which they embedded their individual voices, writers identified how they wanted to be heard. Table 6 indicates the frequency with which writers of a sample of letters to Hamilton named a particular experience. When Americans named the places where they wanted to be recognized by naming the experiences through which they conveyed their individual conclusions, three-fifths chose the most intimate voices of family and friends (50.3 percent) and of firsthand experience in the military or Nicaragua (9.9 percent). Another 17.1 percent chose the infinitely malleable voices of citizenship and patriotism into which individuals could pour almost any meaning or experience as they tried to create a personal bond with a congressman. The writers were strikingly reluctant, by contrast, to use the large voices of race and ethnicity (2.1 percent) and gender (1.1 percent) and only slightly less so to use those of occupation and class (6.6 percent), religion (5.5 percent), and political partisanship (4.5 percent) that many scholars have assumed to nurture the capacity for autonomous interpretation in American culture. In making sense of the hearings writers thought, not of groups to which they could be said to belong, but of the individuals with whom they watched and discussed the story. The variety of different identities that writers selected and the preference for voices of intimacy and firsthand experience over larger ones of background or circumstance give only a limited sense of the rich individuality with which they expressed those identities. Individuals drew dramatically different conclusions from their shared experiences. Social background neither predicted nor determined the conclusions they sent Hamilton. Far from being uniform pieces of an abstract mass or interchangeable members of a social group whose collective experience had nurtured homogeneous thoughts, Americans spoke in unique voices. The identities they named might be recognizable, but the conclusions they drew were distinctly their own.

By far the most frequently heard voice grew from the most intimate experience of all, the bond that united husbands and wives. Nearly one in every four communications to Hamilton was signed jointly by husbands and wives, their common voice. They reported feelings, facts, and conclusions almost as if the writers were experiencing them as one:

> We have been watching the Iran Contra debacle and feel very pained with what we have heard so far. The speech you made . . . was the most moving speech we have heard in years. . . . If you decide to run for President we would exert all our efforts to elect you and be part of your administration. (Husband and wife and "families (9 people)")

> We agree with the enclosed editorial, and we look forward to your response, and to your *action*. (Husband and wife, Santa Cruz, Calif.)

> We compliment you and Senator Daniel Inouye on the well conducted hearings. We are amazed at Col. North and Admiral Poindexter testifying of their covert and illegal acts and yet feeling they did nothing wrong and are good patriots. We believe our big country should show leadership and help small countries. We were pleased with the testimony of Secretary of State Schultz. (Husband and wife, Ventura, Calif.)

> We just can't rest until we tell you both how very embarrassed we were for both of you this afternoon. (Husband and wife, Scottsdale, Ariz.)

Because writers most frequently identified their political views with their primary relationships, many parents and grandparents approached the hearings with deep concerns about how they would be able to provide secu-

Table 6 Experiences Named in Letters to Hamilton

Experience	Frequency	Proportion (%)
Family or household relationships	**456**	44.4
Husband and wife	255	24.8
Man and woman, living together, different last names	11	1.1
Three or more, living together, different last names	29	2.8
"My family," no further specifics	40	3.9
Voice of parenthood	70	6.8
Voice of grandparenthood	29	2.8
Voice of child- or grandchildhood	18	1.8
Voice of "housewife"	4	0.4
"Friends" and/or "neighbors"	**61**	5.9
Occupational or class identities	**68**	6.6
Colleagues and coworkers	1	0.1
"Working class" or "working people" or "union member"	4	0.4
"Common" or "ordinary" people	2	0.2
"Middle class"	4	0.4
Unemployed	2	0.2
Voice of particular occupation	55	5.3
Teacher	21	2.0
Job with expertise in hearing	8	0.8
Clergy	7	0.7
Lawyer	6	0.6
Business	4	0.4
Farmer	4	0.4
Doctor	3	0.3
Nurse	1	0.1
Secretary	1	0.1
Social identities	**108**	10.5
"Christian" or specific religious beliefs	57	5.5
Retired or senior citizen	13	1.3
Immigrant or descendant of immigrants	13	1.3
Woman	11	1.1
White/Anglo/WASP	7	0.7
College educated	6	0.6
Black	1	0.1
Particular experiences	**101**	9.9
Military service	89	8.7
Visit to Nicaragua	12	1.2
Political identities	**234**	22.8
Citizenship	175	17.1
"American"	78	7.6
"Citizen"	68	6.6
"Voter"	16	1.6
"Taxpayer"	13	1.3

(continued)

Table 6 continued

Experience	Frequency	Proportion (%)
Mass	13	1.3
"People" or "Public"	7	0.7
"Silent Majority"	6	0.6
Partisanship	46	4.5
Democrat	28	2.7
Republican	18	1.8
N (experiences)	1,028	

Note: Identities were included and tabulated when writers used a particular voice or experience to explain their interpretations, not when the identity appeared on their letterheads. There were obviously more whites or citizens or women or lawyers (to judge from the letterheads) than people who embedded their views in those particular experiences. Some writers used the authority of several experiences, and I counted each experience in such cases. When writers used adjectives to precede nouns, I only counted nouns. I counted "American citizen," the most frequent such case, as "citizen," not as "American." I excluded orchestrated form letters from the sample.

rity, autonomy, and values for their children and grandchildren. They worried first about their children's physical survival. "We have a son fourteen years old," wrote a couple from Cypress, California, "and we have no desire to have him sent off to war because someone 'blundered.'" "I am a grandmother with 14 grandchildren, 10 of whom are boys, all under 12 years of age," explained a woman from Camano Island, Washington: "I therefore shrink from any action that may affect their lives and involve them in a conflict that might snuff out their futures." The passion to shield their children from war led some writers to favor and some to oppose aid to the Nicaraguan contras. Failure to vote funds for the contras meant that "you'll be sending my two sons down there to fight a war in ten years," feared a woman from Almond, New Jersey, and "the ultimate necessity of my two-year-old grandson becoming engaged in combat somewhere between Ohio and Managua in the coming 25 years," came word from Columbus. Support for the contras meant to a woman from San Anselmo, California, that she "may very well see my son drafted to fight in another jungle." A Latina mother from Long Beach implored Hamilton: "I do not want anyone fighting in Latin America. . . . Help us not to send money for my *brown* son to kill his cousins or ancestors."

Even deeper than fears about war were concerns about their ability to pass along cherished values. For many writers the most basic responsibility of parenthood was to teach their children values to live by. "I fear for the future of our democracy and the society my two little children will inherit," declared a man from New York. A mother of two preschoolers from Jefferson, Massachusetts, announced: "I do not want them growing up in a country whose government is run by the likes of North and Poindexter." "We don't want our grandchildren to come to the service of their country thinking that lying and cheating are the way to get what you want," a couple telegraphed Hamilton.

When Congressman Louis Stokes spoke of the pride his mother felt in the prominence he and his brother had achieved in Cleveland and Washington, a woman wrote him from Marietta, Georgia, about how she had lost her pride in her country because of what had happened to her son when he applied lessons he had learned in the military. He had graduated from the Air Force Academy and become a decorated Vietnam pilot. He had learned the honor code "not to lie, cheat or steal nor tolerate one among us who do." When he left the military and entered state employment, her son discovered corruption at a very high level. He decided not to tolerate it. He reported it. He was fired. "So, I find Colonel North's and Admiral Poindexter's deception and lies destructive not only to our national security but also to the cadets and midshipmen who have continued to allow the honor code of the academies to govern their behaviors and actions." She regretted to report that she could "no longer feel the sense of pride" in the accomplishments of her son. "Rather, I feel there is really no place in America for honorable men and I am ashamed."

Because Americans formulated their interpretations as they talked with those around them, they spoke most frequently in the voice of these intimate associations. While their families were at the center of most of these worlds, writers frequently widened their voices a bit to include others. They embedded their conclusions to Hamilton in associations with "the many people I've talked with today" (Santa Barbara), "everyone we know" (Michigan City, Ind.), "my wife, grown children, friends (including Republicans)" (Los Altos, Calif.), "I and many of my friends" (Haverford, Pa.; Sewell, N.J.; and Glendale, Calif.), "most of my friends and colleagues" (New York), "a number of my friends" (Charleston, S.C.), "a host of our friends" (Kalamazoo, Mich.), "my many acquaintances" (Belle Harbor, N.Y.), "I, my husband, and everyone I know" (Ventura, Calif.), "our family and friends" (Webster City, Iowa, and Cohoes, N.Y.), and "our many friends" (Fairfield, Conn.).

Some citizens tried to swell their voices, without sacrificing authenticity, by preparing formal statements that they then solicited family or friends to support with signatures. Twelve "people from all walks of life" in San Jose— "laborers, teachers, editors, writers, and manufacturers," some related to each other—signed a "collective opinion" that criticized both the Reagan administration and the Iran-Contra committees for pandering to the contra side of the conflict in Nicaragua. On July 14, 1987, eight residents of Seattle signed a two-page letter. On August 4 they sent the letter again, this time adding the signatures of four more people who wanted to be associated with their conclusions. Five people from Houston signed a petition that condemned the committee for being too critical of North, while five others from Tacoma, Washington, criticized the committee for being too kind to North.

Some writers interpreted the hearings through the experience that had attracted them or their families to migrate to the United States. "As a survivor of Nazi Germany's concentration camps," telegraphed a woman from San Francisco, "I heard an ominous echo in the testimony of Colonel North. His attitude reminded me of the slogan, 'right or wrong, my fatherland.'" The memory of how Russian soldiers had tortured and raped his mother and tormented his sister as they had tried to flee Poland left an immigrant in San Jose with "a perspective which many Americans do not have": "The fact that Nicaragua is now a Communist-dominated nation in our hemisphere should cause all of us great concern and fear."

While the fact that a person's ancestors had emigrated from Mexico or Ireland or Italy did not determine what that person concluded from the hearings, many individuals turned ethnic heritages into important voices for interpreting what they saw. "As a grandchild of Italian peasant immigrants who felt America was great," wrote a woman from Sunapee, New Hampshire, "I feel Col. North went against the very basic tenets of our country's basic foundation." It did not require Italian ancestry to reach this view of North, but the reality of her grandfather's experience was no less a formative part of her view of North. "I feel this threat to liberty most keenly," wrote "a first generation American whose parents were both refugees from tyranny" from Los Angeles: "Imagine my shame as I grew to learn that my country did not practice as it preached."

Religion shaped what many writers saw. But religions offered a wide range of views on political conflicts and on how individuals should respond to authority, law, and conscience. Some churchgoers concluded that God wanted the Marines to battle godless atheism in Nicaragua, while others believed that God sided with the revolutionaries in Nicaragua in their struggles for freedom. A couple from Valinda, California, signed "In Christian Love" to their praise for Hamilton's "fantastic job," while a woman signed "In Christ's Love" to her promise never to for vote for anyone who treated Oliver North as Hamilton had. Although religious viewers reached very different conclusions, they shared a faith that congressmen should ignore abstract masses created by polls and pay attention instead to real individuals who tried to live by God's authority. Since "our Congress is prone to be guided by any and all polls of Americans to undo what God directs them to do," a woman from Gurnee, Illinois, urged congressmen instead to follow God's will and ignore the "opinions of millions of our Godless subculture who must belong to the Devil psychologically and physically and should not be listened to."

Lee Hamilton's close association with the Methodist Church became a source of both pride and crisis for many members of that sect. Methodists often knew—he was profiled in a denominational magazine during the hearings—that he was the Methodist son of a Methodist preacher. Many were angry and bewildered, therefore, when he reached very different conclusions from their own. A South Carolina woman who served her church for thirty-two years, many of them as the church organist, explained to Hamilton: "I love my Lord and seek to do His will." Descended from a Methodist bishop, she was a "life-long Methodist." She was deeply disturbed to discover that Hamilton was "also of this denomination and [had] relatives in high places in the church." Since they were both Methodists, she demanded, "how can we be so different in our views?" Lamenting that "I'm not proud of you" even though they were both Methodists, a woman in Hutchinson, Kansas, imagined a way of returning the erring Hamilton to the true faith: "I hope your Father and Brother are praying for you that you will not continue being so biassed against all the ones you treated so shabbily and also the President."

While some viewers invoked political allegiances they had carried since childhood, they worried when people from their parties expressed repugnant views. As voters watched twenty-six legislators express more diverse views than they usually heard from politicians, they found some Democrats with whom they felt closer than usual and others from whom they felt more alienated than usual. Listening to Hamilton address North, a woman from Los Angeles wrote that "I am proud to be and always was a Democrat," adding that she hoped he would run for the presidency. A Democratic couple from Claremont, California, protested from the Left against "the shameful way in which Democrats . . . allowed right-wing Republicans to use them as a platform" for contra propaganda. "I have been a Democrat for 45 years," explained a woman from Absecon, New Jersey, who was so disturbed by Hamilton's treatment of North that "after this charade I will change my political affiliation."

The experience of watching the hearings as women inspired writers to draw a wide variety of conclusions. By far the most common perspective shaped by gender was motherhood, the writer's concern for her children. To other women, the absence of even a single woman among the twenty-six committee members reminded them of their private struggles in a male-dominated world. "Not one woman participated in the hearings!!!" observed a woman, reminding Hamilton of his criteria for judgment: "Remember what you said about accountability and personal responsibility."

The personal experience on which writers drew most frequently was service in the military. One out of every twelve writers in one sample of letters to Hamilton referred to military service by themselves or members of their family. Again as individuals, however, they reached dramatically different conclusions from those experiences.

"How proud I am to be a Marine, even though it was forty years ago!" exclaimed a man from Longview, Texas, to Oliver North: "You made me even more proud as you withstood the pounding of the very men who have placed our country in jeopardy." To other writers, North's and Poindexter's performances kindled feelings of shame, embarrassment, and anger that grew from their own military experiences. "This 62 year old Grandpa, who volunteered for the 2nd W. War and served 3 years in the Navy's landing craft in 8 invasions, did not appreciate North and Poindexter making it seem that I was not a good American or did not believe in God if I disagreed with Contra policy," protested a man from Winslow, Pennsylvania. And from Florence, Kentucky, a man wrote: "After spending 27 years in the Marine Corps, it pains me to see and hear the likes of Secord, MacFarlane, North and Poindexter lecture me on the 'joys' of illicit covert operations."

Because people valued firsthand experience above other sources of perspective, writers often grounded their conclusions in things they had seen and heard for themselves. As she listened to North explain why he did not trust Congress, a woman from Jackson, Mississippi, remembered her visit two years earlier to the gallery of the House of Representatives. "It was a circus," she reported: "Tip O'Neill was up there hammering away with his gavel and no one paid a damn bit of attention. We sat there and thought God is this what we have elected to make the laws of our land. It was gross." From this experience "it certainly is not hard for me to understand why Adm. Poindexter and Col. North did what they did."

A remarkable number of visitors to Nicaragua reported their experience as authority for refuting the anti-Sandinista stories of most government officials. "The Nicaragua I saw bore no resemblance to the reports coming from the Reagan Administration and conservative 'experts,'" reported a minister from Glassboro, New Jersey. From Lakeland, Florida, a woman looked to Hamilton "to help get the true story told," which she and her husband had observed firsthand: "We lived with the people in their poor little homes, we picked coffee with them in the north, we travelled the often mined roads, we listened to their pain and heard their plea, 'Stop the war, stop the killing, stop the lies.'" From Tallahassee, Florida, a man answered North's claim that there was no religion in Nicaragua with firsthand observation: "I was there 4 weeks ago and testify that there is *much* religious freedom there."

To refute stories that viewers were mindless and passive spectators, writers wanted congressmen to understand how firsthand experiences gave them authority. The voice of experience was what politicians most needed to hear. If North could "show his slides" of Nicaragua on television, "why can't my daughter show hers?" demanded a woman from Fergus Falls, Minnesota: "She was there just this past March for three weeks, working near Matagalpa picking coffee on a farm. She interviewed the people themselves, played with the children, ate their food, saw their poverty." The next step was to turn her daughter's experience into the voice of a larger group: "Why don't we listen to those thousands of Americans who have gone to Nicaragua in the past four years in order to 'see for themselves'?" "It is only through visits between our people and the Central American people that we get honest reports of conditions there," explained a man from Venice, Florida: "We cannot rely on reports from this Administration." With a faith that firsthand experience would overcome even the strongest preconceptions, a man from Cardiff, California, wrote Hamilton: "I have just returned from a six week visit to Nicaragua. I wish all of our Congressmen would do the same. If they did, they most surely would vote against any further aid to the Contras."

Although they presented themselves in voices they hoped would make them recognizable, writers drew radically different conclusions from others who wrote in the same voices. Instead of speaking for the cohesive or monolithic ethnic or regional or partisan cultures in which Americans once made political claims, citizens in the late 1980s formed conclusions with those who shared their daily lives and added larger allegiances more often to give greater visibility or authority to their individual conclusions. Citizens knew that they would be more recognizable if they spoke in larger voices, but they still spoke most often in the intimate voices of their primary relationships. Even when they referred to ethnic, gender, partisan, religious, and other larger allegiances, they did not enter the public forum to express the common creed of "Irish Catholics" or "Republicans" but instead to report how they had individually reshaped their group experiences with the help of family and friends.

▌▌ Pressure groups and mass movements inherited older institutions and cultures that mobilized individuals to take part in politics. For members of these kinds of groups the hearings were not so much an opportunity to converse as the latest occasion to mobilize longstanding commitments to ideologies, programs, or partisan goals. Wanting to advance their group's goals, these citizens easily responded to organized appeals to write and call legislators to support or oppose contra aid, to support military officers or peace initiatives, to support liberal Democrats or conservative Republicans. Sometimes they spoke in the formal voice of the group. The Trumbull Peace Council of Warren, Ohio, formally thanked Hamilton because his "statements on television summed up our feelings about this whole tragic affair" and then went on to urge that United States obey the World Court's verdict that the United States should compensate Nicaragua for damages it had inflicted. Senator William Cohen received communications that supported the committee's investigations from the Institute for Peace and Justice in St. Louis, the Peace Council of New Haven, Coalition for World Peace at Arizona State University, Ecumenical Peace Committee of Albuquerque, Peace Education Forum of Benzonie, Michigan, Ministerios Hispanicos of San Antonio, Habitat for Humanity of Americus, Georgia, and the Westwood Friends Meeting of Los Angeles. From the other side, Cohen heard opposition to public investigation of military and Republican figures from the Republican Town Committee of South Berwick, Maine, the Young Republican Club of North Towanda, New York, and American Legion Post No. 84 of Orono, Maine.

In contrast to the American Legion posts, partisan political committees, and peace groups, whose meetings often provided important places for members to shape activities and voices through face-to-face exchanges, modern pressure groups also entered the debate. These "groups" never met. Their members' only activities were to contact legislators and contribute money upon the request of someone they had never met. Through newspaper ads, telephone appeals, or direct mail requests, merchandisers of political opinion simply recruited large numbers of communications to Congress. The "Lt. Col. Oliver North Support Committee" joined with the Saturday Morning Breakfast Club of Tucson to pay for a large newspaper ad that urged readers to write to legislators in support of contra aid. Even this instruction was not concentrated enough for some organizers. They asked people to check a box or two on a form and sign their names. The American Freedom Coalition circulated a "National Opinion Poll" that asked people to check whether North should be jailed or given "a patriotic medal," and to check whether Congress should or should not spend "over $5.3 million tax dollars to persecute Colonel North." People were then asked to sign the "poll" and an accompanying postcard that was already addressed to congressmen. Citizen Action in the Courts to Conserve American Freedom asked people to sign a "Congressional Petition to Grant of Immunity" for North and mail it to Hamilton and Inouye. Taking no chances that its supporters would get the message wrong or send it to the wrong place, the Moral Majority told supporters what their messages should say and asked them to return their communications to the organizers who would forward them to the congressmen they wanted to target. From the Left a group asked people to sign a printed "Citizen's Complaint" to Inouye and Hamilton that called for an end to all covert operations and the impeachment of Reagan. In this new world of direct mail technologies it was a good question whether a "member" was a person whose name was on a computerized list as a likely target, a person who received the appeal, or a person who answered it. The deepest experience that connected these supporters was signing the same form and appending their names to language written by others.

Direct mail organizers developed elaborate ways of recruiting people and resources to concentrate what looked like citizen pressure on legislators. Hamilton received a single anticommunist "opiniongram" on scores of pages with the identical message but 1,289 different names. "Within hours" of North's first appearance, direct mail specialist Richard Viguerie recalled, "our copywriters, graphic artists, and account people were putting together the first of what has become a 10 million letter, multiclient campaign" to renew contra aid. In the three weeks after North began to testify the Oliver North Legal Assistance Fund claimed to have raised $1.3 million from individuals in amounts that averaged $40 each. The National Conservative Political Action Committee reported that its direct mail fund-raising response had improved by 200 percent when it developed and sent a letter that referred to North eleven times in fourteen paragraphs.[2] While conservative and Republican groups earned deserved reputations for their abilities to stimulate political communications, Senate and House aides were impressed by the ability of the Christic Institute to get results from the Left. Senator Cohen received 511 communications that urged the Iran-Contra committees to follow leads unearthed in the Christic Institute's lawsuit. And nearly four-fifths of those communications came from Cohen's home state of Maine.[3]

While narrowing the range of everyday interpretation to a single message and concentrating pressure on a single point, organized groups used voices that they hoped would exaggerate the size of their followings and the representativeness of their members. While individuals ordinarily spoke in the first person singular of personal experiences, pressure groups sought signatures on messages phrased in the first person plural, in which the writer subordinated individual expression to imaginary aggregates with low common denominators.

Even more common than the preference for mass expression over individual voices of personal experience was the substitution of threats, particularly of electoral defeat, for cautious everyday voices of doubt, hope, fear, and affection. Threats were as uncommon in the spontaneous letters as they were uncommon in everyday talk. Letters that seemed to be orchestrated, by contrast, often threatened retribution at the hands of an abstract mass of voters:

> I also heard Colonel North ask: "Who will investigate Congress?" The answer is: *People like me will*—in the 1988 election—to see if you voted for continued U.S. aid to the freedom fighters to stop Communism. (Printed postcard signed by many)

> The revolt may come—from the silent majority who has seen a vindictive Congress in action. . . . Colonel North is working FOR us and our welfare while Congress is working AGAINST us and our future. How can the voters de-select the "Select" Committee? (Man, San Rafael, Calif.)

> You can be sure there will be contributions and work so after the next election you will have to get a real job. (Woman, Toms River, N.J.)

I am appalled that there are some congressmen who have capitalized on the Iran-Contra affair and have turned it into a political circus to accomplish their own selfish means, and doing so in the name of the people. To those men I say farewell, you have lost the confidence of the American people. (Man, Bolivar, Ohio)

While the writers of spontaneous letters tried to make their individual stories more recognizable to politicians by embedding their voices in larger social identities, the organizers of orchestrated mailings tried to hide the unmistakable fact that these letters existed only to be counted as pieces of a mass, not read as voices of individuals. Organizers of direct mail campaigns tailored their letters to appeal to politicians' traditional faith that spontaneous voices were more authentic and more representative than orchestrated ones. Organizers hoped that politicians would be more likely to interpret the orchestrated letters as evidence of the mass in motion if they sounded like the voices of unaffiliated individuals. Some results were more obvious than others. Hamilton received the following letter in handwritten form from a man in Edmonds, Washington:

> Your televised Iran/Contra hearings have now become a national disgrace! I am disappointed you have allowed these hearings to go on for so long.
> And I am downright angry at the way most committee members have treated Lt. Colonel North and many of the other witnesses!
> Liberals in Congress seek to destroy the President we American voters elected in 1980 and 1984.
> I have read what Pat Buchanan wrote in the July 13 Newsweek magazine, and I agree:
>
> "The Democrats [want] to slowly bleed Ronald Reagan of his popularity, to break his presidency. . . . The liberal wing of the Democratic Party has made itself the silent partner, the indispensable ally, of revolutionary communism in the third world."
>
> I urge you to end these disgraceful hearings at once! Focus instead on how to protect Americans like me, and the rest of the world, from the dangers of communism!

The author used the first personal singular to convey what seemed to be his own feeling and conclusion, buttressed by Buchanan's words, which had apparently jumped out at him while he was reading *Newsweek*. A few days later, however, the same letter came in typewritten form from a man in Point Lookout, New York, with the exception of four changes in punctuation, three in capitalization, and "ic" subtracted from the name of the Democratic Party. And then the letter arrived with a single change in punctuation in printed form with a heading: "Mailgram to Co-Chairmen of Hearings Senator Inouye and Congressman Hamilton." And it contained a new line at the bottom: "[Your name goes here]." In this case a woman from Chilicothe, Missouri, signed her name. Hamilton received over a thousand signatures on this message in its incarnation as a mailgram. The only originality was in punctuation and capitalization.

Some organizers apparently allowed writers to display a little more imagination, but barely:

> Why don't you lay off of Oliver North and get busy defending America against Communism like you were elected to do? (Handwritten; woman, Rayville, Louisiana, July 10, 1987)
>
> Get off Lt. Col. Oliver North's back and get out and defend America from Communism. (Handwritten; man, Corpus Christi, Tex., July 9, 1987)
>
> Why don't you all get off COL. O. NORTH'S BACK and help defend this country against Communism, as you all were elected to!! (Handwritten; husband and wife, no return address, July 10, 1987)
>
> We support Col. North! Get off his back and get back to the business for which we elected you!! (Husband and wife, Lakewood, Calif., July 10, 1987)
>
> So I implore you to get back to stopping communism, and get off Col. Oliver North's back. (Handwritten; man, Santa Monica, July 9, 1987)
>
> Get off Lieutenant Colonel Oliver North's back and begin doing something worthwhile with your time. (Typewritten; man, Exton, Pa., July 10, 1987)
>
> You people need to get off his back and concentrate on fighting communism. (Typewritten; husband and wife, Tyler, Tex., July 9, 1987)

Because the very issue that had opened the vital conversation around the hearings was for many the right and capacity of citizens to speak as individuals, many citizens protested mightily when organizers tried to recruit them. They lashed back, turning orchestrated campaigns themselves into battlegrounds in the struggle to define where and how Americans should take part in the public forum.

Many Americans were infuriated when others presumed to know what they were thinking and protested loudly when political merchandisers incorrectly identified them as likely sympathizers and solicited their support. Organizers and their computers targeted people who had supported related causes in the past or who came from a demographic group that disproportionately supported the cause. The basic problem was that these statistical and historical probabilities were fictions that completely ignored the reality of tremendous diversity among people. The method produced many letters to congressmen, but it also deeply angered people when its approach did not fit them. "I wonder how you got my name," demanded a man from Cocoa Beach, Florida, when the American Freedom Coalition's solicited him for a contribution to the contra cause. Resigned about commercial techniques of opinion aggregation, he mused: "Probably you had your computer sort on retired military, who are often politically conservative." A man from Brookline, Massachusetts, sent Hamilton a copy of the same "nauseating document," adding: "How my name got on their mailing list is a mystery to me, for my views are as unlike those of the proponents of this 'cause' as can be imagined." To a man in Tucson this "poll" was simply the latest conservative attempt to mislead Congress into thinking there was popular support for their cause: "I have gotten similar letters on a number of occasions when President Reagan wanted to give an impression that he was being backed up spontaneously by the American people." When Guy Vander Jagt of the National Republican Congressional Committee signed a direct mail appeal to support North's legal defense, a man from San Diego was "shocked" to be approached, because North "should be behind bars," and a man from Houston snapped to Vander Jagt that he was "both astounded and appalled that, apparently, you do not have even a nodding acquaintance with the United States Constitution." Even when recipients of such appeals were willing to check a box or lend a signature, they sometimes felt that organizers did not respect them, because they listed their names incorrectly. A woman from Temecula, California, wrote Howard Phillips of the Conservative Caucus that she was willing to lend her name to a Caucus communication to legislators, but she insisted that it bear "my signature," that is, all three of her names, not the two he had listed.

Many writers were particularly galled when organizations that professed to represent their interests committed the resources and name of the organization to a cause they rejected. A retired army lieutenant colonel in Everett, Washington, protested when the Reserve Officers Association (ROA) used its publication, the *Officer*, "to ridicule the Congressional Investigating Committees *and to solicit funds for what appear to be right-wing causes.*" "As a life member of the ROA and writing solely for myself," he wrote Hamilton, "I apologize for such irresponsible copy and commend you for your fairness and restraint under difficult circumstances." To the offending editor he wrote: "You do *not* speak for this life member of the ROA." He added that he wanted the *Officer* to publish the closing remarks by Inouye, Rudman, Mitchell, and Hamilton, citing his criterion for what a reserve officers' association should value: "*That* is material I would have my grandchildren read."

Some writers who were not solicited expressed anger that pressure groups distorted authentic opinions. "I do not belong to an organization!!" proudly proclaimed a woman from Lavallette, New Jersey, who explained that orchestrated campaigns eroded the voices of real citizens: "This is not a planned writing campaign. It is one person expressing opinions!" "WE'RE REALLY MAD!" began a husband and wife from Gates Mills, Ohio, who conflated pollsters and pressure groups into a generalized menace that distorted by intervening in communication between voters and politicians: "We resent pollsters and political commentators saying that they know what we think. No one has asked *us!* . . . *Please do not think that this is a mass mailing sponsored by some crank interest group!* These are our own personal thoughts." Personal thoughts were authentic thoughts.

For other writers pressure groups were a menace because they existed precisely to reshape the forum so that politicians would listen, not to ordinary citizens, but to special and privileged interests. New political methods to identify and present opinion were so expensive that politicians were thrust into the arms of eager pressure groups that contributed both the money and the expertise in opinion management that politicians considered necessary for their survival. A woman from Ashland City, Tennessee, was infuriated by the American Freedom Coalition's mass appeal because "the sophisticated nature of this mailing" meant that expensive and outside professionals had interjected themselves between voters and representatives: "Someone had to pay for the creation, editing, printing and mailing of this solicitation," she observed. And that was the precise point where democracy was threatened. The cause of "the massive corruption" that was leading the United States down "the way of the Roman Empire," believed a man from Beverly, New Jersey, was the emergence of new political methods whose owners and handlers needed lots of money: "A new, corrupt-free political system must be devised that will base a candidate upon the ideas that he has to solve our problems out here and not upon the amount of money he can raise to keep himself in office despite the fact that he is incompetent and/or corrupt." In order to get "the PAC money that you people stuff in your pockets" (St. James City, Fla.), politicians were routinely "selling their souls to PAC's desires" (Menlo Park, Calif.) or "selling out to PACs, lobbyists and special interest groups" (Hurst, Tex.). The new methods distorted voters' voices, and their costliness contributed to the reality, as described by a man from Berryville, Virginia, that "the Congress no longer *represents* the wishes of the common man but that of the special interests."

III As they imagined how they wanted to be heard and counted by congressmen, writers of these letters illustrated the difficulty of combining experience with conclusion, individual voice with cultural or institutional identity. Writers derived different but formative conclusions from their experiences as Methodists or parents or Democrats, but those identities did not predict those conclusions. Some writers claimed those identities as their own in hopes of making themselves more recognizable and adding weight to their individual views. Others chose to subsume their identities entirely in a single opinion by adding their names to hundreds of others on a mass mailing. Even these writers were individuals, however, trying to be recognized and counted.

The challenge of conversation between citizens and representatives was to reconcile the need to be heard and respected as an individual with the need to find common ground. By the late 1980s Americans made sense of and took part in politics through their primary relationships and deeply resented the conventions of the forum that defined them as data from which to produce aggregates that could then be easily interpreted by experts. The institutions and cultures that had once unified and mobilized people—Methodism or the Democratic party—were now more likely to be direct mail groups that existed by virtue of computer sorting, no longer places where people could talk about what mattered. For this, they turned to everyday conversation.

Once they could be seen and heard in the intimate voices of their primary relationships, writers could reveal how these relationships were not passive or isolated places for absorbing what others told them but were instead noisy and active places where they formulated the conclusions they wanted legislators to heed. In these relationships Americans discussed and forged their political views.

Six

❖ ❖ ❖ ❖ ❖ ❖ ❖ ❖ ❖ ❖ ❖

Interpreting Politics
in Everyday Life

Interpretation is so deeply embedded in everyday life that it is almost as hard to describe as breathing or eating or talking. The particular experience of watching and making sense of television is such an everyday occurrence that it is easy to overlook. But at a time when Americans were overwhelmingly depicted as mindless and passive escapists who confused politics on television with entertainment, there may well be no more urgent need for improving conversations between citizens and politicians than to step back and look anew at things we take for granted.

This chapter brings into view the primary relationships where viewers made their own sense of the stories that were unfolding on their television screens. Turning from the defenses that viewers had developed against the marketing, entertainment, and pontification they saw on television, explored in chapter 3, we focus here on how viewers used their primary relationships to forge their political interpretations. The crucial stage in making interpretations occurred when they took things from the world of television, where they were presented to meet the needs of performers, and brought them into their everyday worlds, where they could use their own skills and experiences, their own families and friends, to help them decide what was at stake and what they believed about it. In order to illustrate the active, diverse, and open-ended ways they drew political conclusions, we examine both the personal relationships where they did the interpreting and the individual experiences, authorities, and skills they brought to the task.

Writers made sense of things on television as they met a variety of needs with different people in ways that produced swings of direction, emphasis, mood, and confidence. They even projected what they liked—and missed—in relationships with people around them into both their political ideologies and the issues they saw at stake in the hearings. From these relationships they drew both the content and inspiration to challenge the agendas that drove politics on television and to imagine and prefigure a more responsive political forum.

▌ "I was caught up in the North mania," a teacher from Vero Beach, Florida, wrote Lee Hamilton, "until I started to think how I was going to explain it to my second graders." "One of the hardest lessons I have to teach is that liars never win," she explained, and "I also teach them the beauty of law and the constitution." "How can one do that," she asked herself—and Hamilton—"and still think Col. North a hero?" The tremendous chasm between watching North's performance on television and talking about it with her second graders separated expectations nurtured in the worlds of everyday life from those bred in the staged world where actors performed for unseen viewers.

Like this teacher, many viewers described a vivid line that separated how they felt as they experienced performances on television from how they felt as they experienced life with the people around them. They could choose to leave things in the land of escape where they were an interchangeable voice on the sound track of laughter and applause, or they could bring things from television into their intimate worlds where they would evaluate them by the standards of everyday life. A woman from Albuquerque "found myself hanging on [North's] every word" until she reflected later that his plan to aid the contras would eat up in new taxes the "nice raise" she had just received at work. "I caught myself," she told Hamilton. A man from Dallas "experienced a feeling of euphoria" as he listened to Hamilton and others reaffirm constitutional government, but "then the question hit me. Are these the same very intelligent and capable people that permitted our National debt to escalate?" "The euphoria has left me," he explained, "and I am dumbfounded and bewildered. How can this be? What is wrong?" To move from a world where interpretation paused in questions to one where it began and ended in performances to the mass was as easy for a citizen of Bradfordsville, Kentucky, to feel as it was hard for him to describe: "I know my feelings and wish I could convey them so they would be understood" by people he knew only from television.

Television was ordinarily a place where Americans went to be transported far from their everyday lives, a place to find out about remote leaders and exotic places, a place for escape and diversion from real life. Americans kept television away, and they particularly screened out staged talk by politicians, by dismissing them, talking back at them, making fun of them, ignoring them, and, perhaps most devastatingly, by slipping into a trance that television offered as escape. "Everyone's misled by . . . those crocodile tears"

North "weeps" on television, believed a man from New York: "When the lights on the TV cameras are turned off, and the record looked at, this guy will fade." "What the Colonel and the Admiral are experiencing is mainly an immediate emotional response," concluded a husband and wife from Arlington, Virginia, who thought that when Americans discussed with people around them what North and Poindexter had done they would create "a second wave of public opinion" that would criticize them. Since the need for diversion that inspired what the Virginia couple called "an immediate emotional response" to a television performance was as authentic as the "second wave" of greater reflection, many viewers described crossing the line between them as awakening from a trance. When they suddenly did wake up in their everyday worlds, however, they were appalled to discover that they had been cheering or laughing along with the sound track, at things they now found stupid and unfunny.

Writers explained that the autonomy of their interpretations depended on remembering that political talk on television followed different rhythms from everyday conversation. John Poindexter and Elliott Abrams had successfully used arts associated with television—selling, acting, lying, packaging—to hide and escape responsibility for what they were really doing. Americans wrote congressmen to assert capacities journalists had denied them with the story of Olliemania. Angered by "political grandstanding" and "free advertising by some politicians," wrote a woman from Chicago, they wanted to start up real conversations to cut through the atmosphere of make-believe and the haze of sales pitches and spin doctoring, the appeals to low common denominators that seemed to divert both witnesses and legislators from serious talk. ("When all else fails, you resort to civics cliches, invoke god and country or point to the polls," fumed a man from Port Ludlow, Wash.)[1]

When Americans brought material from the hearings to interpret in their everyday worlds, they ripped that material from the commercial and entertainment imperatives that drove it on television and subjected it instead to the criteria they used in everyday life. North should be judged not as a performer or salesman but by questions a teacher had to answer when she talked with her students or by choices a person had to make when she went shopping to spend her raise. The key to sorting what was authentic from what was made to sell or amuse, to escape the feeling of being manipulated, isolated, pitched at, condescended to, to think and assert for themselves, was to keep the agendas and values that inspired producers and performers from infiltrating and distorting the standards people had developed to interpret life around them.

■■ "I'm so happy to be able to have you and the whole Committee at my breakfast table each morning," a woman from West Covina, California, wrote Hamilton. The hearings dropped out of the airwaves and into the middle of people's lives where they lived them with others, at the breakfast or dinner table, on a couch in front of the television, laced together with conversation about the day's activities. "I've watched the Iran-Contra hearings with one ear as I've gone about my business," explained a woman from Katy, Texas. Active interpretation emerged naturally from the experiences of relaxing with friends, raising families, worshiping God, or working. By exchanging experiences and observations in conversations with the people they knew best, participants shaped topic, pace, and mood, cross-examining claims and evidence, generating authorities and knowledge they could trust. They tried out and modified tentative conclusions before expressing them to acquaintances. They built confidence in their abilities as interpreters.

Because intimacy encouraged the trust people needed to explore the unfamiliar, the most cherished relationships spawned the largest number of interpretations. One-quarter of all communications to Hamilton were signed by husband and wife. Only people who knew their spouses well would introduce their letters with explanations like "I regret the need to write you, but my wife has now insisted upon it" (Chevy Chase, Md.) or "I'm writing to you" because "my husband has poor penmanship."

Families deepened their relationships as they interpreted the hearings. In Laguna Hills, California, a woman came to know her eighteen-year-old grandson much better by watching and talking about the hearings with him. During a family discussion in St. Clair, Michigan, to help a young man decide what to do with his life, a woman drew on the hearings to counsel against a military career. "Don't!" she said: "Look how little value the leaders of our country . . . place" on military service.

Since comments on the outside world became object lessons to guide personal conduct, family members pointed to developments in the hearings to define values to live by. At a home in Butterfield, Minnesota, three fifteen-year-olds were watching the hearings with a parent. "Wow!" they exclaimed in response to North and Poindexter: "Let us try that answer in school! That guy was lucky he doesn't have to obey the law." Soon the conversation turned to Richard Nixon. One of the teenagers declared that Nixon had been "a crook and he got by." Appalled by these conclusions, the parents tried to persuade the children that they had learned "very dangerous" lessons as guides to action. A very similar conversation with his parents led a twelve-year-old to write from Washington: "If I get a poor report card, I am going to ask my father grant to me deniability so I can be a hero and go to West Point. My father would brain me and ground me for life."

Wherever people gathered that summer, they tried ideas on others, sometimes defending initial conclusions, sometimes discarding them, sometimes modifying them, but often aiming at least toward a summary of the conversation that all could accept. A woman from Marina del Ray, California, told

Hamilton that some of her friends were at first attracted to North as a "self-sacrificing hero" while others feared him as "an articulate fascist." After discussing the subject, they "agree[d] that he is a handsome soldier who doesn't understand democracy." From Amsterdam, New York, a woman reported that conversations with friends were drawing them closer to her political perspective. "Most of our friends are Reagan supporters," she told Hamilton, "causing many heated, but friendly debates over the years. We are not debating much anymore. Not one of our friends believes that Reagan didn't know about the transfer of funds to the Contras." The fun of getting to know acquaintances better was often accompanied by the thrill of finding or reaching shared perspectives on the hearings. Employees gathered around a television set in a Seattle office, surprising each other as they discovered "how many of us are of the same mind." The discovery was particularly thrilling because this "mind" was quite different from what interpreters said "Americans" were thinking. Breaks in the coverage became the time for friends at Leisure World, Laguna Hills, California, to call each other and discuss what was new on the hearings and in their lives.

Americans interpreted the hearings as they tried to meet each other's needs. In Hot Springs, Arkansas, a woman told a group of friends that "she was 1000 per cent in support of Lt-Col. North." Her son, after all, was himself a lieutenant colonel. But as the hearings wore on, "she changed her mind, saying, 'He is wrong. No U.S. military officer should lie to the Congress and the American public and thus violate his oath to the U.S. Constitution.'" Her friends knew that this had been a painful change of heart for her. They wanted to support her. So they drafted a formal letter to Hamilton and Inouye, with copies to their Arkansas congressman and senators, commending the hearings and condemning those who had lied to Congress. It was a way to support their friend.

Using their closest relationships as places to form interpretations, Americans looked to casual encounters as places to test those conclusions. Help might come from anywhere. At Warminster, Pennsylvania, it was a sermon at Mass that "invoked my silent Amen" in a man who left church reinforced in the belief that congressmen were using McCarthyite tactics. A woman in Oakland, California, felt rededicated as a citizen when she heard a young friend comment that the hearings gave "us some hope for getting back to democratic government and caring for the needy at home." A man in Corvallis, Oregon, felt "much the same way" as a businessman who had said that "he would have to prefer anarchy to what the Reagan Administration was practicing" and "would not submit" to North's and Poindexter's "militarism and fascistic disregard of Constitutional principle." A woman in Albuquerque had "to bite my tongue" sometimes when surrounded by North admirers, but she felt relieved when she "played bridge Sunday with some gal who thought Reagan a liar, Ollie a nut."

Making sense of hearings became the opportunity to get to know other people better in interactions that sometimes broadened into miniature town meetings. The travelers who crowded around the big television screen at Gate 1 of Robert Mueller Airport in Austin, Texas, were, according to a journalist, "strangers to one another who nevertheless develop a sense of community as they witness this national event." Almost any gathering of Americans, however artificially constructed, could turn into an impromptu forum. Several passengers on United Airlines Flight 399 from Denver to Seattle cajoled the crew into showing the hearings on the plane's movie screen. Across seat backs and aisles passengers and crew fell almost immediately into talk. A white-haired man in 4C began: "You know, I just love that guy North." "Really?" asked a flight attendant: "What did you love best— when he lied to Congress or when he sold missiles to the ayatollah?" From two rows forward a middle-aged man in a green golf shirt leaned back to complain: "Lay off the guy."[2] And so it went.

The experience of watching the hearings with strangers led many people to discover a sense of community with people who turned out to agree with them. As they watched the hearings together, the Elderhostlers who gathered at Colgate University for the week of July 12–17 discovered a bond that united them "to a man—and to a woman." They felt "gravely concerned" about "the ominous implications for our democracy" in North's testimony. Meanwhile, not far away, at Troy, New York, twelve retired men completed a morning round of golf and settled down around a television set in their country club to watch North's testimony. They began to talk and soon discovered that before retirement they had worked at jobs as diverse as lawyers and laborers. They also discovered a shared anger at "the politicians in Congress" whom they believed to be tormenting North. Someone suggested that they convey their opinions to Congress. So they took formal votes. All voted support for North and the contras. Eight voted for bombing Teheran if necessary to free American hostages remaining in Iran.

Other viewers brought their interpretations into the clubs where they had long congregated. Conversations about the hearings sometimes turned to proposals that the club venture into the unfamiliar terrain of political participation by conveying common concerns to legislators. Some thirty members watched the hearings at a senior citizens' club in North Bay, California, and decided each week to vote one of the participants "Biggest Donkey of the Week." One week they awarded the prize to Congressman Jack Brooks because his mouth was "big and foul like the State of Texas."[3] The Thursday Morning Study Club of Glendale, California, formally protested the committees' treatment of North: "Well, we are only some of the little folks from out California way, but we know that 'for everybody comes a payday' and that (to quote a song title) 'Somebody Bigger than You and I' will see to it that we all receive our just rewards for our actions here, sooner or later—including offensive and hostile congressmen."

▍▍▍ Instead of judging what they saw on television by the values that shaped what appeared on television, writers turned the tables, asserting that the values that shaped their everyday relationships ought to shape the conversation. Making their interpretations with the people who shared their lives, viewers turned the standards they wanted to guide their primary relationships into their criteria for evaluating the hearings they watched, indeed into principles they wanted to shape governance. Relationships with others thus became the places where viewers forged their political ideas even as they made those relationships into the content of their ideas.

The core of all strong relationships, they believed, was trust. "When trust is broken relationships fail," declared a man from Gresham, Oregon. Because many viewers had at one time or another been less than fully candid with someone else, they often empathized with the agony that accompanied a lie and then the agony that accompanied the confession of the lie. "I do not believe in lying, and seldom ever have," a woman wrote Hamilton from Marion, Indiana, "but I recall confessing a lie to one person, and that was hard." Many writers feared what would happen to personal relationships when public standards for conduct fell "so lowdown that we should accept lies, instead of truth or honesty," as a Floridian wrote. Once lying became accepted, once people no longer said what they meant, writers feared, relationships would no longer provide the candid feedback people needed to participate in daily life and individuals would no longer be accountable for their actions.

Viewers projected personal qualities they admired and disliked into standards they wanted to guide their government. Different people looked for different qualities. Writers who were offended by arrogance in people around them tended to advocate political principles that placed community rules or negotiations ahead of individual ambitions. To behave in an "arrogant" manner, wrote a couple from San Mateo, California, was to behave as though one was "above the law" and to deserve only criminal prosecution. The "arrogance of Reagan's appointed administrators," declared a man from Ithaca, New York, "violated our laws to achieve ends that they believed best. . . . They have sabotaged the democratic process." The "supreme arrogance," wrote a woman from Venice, California, was to violate the Constitution.

What appeared as "arrogance" to some writers appeared as "courage" or "bravery" to others. These writers admired people who were not intimidated by people or deterred by institutions or laws or customs that stood between them and the accomplishment of their goals. "An Angry and Concerned American" from Fresno admired "people with more guts like Casey, North, and the other brave men who took great risks to do something besides sit on their diplomatic butts. . . . They sure had the guts to try to make something work." Viewing politics as struggle, a woman associated "bravery" with the "fight against Communism."

Writers who admired patience, dignity, and fairness in others tended to support moderating mechanisms like checks and balances and the rule of law as guides for relations among people in the larger society. "Your calm and fair approach," a woman from Houston wrote Hamilton, would help "in preserving our treasured rule of law both in spirit and in action." Hamilton's personal qualities of "patience and dignity" gave a man in Bennington, Vermont, "hope that the system of checks and balances assured in the Constitution are still working and are in a robust state of health." "Fairness and grace" were personal qualities a man in Hudson, New Hampshire, associated with "the rule of law." And a woman from Kensington, California, associated "calmness" with "legality" and "due process."

The standards by which viewers judged the behavior of individuals helped them to define rules they wanted to govern their communities. Hamilton's "obnoxious statement levelling unjust criticism" at Poindexter was "character assassination" and thus "cruel and unusual punishment of a citizen," to a man from Potomac, Maryland. Hamilton's "biased and unfair" demeanor struck a family in Northridge, California, as a violation of "our faith that Americans are presumed innocent until proven otherwise." Since the "smug" Poindexter was "so self-centered that he is not willing to consider that he is wrong," a writer from Washington concluded that his behavior "would lead to the end of our democracy."

Writers challenged congressmen to place the values that guided their personal relationships ahead of their institutional agendas. Of fifty-six themes that writers brought up in a sample of 1,206 letters to Hamilton, the two most common were both principles for how people should relate to others: the accountability of individuals for their actions (mentioned by 42 percent of all writers) and the right to be treated with fairness and respect by others (mentioned by 39 percent).[4]

The most common theme that writers raised to Hamilton was the belief that people were responsible for what they did and should be held accountable for their deeds. Writers were outraged when they discovered that officials seemed to be hiding what they were doing behind dramatic performances, public relations facades, outright lies, and destruction of evidence. Public officials seemed to be acting beyond the reach of anyone. Since the president of the United States denied knowledge of what had happened, the basic challenge of the hearing was to find out who had ordered whom to do what, who had lied about it to whom, and under whose authority the coverup was taking place. In a nation that proclaimed the right of people to govern themselves, the challenge of establishing accountability was also the challenge of discovering whether citizens retained the capacity to make and enforce the rules they wanted to guide conduct:

> Comforting to hear someone [George Shultz] coming on the side of truth, responsibility and accountability. So different from the Poindexter-North philosophy of deceit, destroying evidence, putting out false information and deniability. (Man, Loveland, Colo.)

> Our democracy is at risk when things like this are allowed to occur. When one person whether president or colonel or an advisor to the president can send aid to the Contras in direct disregard to the wishes of the elected representatives of the people, then this great country ceases to be a democracy and becomes a dictatorship. (Husband and wife, Glen Ellyn, Ill.)

> I am frightened and angered by those people in government, like Oliver North, who feel themselves to be above the law and unaccountable to our democratic process. (San Francisco)

The first question was whether Oliver North and others had acted on their own. "What scares me," wrote a man from Tulsa, "is the fact that there is no governmental control at all." "Reminds me of the old skit that Bud Abbott and Lou Costello used to go through: Who's on first? Seems no one knew!" commented a woman from Wichita. "Just where was everybody while these two were conducting foreign policy? Breaking laws, shredding, selling arms to terrorists, felonious acts all!" began a woman from Grants Pass, Oregon.

To other writers the issue of accountability was the issue of holding individuals responsible for illegal acts. In fact, one writer in eight mentioned the theme of upholding the rule of law. Because North acknowledged that he recruited and distributed resources for the contras in order to circumvent the Boland Amendment, many writers began with the issue of criminality and the proposition that the legitimacy of all law depended on prosecution of lawbreakers. "Some legal punishment should be administered to preserve morality in the nation," explained a writer from Weston, Connecticut.

> We cannot afford *not* to enforce the law in such a case, when the very foundations of our democratic political system are called into question. ("An 'Independent' from the State of Arizona")

> The simple fact is that "Lt. Ollie" *and* his superiors broke the law of the United States. This in our eyes makes them criminals, not heroes. North and his superiors should be punished, not deified. (Woman, Jacksonville, Fla.)

> Ours is indeed a government of, for and by the people. Please sir, keep beating this drum so all the Norths, that whole basement crew and everyone who wants to live in this country will get it through their heads that NOBODY is above the law. (Woman, Sacramento)

One of every twenty-five writers specifically urged criminal prosecution or a court-martial of North. Several, like a man from Monterey, California, complained that the committees had granted too much immunity from prosecution to North and Poindexter as the price of their testimony. A crime was a crime, these writers insisted, and its perpetrators should be punished.

North and Poindexter, many writers claimed, were doing just what President Reagan wanted whether or not he knew the details of their activities.[5] Therefore, the responsibility rested with Reagan. "How can Ronald Reagan avoid responsibility for the Iran-Contra outlaw activity?" demanded a couple from Parma Heights, Ohio. Such questions led one in thirty writers to call for impeachment of Reagan as the only way to establish accountability for what had happened:

> The president of the United States allowed a system to be set up which circumvented the normal process of accountability. A mechanism by which Mr. Reagan could encourage his subordinates to act (contrary to the law) in order to gratify his oft-expressed wishes while shielding him from responsibility for their actions was clearly in operation. This represents an obvious outrage, but further indicates that this administration is incapable of being even courageously unlawful!! (Man, Hawthorne, N.J.)

> I hold the President accountable for creating such a lawless climate that gave to "the King's men" to carry out the "King's" orders. (Woman, New York)

> What harms the presidency is a president acting as a law unto himself, a president whose appointed agents break the law, lie about it, and then, when called to account, blame Congress. What harms the presidency, what disgraces it in this case, is the President. The best thing you can do for the presidency is impeach him. (Man, South Pasadena)

Congress, too, had failed to assume responsibility to govern. "Members of congress as a whole are so enmeshed in personal political ambitions and partisan political intrigue they have paralyzed the processes of government," observed a man in Crescent City, California. Since each congressman was pursuing a separate agenda, Congress reminded a man from San Francisco of "535 cats in a gunnysack." "I am sick to death of your petty politics, congressman," wrote a man from Montrose, Colorado.

Writers complained in particular that Congress had failed to take responsibility for foreign policy. "It is about time that Congress does something real strong to stop Communist aggression on the American Continent," declared a man from Portland, Oregon. A man in New Haven, Connecticut, criticized congressional inaction from the opposite perspective, for "failures over the past two years to provide militant overseership of the operations of our foreign policy when the Boland Amendments mandated it to do so." Congress, he believed, was afraid of taking "'unpopular' stands against powerful and popular presidents" who have "blatantly and publicly thumbed their noses at and effectively circumvented the law of the land."

Critics of the investigation argued that Congress evaded its responsibility, not by hiding its activities, as North had done, but by failing to act at all. Indeed, many Americans explained that it was this failure that inspired them to become a reserve army to reclaim citizenship and by their letters restore responsibility to the forum.

> Congress does not act to solve major problems. . . . I perceive Congress as factionalized, partisan, parochial, and without leadership. . . . I have been amazed at how slowly progress is made. The process seems designed to frustrate "good" rather than encourage it. (Man, Houston)

> The old cliche "the ball is in your court" does not apply. Too many in Congress would puncture the ball and hide its remains. (Woman, Taneytown, Md.)

Drawing political conclusions from the ways they related to people around them, writers derived the second most frequent theme from their faith that people were entitled to be treated fairly by others. In their haste to advance their institutional agendas, hearing participants forgot this. By far the most common complaint about the Iran-Contra committees was that they treated witnesses (particularly Oliver North) unfairly:[6]

> I feel you were very cruel in your revenge against O. North. ("Florida")

> No man should have to be put through what Lt. Col. Oliver North has been put through. ("A Citizen")

> For the eyes of Texas and the entire world to see your venomous, vulgar verbal attack of Col. North was outrageous, undecorous and repugnant. (Woman, Newton, Tex., to Jack Brooks)

> I have not written a political letter of any sort in ten years. However, I am so outraged at the abuse of Col. North I cannot stand still any longer. (Woman, Chino, Calif.)

Many writers were so shocked by Hamilton's violation of everyday standards that they assumed that he would feel guilty afterward. "I hope you can face your own family after such a public display of a personal degrading action," a man from Houston wrote him. After watching his "great effort to ruin a man and his family," a man in Los Angeles wondered whether Hamilton would "sleep good at night."

The treatment of North reminded many writers of McCarthyism, the Spanish Inquisition, and other times when people in power had placed partisan objectives above standards of decency that people upheld in personal relationships. Calling the hearings "the Great Show Trials of 1987," a man from Columbia, South Carolina, remembered: "Just 50 years ago Stalin conducted similar trials in the USSR for the same purpose—partisan political expediency." A woman from Fairfax, Virginia, summarized widespread sorrow and anger at how the desire to win elections and control agendas had led politicians to use methods that would be unacceptable in everyday life: "I guess you are more interested in your political party than human beings. It makes me very sad."

Because arguments about fairness and accountability were not over their desirability but over how to interpret and when to apply them, many writers upbraided congressmen for applying those standards wrongly. Many writers turned the tables on judges of others' acts, accusing judgmental critics of hypocrisy in tolerating similarly unfair or irresponsible behavior in themselves. The charge of hypocrisy, as in everyday life, allowed writers to uphold the principles of fairness and accountability while rejecting a particular application and challenging the moral authority of the accuser:

> The eloquent dissertation on morality, honesty, integrity coming from men who "voted" themselves an increase in salary "through the back door." Is that called lying, or cheating, or a cover-up? Or just secrecy? The sharing of breakfast with lobbyists at $1000.00 a meal. Is that integrity, honesty? Or can it be a cover-up? Congress must clean house before it casts stones. (Woman, Lewiston, Mich.)

> When I heard Senator Inouye use the word "chilling," I wanted to tell him that many people felt "chilled" at the way Congress engineered their recent substantial pay raise. This is a slap at the many people who were taking paycuts and losing jobs. . . . Their self glorification did not sit well with me. They, too, have feet of clay. They are subject to making mistakes just as Oliver North did. (Woman, Lafayette, La.)

> It's too bad that you all can't be put under the magnifying glass as he and others have been. I would venture to say there would be a lot exposed that wouldn't be very pretty either. I do believe some day, some how (maybe not until our final judgment) you will have to answer for what you have done. (Woman, Provo, Utah)

> Congress with its money misuses, pork barreling, censures and sexual use of page boys is disgusting and needs the investigating. (Woman, Columbus, Ohio)

Never in their conversation with legislators did writers forget that the forum was grounded in their relationships as individuals. Even when they conveyed messages about issues of principle and partisanship, many writers clearly turned standards of their everyday relationships into values that they used to make sense of the hearings and wanted to see prevail in government.

IV Viewers tested what they saw on television against experiences and authorities they had learned to trust over time. Something on television might remind them of things they had learned as a child, or read recently in a book, or heard on a radio newscast. Most people recalled favorite expressions that encapsulated their approaches to life or at least to particular issues. They had books, periodicals, newspapers, and radio or television programs on which they relied for information they could trust or at least for a perspective they could anticipate. And, belying the story of the monolithic crowd invented by journalists, Americans chose authorities that stretched across a wide spectrum.

Because people rooted their quest for autonomy in their everyday associations, they more readily believed things they had seen for themselves or heard about from people they trusted. Parents, teachers, and sometimes preachers were the most influential authorities. Their influences were so obvious that few writers stopped to explain where in childhood they had formed a basic belief in the way that a San Diego man recalled that "as a boy in elementary school I was taught that we had a government in which checks and balances kept one branch from dominating any of the others." Indeed, many writers sounded as though they were imagining how trusted authorities from their pasts—parents, teachers—might have reacted to a claim they heard in the hearings. Some writers sounded as though those people were present as they watched the hearings.

Writers trusted people they could cross-examine actively about what appeared on television in ways they could not probe presentations of entertainment by actors, products by salesmen, or expertise by pundits. A woman from Lafayette, Louisiana, *knew* that Oliver North was an "outstanding instructor and a dedicated Marine" because her son had personally encountered North as an instructor at a Marine training school. A couple from Reynoldsburg, Ohio, gained more confidence in North after hearing him praised by another Marine lieutenant colonel they knew. A woman from Topeka warned Hamilton that the press could not be trusted because a friend's husband, by occupation a lobbyist, said that he could "hardly recognize" meetings he had attended in accounts of those meetings by journalists.

The claim from the hearings that writers most often refuted with firsthand observation by people they knew personally was the claim that the Sandinistas were a threat to American interests, the basic justification Reagan's appointees presented for making the Iran-Contra deals. These officials justified their attempts to overthrow the government of Nicaragua because, they said, that government was totalitarian. Many writers answered with firsthand reports from family and friends. "I have friends who have visited Nicaragua and Central America several times in the last few years," reported a woman from Port St. Lucie, Florida, "and what they say is not what the Reagan Administration is saying." A man from Van Nuys, California, enclosed a six-page description of Nicaragua from a friend's son who had spent a year there because "this is 'first-hand information' and not 'second-hand' hear-say." A man from St. Helena, California, explained why he trusted friends who had lived in Nicaragua and whose "stories are exactly the reverse of tales we get from Washington": "My friends have no reason to lie to me."

Other writers trusted authorities who shared their ideology, religious commitment, political loyalty, occupational affiliation, or local residence. Instead of believing politicians or pundits, a couple from Glen Ellyn, Illinois, insisted that committed participants from their religious sect "are much more reliable when it comes to learning the true story." Their claims to authority came from their participation as "missionaries who live and work among the people of these countries and are involved in their daily lives."

From local newspapers, writers seized on—and enclosed for Hamilton— perspectives that echoed their own. "I'm enclosing the clippings because they say better than I would be able to do it," wrote a woman from Louisville. Others sent clippings that "say it better than I can" (Santa Barbara) or "express far better than I can" (Oldwick, N.J.). To make a particular clipping their own writers often underlined, highlighted, starred, added exclamation points, or drew arrows to the points they especially wanted Hamilton to read. A writer from Laughlintown, Pennsylvania, drew an arrow to a Reagan quote in a clipping and wrote in the margin: "I am critical of him for this." "What's so funny?" a writer from Pittsburgh scrawled beside a picture of a smiling Reagan. To underscore his conclusion that Reagan "should be negated and ignored," the writer marked a big X across the president's picture. The thoughts were the writers', but the words were often those of wordsmiths that they expected would more effectively persuade the likes of congressmen. And because the debate was over what Americans thought, not what North had done, writers more often enclosed columns, editorials, and particularly letters to editors, than news reports. In one sample of letters, eight writers enclosed news reports, twenty-two enclosed columns and editorials, and twenty-seven enclosed letters to the local editor. As the forum that was most accessible to citizens, letters to the editor that criticized North were the best refutation of Olliemania.

Writers overwhelmingly preferred local newspapers to radio or television as sources. Newspapers provided readers the chance to choose what they wanted to think about and the occasions when they wanted to read. They could stop reading a story whenever they wanted. The range of perspectives was wider in newspapers than on television. Newspapers included local voices in their editorials and letters from local residents. Newspapers, in short, offered a greater selection of information and perspective and more familiar local grounding and voices than did television. The few writers who cited radio and television reports—like the man from Grass Valley, California, who liked Paul Harvey, and the man from Chicago who relied on NPR reporters such as Cokie Roberts—chose commentators with distinctive perspectives and specialized audiences over network news shows aimed at mass audiences.

Diversity of perspective was even clearer in the range of magazines from which writers selected material to send Hamilton. They ranged across a continuum from *National Review*, the *Spotlight*, *World Economic Review*, and *Ruff Times*, on the Right, through *Readers Digest*, *Newsweek*, *Time*, and the *New Yorker*, to the *Nation*, *In These Times*, *Mother Jones*, and the *Progressive*, on the Left. Service veterans looked to periodicals that focused on an experience that had been important in their lives. They sent *VFW Bulletin*, the *Retired Officer*, and the *Officer*. For perspectives on American foreign policy readers turned to magazines that ranged from the Catholic social justice *Maryknoll Magazine* to the establishment-minded *Foreign Affairs*.

Choosing a book was like choosing a friend who could bring fresh information, depth of coverage, and a compatible perspective on precisely the topic a reader wanted to explore. The books people recommended to Hamilton reflected the range of perspectives and interests writers brought to the hearings. They chose the topic, chose approaches that ranged from scholarship to firsthand observation, from fiction to nonfiction, from Left to Right. A writer from Seattle believed the committee should move beyond the Iran-Contra topic to the more general ways that the theory and practice of "plausible deniability" camouflaged covert actions all over the world: "I would like to refer you to" R. W. Johnson's *Shootdown: Flight 007 and the American Connection* "to determine to what extent the NSC staff has been involved in other 'plausibly deniable' covert operations." A writer from Jacksonville Beach, Florida, commended Garry Wills's *Nixon Agonistes* for insight into Reagan's "closest friends." "You are a very busy man and I hesitate to bring more research to you," began a woman from Lake Park, Florida, but she thought Hamilton should read *A Man Called Intrepid* by William Stevenson in order to appreciate how Franklin Roosevelt's covert actions had been "a success and Hitler was defeated." A woman from Gretna, Louisiana, recommended three books on Reagan because, she assured Hamilton as though introducing three friends, "you will find them interesting."

Many writers preferred primary sources from which they could form their own conclusions. A woman from Springfield, Missouri, pored over the *Tower Commission Report* and other documents before forming the views she advanced to Hamilton. Others quoted the State Department's official *Sandinista Military Build-Up*, the Nicaraguan Embassy's official *Fact Sheet*, charters of the Organization of American States and the United Nations, constitutions of the United States and Nicaragua, and the Declaration of Independence. Others grounded their conclusions about Nicaragua on firsthand observations by the Latin American Studies Association, Freedom League, Amnesty International, Presbyterian Church, Americas Watch, and Christic Institute.

Many viewers were reminded during the hearings of expressions that re-capitulated their basic outlooks on life, sayings that helped them sort the significant from the insignificant, the true from the false. Writers seemed to carry around a quotation from the Bible, a line from a popular song, a poem, or a folk expression that encapsulated a timeless principle that or-dered the past and projected the proper course for the future. The expressions might have originated from a desire to provide identity and continuity for particular relationships ("our song") or to make sense of a formative experience in the past (like the sudden death of a loved one). These expressions helped writers explain human nature or apply moral principles or political philosophies in the face of new circumstances or conflicting voices.

Writers quoted expressions that had clarified particular experiences in the past while seeming timeless and universal. "All of you gentlemen on the Iran-Contra Committee used quotations from famous people," observed a woman from Victoria, Texas: "My favorites are 'What Fools These Mortals Be,' and my best is 'What Evil Lurks in the Hearts of Man Only The Shadow Knows.'" These expressions supported her conclusion that "none of us knows what the other person is thinking, regardless of how nice they appear on the outside." A woman from Oakhurst, California, quoted at length from George Washington's farewell address: "Knowing from *many* former experiences that it is a 'sure-fire' way to generate a passionate fervor, I've this morning reread" the address, and "O, how I long to copy it here entire! (Won't you *please immediately re-read* it, too?!)" The witnesses' testimony reminded two people independently of Scott:

> O, what a tangled web we weave, When first we practice to deceive.

Writers drew on such expressions, not to demonstrate erudition—for they rarely cited chapter, verse, or page, or worried about the original or accurate form of the quotation—but because the sentiment seemed to distill the wisdom of ages. "Concerned Citizens" began a four-page, single-spaced letter with phrases from a poem and a nursery rhyme that by 1987 had acquired the standing of authoritative wisdom. The expressions helped the writers make sense of Hamilton's behavior: "You have heard the saying 'if we could see ourselves as others see us.' Well, you have not heeded it in these hearings. . . . You obviously are feeling like Little Tom Thumb when he put his thumb in a pie and pulled out a cherry and said what a great boy am I. . . . You are just as immature and unqualified and lacking in common sense as Tom Thumb." Believing "it's pathetic to see how you deferred to North," a writer from Oakland, California, quoted "that great American philosopher James Thurber, 'You might as well fall flat on your face as lean over too far backwards.'"

The writers quoted expressions to describe everything from political principles to human nature:

"There is nothing more dangerous than ignorance in action." Goethe. Impeach the president for his claim of ignorance. (Clearwater, Fla.)

Listen to Franklin's words: "I have lived, sir, a long time; and the longer I live, the more convincing proofs I see of this truth, that God governs in the affairs of man." (Man, Newhall, Calif.)

Power corrupts. Absolute power corrupts absolutely. (Spokane, Wash.)

"No act of kindness, no matter how small, is ever wasted." Aesop. (Woman, New Buffalo, Mich.)

The old adage of "money is the root of all evil"—could this be? (Woman, Hollywood, Calif.)

"Luegen haben kurze Beine." (German phrase meaning "Lies have short legs") (Man, Montclair, N.J.)

Samuel Johnson said about 200 years ago: "Patriotism is the last refuge of a scoundrel." It should point out to all of us that we do not need the military running the government. (Man, Clover, S.C.)

Simplify. Simplify. H. D. Thoreau. (New York)

Our fears do make us traitors. Macbeth. (Pasadena)

As your illustrious namesake declared in No. 15 of The Federalist: "Why has government been instituted at all? Because the passions of men will not conform to the dictates of reason and justice, without constraint." (Man, Vernal, Utah)

I'm reminded of something a distinguished senator said some time ago, as I remember: "When I see something coming down the road that looks like a skunk, waddles like a skunk, smells like a skunk, and somebody tells me it's a lamb, I'm not reassured." (Man, St. Charles, Mo.)

Remember: the evil men do lives after them, the good is oft interred with their bones. Let's all work together for good and the brotherhood of man. (Man, Dallas)

In times of doubt writers returned to cherished and founding principles. They quoted and cited the wisdom of Lenin, the Boy Scout Oath, George Washington, P. T. Barnum, Edmund Burke, John C. Calhoun, George Bernard Shaw, Reinhold Niebuhr, John Adams, "Doonesbury," Nostradamus, Franklin D. Roosevelt, Machiavelli, Abraham Lincoln, Will Rogers, Shakespeare, Daniel Webster, Sam Donaldson, Dorothy L. Sayers, Sir Walter Scott, John Quincy Adams, Hannah Arendt, Barry Goldwater, Judge Roy Bean, William Gladstone, Patrick Henry, Winston Churchill, John F. Kennedy, and Graham Greene.

The desire to find and apply universal principles to explain the unfamiliar led many writers to draw on religious teachings. The most popular single authority by far was the Bible. But because the Bible contains a variety of morals, writers naturally drew different conclusions from their readings. What these principles had in common was the quest for eternal authority to guide everyday life. The large numbers of writers who expressed themselves in a religious voice agreed with a writer from Julian, North Carolina: "You who speak of the rule of law, . . . remember that God's law takes precedent over man's law." "I assure you that God is not mocked" and that "His will pertaining to humanity will happen irrespective of what you do," a man from Moline, Illinois, advised Reagan and Gorbachev, reminding them that "God's intended will and program for man, revealed in His inspired holy scriptures, given through instrumentality of angels and man, is available for anyone to discern by careful, reflective study of the Bible."

God alone would judge right from wrong. The challenge of interpretation and conduct was to accept, apply, and obey God's authority:

> The matter is in the hands of the eternal, all knowing Creator who established this nation. I most highly recommend that you . . . bow and repent before your Maker and humbly ask Him to take away your sin. (Man, Westminster, Calif.)

> If you love the God of the Bible why don't you *obey* Him? The God in whom we trust has a higher law than you liberals. Not a sparrow falls without His notice. . . . You liberal law-makers . . . have given more heed to the hippie protesters than to the voice of Almighty God found through Bible study and prayer. . . . We conservatives know that God's judgment day is coming when His books will be opened. His decisions as to "right" and "wrong" will not be based on the Boland Amendment. (Man, Waco, Tex.)

> Good has come of the hearings, for hundreds of thousands of us needed desperately to know that God was still with us and that the government is indeed upon His shoulders and that He shall deliver us. (Woman, Memphis)

> "It is time for Thee, LORD, to work: for they have made void Thy Law." Psalms 119:126. (Corpus Christi, Tex.)

> The Lord has spoken. He took Casey! He took Malcolm Baldridge. (The latter lied about economic statistics.) Hatch, Hyde, Fitzwater, Baker, Greenspan could be next! Reagan must stop lying. (Man)

The methods for understanding and applying God's will were through meditation on one's conduct and through prayer in which the interpreter asked God for forgiveness and guidance. "There is a way out," a woman from Shawneetown, Illinois, promised Hamilton: "You can ask Jesus into your heart and ask him to forgive you." Another woman was more insistent: "What all of you should do is get down on your knees and pray, asking the Lord to come in and take over your life."

Writers quoted the Word of God to remind participants of eternal laws of conduct they had apparently forgotten. Although writers referred to many different stories and maxims from the Bible, they most frequently extracted and applied one principle of judgment. The principle was that a person should judge and act toward others as one wanted to be judged and treated by others. Writers identified two different ways—drawn from different parts of the Bible—of expressing this principle. The first was for people to treat others as they wanted to be treated in return, and the second was to suspend judgment and censure of others until they were themselves blameless:

> Whatever happened to the age old saying, "Do unto others as you would have others do unto you"? (Man, Altoona, Pa.)

> Jesus said, "Let him who is without sin among you be the first to cast a stone." That would eliminate all of you. (Woman, San Francisco)

> Had you been on the scene when the words were spoken "Those among you without Sin, cast the first stone" it would show . . . that not only did you throw the first stone but the last one, while utilizing a large pile of stones in the process. (Man, Mason, Ohio)

> I only wish my god would take over these hearings. I just wonder how many of you have not sinned. None of you, for there is only one person that did not sin and that was Jesus Christ. As it says in the Bible, we are not to judge our neighbors. (Unidentified)

Writers cited precepts from the Bible, other traditional sources of wisdom, or more individual authorities, not as abstractions but as guides to shape personal conduct and relationships or as lessons won hard from firsthand experience. Writers were confident that, just as these had value in their everyday lives, they would help committee members in a difficult task.

V "Listening very carefully to these hearings and trying to make heads and tails of it"—a woman from Huntington, New York, spoke for many others as they formed their conclusions. Each interpreter not only applied experience and invoked authority but also brought a unique cognitive style that distinctively combined values, temperaments, habits, skills, prejudices, and senses of humor. Viewers developed their own ways of asking, deducing, testing, affirming, rejecting, imagining—in short, of interpreting.

Instead of the slick appeals of marketing and the rehearsed lines of punditry, writers described their own processes of forming conclusions as similar to the open-ended rhythms of everyday talk. They started and stopped, meandered from one direction to another, shifted in mood, voice, and confidence. What most impressed aides for Jack Brooks, William Cohen, and David Boren was how much the telephone calls resembled ordinary telephone calls in which callers spoke as they did in everyday conversations. Instead of the usual communication to a legislator in which people asserted a position to be counted, these callers cared as deeply about the conversation as about the opinion they initially called to express. They often reversed direction, sometimes in response to new information or perspective from the aide. They did not want to hang up until they could reach some shared understanding with the aide. Some letters conveyed this open-ended, responsive interpretation. "Yesterday I wrote you a 'hate mail' letter for which I am sorry, and I apologize for its content," a "Concerned Citizen" wrote Hamilton from Maryland. "Please delete [the] last paragraph—I may be in error," a man from Nashua, New Hampshire, added as a postscript to his letter. As in everyday talk, habits of apologizing, of adding and subtracting, accompanied active interpretation.

Writers often evaluated what witnesses and congressmen said on the basis of their reactions to them as people they might encounter around them every day. "Admiral Poindexter . . . shows his contempt for the rights of others by smoking constantly," wrote a woman in Turlock, California. "I could have told you people not to mess with a Marine especially one that went through the Naval Academy," began a woman from Portia, Arkansas: "They are just too well equipped for a normal person to deal with." A man from St. Louis concluded from his five years of working for "'cowboys' like North," particularly a lieutenant colonel who had served in Vietnam, that "they operate on an entirely different channel from the constituted Civil Gov't." "I can relate with Lt. Colonel North's ordeal," began a retired Air Force sergeant in Florida, because "I once was a fall guy for five officers." A man in Van Nuys, California, did not believe Fawn Hall's claims of ignorance about North's activities because "she is the only person I know who does work and doesn't know what she is doing." A man in Gresham, Oregon, was inclined to trust North's judgment because "the players who know North best Love this man."

Many writers tried to make sense of what they were hearing by imagining themselves in the position of the witness. As he listened to Poindexter, a man from Tyler, Texas, "kept asking myself, 'what is going on in his mind?' If I could look through his eyes, what would I see? I have fantasized his answers and have written what I believe he would say." From this empathy he wrote four single-spaced pages to indict Poindexter's critics. A woman from Marina del Ray, California, "known among my friends for having an unusually accurate memory," told Hamilton that she could "not remember everything that happened a year ago" and so she thought committee members were unreasonable in the details they expected Poindexter to remember. "If I was a hostage I wouldn't care what they did to get me out," wrote a man: "Put yourself in the hostages' shoes for a moment," he advised.

Writers brought their own methods for evaluating what they heard. A woman in Quitman, Texas, wanted to study the testimony before deciding what she thought. She videotaped the hearings on fifteen six-hour tapes which she played and reviewed "to form my own opinion." Others judged what a person said on one occasion against what the person had done in the past. North "has lied before—why not now?" asked a couple in Big Arm, Montana. They considered the source. "When people talk to the President they might do well to remember that he was an actor by profession," wrote a woman from Upper St. Clair, Pennsylvania. What they learned at one moment left them with more—and less—confidence in something they had heard earlier. "I laughed when I first heard the allegation late last year [that Reagan campaign aides had made a deal with Iran to send arms if the Iranians waited until after the 1980 election to free the American hostages]. Now, after hearing what you uncovered, this sounds no more mind-boggling than the rest," wrote a woman from San Leandro, California. While few matched the formal rigor of the writer who specified seven assumptions and sets of facts before drawing a conclusion, many constructed their interpretations by applying rules of logic.

When viewers saw a strange juxtaposition of elements—internal inconsistency, paradox, incongruity, hypocrisy—many tried to reconcile the contradiction. They wanted to reconcile the discrepancy in order to decide whether to take more or less seriously something or someone they had estimated differently in an earlier evaluation. "I was amazed to find that Chairman Inouye voted against aid to the Contras," wrote a couple from Greenville, South Carolina, who explained the reason for the amazement: "Anyone who contributed as much as he did in WW2 certainly must see the dangers involved in a Communist takeover in Central America." With all the media talk of Oliver North as a hero a writer in Des Moines was struck by—and sent to Hamilton—a local news story, "Modesty becomes 2-time hero," that described how a Waterloo truck driver had rescued a child from choking and a swimmer from drowning. The truck driver, not North, was the "*authentic American hero*," the writer explained.

Contrasts demanded attention. After listening to Hamilton's "personal attack" on North and then hearing the congressman tell Tom Brokaw that he had not prejudged North, a man from Vero Beach, Florida, heard hypocrisy: "That was wrong saying one thing in the hearings and then saying something different outside the hearings." A woman from Riviera Beach, Florida, imagined how Hamilton had escaped censure for supporting the Boland Amendment: "You surely must have given some good Methodist prayers for never being called to task when the sieve-like Boland Amendment was passed." The hearings introduced viewers to one group of politicians at the same time that another group was campaigning for the presidency. The contrast struck many. "The only thing that still puzzles me is why people like you (and Senators Nunn, Rudman, and Cohen) are content to sit back and let a sad and sorry parade of incompetents, poseurs, and ego-trippers seek the presidential nominations," wrote a man from Alexandria, Virginia: "The country sorely needs leaders of your quality."

Most writers brought a wide assortment of experiences and principles that eased the task of making sense of the unfamiliar. The great authority of common sense, as Clifford Geertz has observed, is that it is "capable of grasping the vast multifariousness of life in the world," the full range of possibilities and contradictions that exist in individuals and cultures.[7] From one perspective the hearings were about lies and lying, and writers had ready principles:

> Lieing is a form of contempt and disrespect and a person that lies does not deserve one bit of respect from anyone. (Man, Burlington, Vt.)

> To deal with rats you have to be a rat. There is no alternative. Hence the "lies and deceit" of North and Poindexter were conceivable; yes, even warranted. (Man, Fox Lake, Ill.)

> We all make mistakes, but they shouldn't be based on deceit. (Woman, Betheda, Md.)

From another perspective the hearings were about the proper relationships between employees and supervisors. Here, too, writers applied principles. "Subordinates only take matters into their own hands when the 'The Boss' is weak and cannot lead," explained a woman from Santa Ana, California. A man from Alexandria, Indiana, applied a different maxim of management to explain why North and Reagan should have ignored the Boland amendment: "You cannot have 535 persons running the show. One person has to be top man." And a woman from Fort Myers, Florida, applied a third perspective on managerial accountability in the form of a question: "Why are you going all out for a subordinate when the Big Cheese is right there—put the blame where it [should be]."

Writers also eased the task of interpretation by using metaphors, similes, and analogies that recapitulated in their distinctive—and diverse—ways their standards for judging how people should act:

> Rome burns while you're fiddling. . . . While you're vilifying Oliver North Communist Russia gains ground in Nicaragua. (Husband and wife, Fair Oaks, Calif.)

> To use a commonplace analogy, when a surgeon performs a cancer operation, but fails to excise the cancer, how can the patient's health be restored? Ronald Reagan's presidency is the cause of this Nation's demise, and the Iran Contra scandal is its outstanding symptom. (Woman, Canoga Park, Calif.)

> My impression is that these Reagan people travel at the drop of a hat, circling the globe, rather than thinking. They seem to me to travel about like warrior ants, flying to far distant countries for just a three hour meeting. . . . Possibly less movement might calm these officials down. (Woman, Haverford, Pa.)

> You will receive back what you have sown. This is a law of life. You will reap what you sow. Remember this in the coming years. (Woman, Colo.)

> The so-called boyish charm is a *calculated act* usually used by children guilty of serious offenses. (Husband and wife, Philadelphia)

Writers often disagreed on how to apply principles that they agreed were important to evaluate people's justifications for their acts. Twenty-four different writers told Hamilton that they believed that a crucial principle of judgment was whether an end could justify any means, but they came up with different answers. A husband and wife from Arlington, Texas, did "NOT believe ends ever justify means," while a woman in Kentfield, California, concluded that "the end justifies the means in this case."

As they began to test and apply conclusions, writers often seized on someone else's view as a place to start. When a statement seemed to be addressing their concerns, they wanted to consider it carefully. "I was driving through a very remote section of Colorado [during the broadcast of Hamilton's speech to North], and even pulled over at one point to better follow your words through the static of poor reception," a man from Denver wrote Hamilton: "I'd like very much to be able to reread your comments." In asking Hamilton for a copy, a man from Hermitage, Tennessee, explained another use: "I want to have as many people read it as I can show it to." They wanted to present his interpretation with others, partly to support their own views and partly to test the interpretation to others before committing themselves fully to it.

When they heard an expression that addressed the present challenge in language they admired, many writers wanted to freeze that statement, to fix it in their memories for future application. Hamilton's remarks to North, wrote men from Tallahassee and Los Angeles, were "timeless." "Your address at the close of Lieutenant Colonel North's testimony was the most eloquent since Lincoln's address at Gettysburg," a woman from Whittier, California, wired Hamilton. An 86-year-old woman from Brooklyn described how Hamilton kindled her memories and inspired her with universal sentiments in a form she wanted to retain for the future:

> Not since the days of Roosevelt have I heard such a delivery of moral, ethical, legal substance. . . . A quality of the above concern is absent in most of our leaders, for, were it not so, we would not have the "goings on" not only in Washington, the "big" men, but also the "little" man in our society. Believe me, please, Rep. Hamilton, I cried when you finished—and your words still linger. How I would love to have a copy.

A woman in Exeter, New Hampshire, had a similar impulse to fix Hamilton's words in her memory: "I heard your closing statement on my car radio and scribbled the quote, 'Democracy is not about objectives but about a means for achieving objectives,' to keep."

Many writers believed that some statements should acquire the authority that parents and teachers used to pass along tried wisdom. By these timeless words Hamilton projected a moral compass that defined what it meant to be an American:

Your words should be printed and distributed across the country, and they should be taught in our civics classes as a modern day explanation of what our system of government is and how it should function. (Man, Houston)

I devoutly wish that your two inspiring speeches could be made required reading for all our young people. (Man, New Rochelle, N.Y.)

Long after the sights and sounds of North's starry-eyed performance has faded from our collective memory, we will be quoting the speech given by Hamilton in our history books and civics classrooms. (Woman, Los Angeles)

By stating lessons that subordinated the personalities and details of this case to more universal principles of popular government, Hamilton helped many viewers formulate in terms of civic legitimacy the personal feelings of exclusion that had originally left them so uneasy and isolated when they heard the stories of Olliemania. Here, then, were words with which to reclaim and reshape the public forum.

Seven

Bringing Critical Issues into the Public Forum

POLICING THE WORLD AND

DEFINING HEROISM

Citizens wrote congressmen to raise the issues they wanted to discuss and resolve in the public forum. They wrote to contribute their deepest convictions to political debate. But before the forum could become a place where citizens and politicians could discuss basic issues that divided them, citizens had to clear the forum of the ways opinion management had distorted both the content of the issues that were raised and the manner in which they were discussed. By insisting that politicians hear and discuss the issues that mattered to them, writers knew that they were challenging customs that opinion management had introduced to political conversation. Politicians seemed to be aiming for and appealing to common denominators they imagined held the audience together as an emotional mass. And by appealing to the most weakly held beliefs at the center of the political spectrum, politicians seemed to prefer to talk about issues on which there was consensus or an acceptable area of compromise—even when neither the issues nor the compromise mattered to most people. Conversely, they sought to avoid issues on which Americans were deeply divided.

The habits of opinion management had so badly distorted conversation in Washington, many writers complained, that politicians had forgotten how to listen to real issues. In their subsequent account of the hearings, two of the most distinguished participants, Senators William Cohen and George Mitchell of Maine, illustrated how the habits of opinion management led politicians to frame political issues differently from the citizens who wrote them. Observing the popular uprising that flooded their offices with phone calls and letters, Cohen and Mitchell concluded that the investigating committees had triggered the revolt by managing public opinion badly. The hearings should have begun, they wrote six months later, with the issue of the sale of weapons to Iran because "most of the Committee members and the American people were truly angry" about that issue. The first rule of opinion management was to appeal to low common denominators. Instead of following that rule and opening with Iran, they opened the investigation with the issue of contra aid about "which the public was confused and the Committee members were divided," a nightmare for opinion manage-ment.[1] In fact, however, viewers wanted congressmen to discuss the issues that really bothered them, not those they did not care about. The senators were right that Nicaragua was more controversial than Iran, but the more important fact was that eight times more Americans wrote Hamilton about Nicaragua than about Iran. More than one out of three writers (36.3 per-cent in one sample of 1,206 letters) raised the issue of Nicaragua to Hamil-ton, but fewer than one in twenty (4.5 percent) brought up Iran. The sale of arms to Iran was a low common denominator media issue—one on which the polls would indeed produce near unanimity of conclusion—but most writers saw the arms sales as an aberration. It was neither deep nor salient to most. Reagan's attempt to overthrow the Sandinistas, by contrast, was a crucial issue that recapitulated the controversies surrounding the develop-ment of American empire.[2] That was the issue they wanted to argue about even if it was too controversial for politicians. The hearings provided an opportunity at last to debate the first principles that politicians had so long deferred.

The Iran-Contra hearings thus provided a rare occasion when viewers by sorting through the details of the moment brought into clear view the underlying and timeless principles that they wanted simultaneously to order the ways they related to the individuals around them and to balance claims for policing the world and maintaining constitutional government at home. While journalists announced that the issue in North's testimony was whether viewers would be swayed by a television performance, viewers thought the debate about North should be about the principles that should govern public policy and personal relationships. While the 1987 debates over covert aid to the Nicaraguan contras clearly belonged to the late years of the Cold War,[3] those debates also illustrated how Americans projected what they expected and experienced in their personal relationships into fun-damental differences about the proper role of government in people's lives and the proper foreign policies for the government to pursue. Because the principles they wanted to uphold in these debates grew from their core val-ues of political ideology and personal relationships, writers insisted on con-veying their needs as clearly as possible in order for the resulting conversa-tion to respond, not to vague rhetoric, but to their basic needs and values. In place of the usual shallow, visceral, blurry statements that politicians hoped would appeal to everyone, viewers insisted on sharp, vivid, profound positions that they knew would widen and deepen debate to address fundamental issues. As writers from the two sides stated their profound differences over whether the United States should police the world, they also revealed two very different ways that they experienced the outside world in their everyday relationships.

When viewers wrote to take sides in a fundamental debate, when they insisted that the forum be a place to debate issues that were salient and controversial instead of those that were safe, writers projected a third way in which they envisioned the public forum in their personal relationships. We have already seen how they wanted to be seen and heard first as distinctive individuals with unique conclusions and second as human beings who believed that universal values of fairness and accountability ought to guide relationships regardless of differences between individuals and groups.

This chapter explores the third way, how the taking of sides, the making of choices, reflected different ways Americans looked outward from their intimate worlds, indeed who they saw as friends and enemies. In stating these differences writers revealed the profound ideological differences that shaped their positions across a spectrum of issues that they rarely felt compelled to bring into the open. In taking sides with such vehemence on this occasion, writers illustrated that however much opinion management assumed that the audience was a mass that could be moved by manipulation at the center, the reality of the public forum for most people was one in which people brought ideologies through which they evaluated the details of new things they encountered. Writing of the particularly partisan arena of presidential campaigns, James Carville noted that "there are only anywhere from 3 to 7 percent of the voters in any election that really decide the outcome. Most people out there are going to vote a certain way, and you know who they are and how they're going to vote before the campaign begins."[4] While taking sides in a congressional hearing was more complex than in a presidential campaign—viewers had to weigh priorities, applications, contradictions among principles, for example, as well as whether to take sides on a particular bill or to state their basic philosophies—many writers still clearly believed that politics was an arena of combat and that the public forum was a place for taking sides, for contributing their specific positions on policy issues or their fundamental ideologies.

In looking at the basic differences that divided writers, we return to the bedrock issues of heroism, foreign policy, and constitutional government that Americans believed were at stake in the hearings. As they explained why Nicaragua was more important to them than Iran, Americans illustrated both the wide divisions of content that split them into two camps and the wide divisions of approach that separated the ways citizens approached issues from the ways legislators did.

❚ Americans wrote Hamilton first to take sides in a political controversy and to influence how he and the House Select Committee would act. Writers wanted legislators above all to know whether they supported the legislator's activity. Because legislators on their side wanted to know whether viewers supported or condemned them, Hamilton directed the staff of the House Select Committee to divide the mail into communications that were "anticommittee" and those that were "procommittee" (which included people who criticized the committee for not probing deeply enough). Because this was the division that made most sense to writers and legislators alike, it is the one we use as the starting place to identify the issues over which Americans divided that summer.

While the letters do not constitute a representative sample of all Americans, they are an excellent window on the issues that mattered to people who wanted to take part in the 1987 debate. Americans wrote congressmen in part because they thought pollsters were asking silly questions. Believing that viewers would (or should) see themselves as an audience at a television performance, for example, pollsters asked whether a performance was credible. Instead of inviting citizens to speak for themselves, pollsters defined the questions and answers citizens could comment on. Only by asking citizens what they had meant by their responses, however, could pollsters have explained why polls produced majorities of Americans who believed that Oliver North was a dedicated patriot whom they would not elect to public office, that he broke the law but should not be prosecuted, or that they "believed" testimony in which he passionately defended his previous lies on the same subjects. Pollsters did not give citizens the chance to explain how they resolved these apparent contradictions.[5]

A study of Americans' political interpretations ought to respect the contexts in which they formed and expressed those conclusions. Politics is an arena in which people could choose when and how—and whether—they wanted to participate. Pollsters, of course, forced everyone to participate, whether they cared about the issue or the pollster's alternatives or not. The most accurate portrayal of a particular political debate may well focus on only those citizens who chose to participate in that forum.

Because Americans tended to write congressmen they admired, the real limit on the representativeness of the letters was whether Americans from all points of view chose to write Hamilton and the House Select Committee. They did. For one thing, newspapers, radio, and television commentators generally presented the House and Senate Select Committees (with their addresses and phone numbers) as places for people to write and call with their conclusions. For another thing, mail to the House Select Committee and its chairman, Lee Hamilton, landed somewhere in the middle of the ideological spectrum of letters to congressmen that summer. Staffers for the House Select Committee and Hamilton filled 56.5 percent of their cartons

Table 7 Themes in Letters to House Select Committee

Theme	Percentage of Letters
Concerns of Anticommittee, Pro-North Writers ($N = 546$)	
(Un)fairness of treatment of individuals	66
Communism	43
Nicaragua	33
(Un)accountability of individuals for acts	29
Communism is a geographic threat	25
U.S.S.R.	22
Oliver North got the job done	19
Investigation is partisan attack on Reagan	18
Investigation embarrasses U.S. in world's eyes	16
(Un)heroism	15
Protection and security	13
Concerns of Procommittee, Anti-North Writers ($N = 660$)	
(Un)accountability of individuals for acts	52
Constitution	41
Nicaragua	39
Democracy	37
(Un)heroism	24
Rule of law	24
Oliver North lied and deceived	23
(Un)fairness of treatment of individuals	17
Contras kill innocent people	17
U.S. has no right to impose its will on others	15
Memory of nazism and World War II war on fascism	15

with procommittee communications that basically applauded the investigation and Hamilton while disapproving of witnesses like Oliver North and filled 43.5 percent with messages that condemned the committee and praised North. Hamilton's mail was more sympathetic to the committee than letters to conservative Republicans such as James Courter and less sympathetic than letters to liberal Democrats such as Louis Stokes.

The sample of letters and telegrams to Hamilton from which I identified the themes to analyze in this chapter paralleled very closely the pattern of all communications to the House Select Committee. After eliminating orchestrated communications and those that were too brief to identify any theme other than gratitude or condemnation, I ended up with 546 anticommittee letters and 660 procommittee letters from which at least one theme could be extracted. The sample thus contained 54.7 percent procommittee communications in an entire collection that was procommittee by a 56.5 percent margin.

From a list of fifty-six recurring topics and themes, table 7 lists the eleven that writers from each "side" mentioned most frequently. Any aggregation of themes identified and compiled by an outside observer must be subjective. Each letter was a unique expression. And yet the list of themes has the overwhelming advantage that these were themes that the writers themselves chose to bring up.

■■ Writers wanted above all to widen the discussion of the Iran-Contra scandal to include the issue that most deeply divided supporters from critics of the investigation: should the United States police the world? Writers argued particularly about the desirability of military solutions to international conflicts and about the proper role for the military to play in an American life shaped by imperial scope. While writers identified political principles as the basic points that divided one side from the other in the debate over whether the United States should police the world, they also often conveyed a sense that differences in principle overlapped differences in how they experienced personal relationships. Writers for one side seemed to face their personal relationships inward, concerned with protecting the right of people to choose how they wanted to live, while those for the other side seemed to face outward, concerned with preserving respect against external enemies. North's supporters embraced his attempts to protect their security from foreign enemies. North's critics feared that his actions threatened the Constitution. Because the public arena seemed so rarely to provide an opportunity to debate the desirability of American military empire and interventions abroad—and because legislators seemed to want to keep the issue narrowly focused—writers seized on this occasion with particular eagerness to explain where they stood and to insist that the underlying principle be debated.

As Americans defined the terms of that debate in their letters, they disagreed both over which values and traditions ought to guide American policy and over how to interpret and apply traditions and values both sides claimed to support. The depth of that division becomes clear by comparing the frequency with which writers on each side brought up a theme (see table 8).

The debate over policing the world pitted the two sides in a conflict over American policy at home and abroad. It was true that different supporters of a position brought different emphases. Some critics of the investigation began, for example, with a fear for the safety of their own children while others began with a partisan vision of a Democratic Congress, a fear of rising immigration, or a preoccupation with Soviet intentions. Some supporters of the investigation began with a concern for domestic American needs, while others began with a reverence for law, a sympathy for people who were fighting dictators in their countries, or a religious commitment to peace. There were clear points where the two sides converged at least in spirit. Both carried a strong isolationist tone in which a strong American

Table 8 Themes in Letters to House Select Committee

Theme	Procommittee (%)	Anticommittee (%)
Communism	3.0	43.4
Anticommunism	3.5	0.2
Democracy	37.3	4.9
Constitution	41.2	8.1
Rule of law	24.2	4.0
Freedom	2.4	4.9
Free enterprise/capitalism	0.6	1.3
Investigation embarrasses U.S. in world's eyes	3.0	15.6
Protection and security	0.6	13.2
U.S. has no right to intervene in internal affairs of others	15.3	0
Political and diplomatic answers are better than military ones	11.1	0.2
Communism is a geographic threat	1.7	24.9
U.S. domestic needs more important than foreign needs	5.7	0.2
Pursuit of democracy abroad erodes it in U.S.	6.7	0
Nicaragua	39.1	33.0
U.S.S.R.	2.0	21.6
Cuba	0.5	7.0
Iran	3.8	5.3
World War II (excl. nazism)	1.8	4.2
Nazism	13.2	1.6
Vietnam	3.3	4.9
Korea	0.9	1.8
Watergate	3.3	1.3
Monroe Doctrine	0.2	2.7
N(letters)	660	546

presence abroad should be pursued, if at all, more with reluctance than desire. Both sides valued principles like accountability and fairness. Both sides agreed on the facts of what Oliver North had done. Neither side conveyed much of a sense of the American mission or American idealism that had inspired American internationalists earlier in the century. Only 1.3 percent of the investigation's critics and 0.6 percent of its supporters associated an American role abroad in any way with free enterprise, capitalism, or a market economy. Still, there were two unmistakable camps.

Critics of the investigation looked outward from their personal relationships, fearing that outsiders threatened the security of their intimate worlds, their children, their jobs, their respect in the eyes of others. The best protection against these menaces was an imposing defense that would deter potential invaders from challenging the critics' worlds. They feared developments abroad that might menace their own children. The United States should

129

seek and arm friends abroad in order to spare American children from having to fight.

Some feared that Americans would have to defend the United States against a menace that was literally approaching the country's borders. For some that threat came in the form of refugees who left their homelands to settle in the United States. "The quality of life in South Florida has deteriorated tremendously," wrote a woman from Boca Raton, Florida, when refugees from Cuba migrated to the United States. The result of the Nicaraguan revolution, according to a woman in San Antonio, was that "we are already being invaded and the political refugees have already started flowing over this border." The sense of an imminent threat at the borders merged with a fear that young Americans would be forced to defend that border sooner or later:

> We will have to draft our sons and grandsons to fight for protection of our very borders. All President Reagan and Col. North want is for the Freedom Fighters (which you mistakenly call "Contra's") to fight for their own country. If they are not permitted to do so, it will be our "boys." (Man, Deerfield Beach, Fla.)

> Will it be necessary for the Communists to start pounding on the gates of El Paso, Texas, before you and your naive cohorts wake up and recognize the danger to this country? (Man, Knoxville, Tenn., to George Mitchell)

> Stop the spread of the horrendous, degrading, and crushing communist wave that is eating up bigger and bigger portions of the world, about to creep through your very own back door here in Texas. (Woman, Houston, to Jack Brooks)

Defense of home and family required the American government to protect friends all over the world against those who might threaten the United States. The word "protection" was the principle most frequently named by critics of the investigation. One in every seven critics brought it up, and in nearly the same way: "You have a *constitutional obligation* to *protect* the people of this country," explained a man from Green Valley, Arizona. "What we want of you who are suppose[d] to represent us," wrote a woman from Sierra Madre, California, is "to protect us and protect our borders," that is, "to defend me and my family from foreign attack." And they wanted people to protect them from external dangers: "Thank God that Oliver North was there to defend me and my family," began a woman from Jensen Beach, Florida.

Fearful of threats from without, critics worried about strangers and enemies who were watching their actions, perhaps with respect, perhaps with ridicule, perhaps with approval, perhaps with disgust or contempt. They conveyed a sense that they were being monitored closely for signs of weakness that rivals or judges might seize to invade or mock their worlds. This view broadened in the age of television into a conviction that people all over the world were watching and evaluating how Americans behaved, watching for things that would command respect or that would signal weakness. They feared embarrassment and humiliation with an acute sensitivity that blurred the personal with the political. The theme that the hearings were embarrassing the United States in the eyes of the world was the ninth most common theme for the investigation's critics. It was mentioned by one in six of them. And the form of disrespect they feared most was ridicule:

> The whole Communist world must be staying awake nights laughing at us. Why we insist on tearing ourselves apart in front of the entire world doesn't make any sense. (Woman, Walcut, Calif.)

> The manner in which they have been conducted creates an atmosphere which must cause world-wide disrespect for the United States and makes us the subject of ridicule. (Man, Granada Hills, Calif.)

> Russia must have been thrilled watching this over the air. (Husband and wife, Burghill, Ohio)

> Our allies look at us as a bunch of nincompoops and our enemies are laughing with glee. (Husband and wife, Roy, Utah)

From these yearnings for protection and respect, critics of the investigation constructed a reading of history in which totalitarian governments developed insatiable appetites for world conquest. Beginning with Nazi Germany's conquests of its weaker neighbors, dictators marched ever onward until stopped by superior military force. The Allied victory over the Nazis proved the necessity for military solutions to the challenge of totalitarian governments, but it also proved that the United States, as in 1917–18, was the military power of last resort that would ultimately, however reluctantly, have to settle any issue in the world.

Stalin inherited Hitler's relentless quest for world conquest, seeking to impose communism on weaker nations. The omnipresent threat of communism was the second most common theme of the investigation's critics. They defined the threat of totalitarianism—Soviet and Nazi alike—as a military one:

> This Communist Cancer Threat does exist and we must fight it with all of our zeal and power, wherever free countries have been and are falling under the slavery of Soviet domination, OR WE SHALL SURELY LOSE OUR OWN FREEDOM. . . . We would like for you to explain . . . why it is that you are so proud of your part in fighting against a Nazi drive for totalitarian control of the world, but are unwilling to even resist with the same zeal against the Soviet Drive for a Communist Totalitarian Control of the World, which, I might add, has progressed further along than Hitler's drive for World Conquest. (Man, Shalimar, Fla.)

The U.S.S.R. is the most land-hungry, power-thirsty empire that the world has ever known. (Man, Indianapolis)

The only way to answer this threat, these writers believed, was a strong military deterrent. "History will teach you that Marxists only listen to force," explained a man from Poinciana, Florida. After crushing Germany and Japan with military force, "American children walked the streets in those countries untouched. They didn't love us, but had fear and respect," wrote a woman approvingly from Pennington, New Jersey. "It is time Congress . . . gets down to business of this country, builds a strong defense and be Number 1 Country, where no other country can boast 'they will take us over without a shot.'"

Since dictators were insatiable in their desires and relentless in their determination, they constantly probed for weakness in their adversaries. The basic challenge to Americans in 1987 was the same as it had been when the Nazis threatened Austria and Czechoslovakia a half-century earlier, to find the will to resist the dictator's drive for conquest, to demonstrate resolve and toughness. That resolve would command respect from dictators and that respect would finally protect Americans' intimate worlds. Resolve now could forestall the need for military action later.

Admirers of Reagan and North believed that the American people had demonstrated that resolve by reelecting Reagan by a popular landslide in 1984. Critics of the investigation justified the administration's pursuit of extraordinary measures to stop "communism" in the name of the majority that had reelected the president. From their point of view—and this theme was the eighth most common one for critics, mentioned by 18 percent of writers—Congress and the Democrats were trying to "tie the hands of our President, with just one interest, their aim to enhance their own powers," wrote a man from Cincinnati. To critics of the investigation Lee Hamilton and Democrats in Congress had often in the past lacked the will to deter communist expansion, leaving American homes vulnerable to humiliation and attack. They were unwilling to provide enough weapons to deter governments that disagreed with American purposes, and they were unwilling to give all-out support when the United States did commit military forces to a struggle. Nicaragua was just the latest example in a long history of weakness:

> I recall as if it was yesterday that John F. Kennedy, another Democrat—refused air cover at the Bay of Pigs—and now we got a Soviet state 90 miles from our shore. (Man, Decatur, Ga.)

> It is Congress who paralyzes the nation so that we cannot act to pursue our legitimate interest anywhere in the world: at home, Lebanon, hostages, Persian Gulf, Central America. You name it. It is the Congress who is directly responsible for the death and maiming of untold thousands of Americans in

this century; walking away from the League of Nations at the end of World War I, refusing to allow the US to arm itself between World War I and II. . . . The Congress required us to wait until the Japanese were able to cremate us at Pearl Harbor. It was Congress who allowed us to commit troops in Korea, but then . . . jerked the rug out from under us. I was there. It was the Congress who allowed us to build up combat personnel in Vietnam, but refused to let them fight to win, and finally deserted those men in the rice patties of Viet Nam.

Congress is to blame for much, Mr. Hamilton. How about our policy of No Win in Vietnam? Congress sat back and did nothing to change that while brave American boys died in vain. (Man, Bronx, N.Y.)

Deserting men to their deaths must come easy to Democrats. Truman did it in Korea and Johnson did it in Viet-Nam. (Man, Hurricane, Utah)

Because the defense of homes and reputations rested on determination to assert American military power, some critics of the investigation found a common pattern to explain why some congressmen failed to support military measures. "Your closing speech . . . must have *thrilled the Soviets!*" wrote a woman in Winnetka, Illinois. The hearings were a "shameful Soviet style, KGB flavored" tribunal (Johnson City, Tenn.) for which Hamilton should be tried for treason (Valparaiso, Ind.; Lookout Mountain, Tenn.; Columbus, Ohio; and Victoria, Tex.). "Lee," began a man from Taylor County, Texas, "our country for sure can not be run nor can it last if it is led by communist lovers like yourself. . . . You are so much like the Reds, you would never know the difference."

The basic difference between the intimate worlds of supporters and critics was that the supporters faced inward and the critics faced outward. Critics wanted protection and respect from outsiders while supporters wanted to live their own lives in peace. While critics brooded about threats from foreign enemies, supporters worried about threats from their own government that left citizens feeling powerless. Supporters were less concerned with whether Americans had the will to stop a rising dictator's possible military challenge to neighboring countries than with whether his own people had the will to preserve and mobilize their own liberties to stop his rise. While parents from both sides were eager to shield their children from foreign combat, supporters believed that the way to do this was not to fund proxy armies but to shun commitments to defend remote governments in the first place. While critics wanted the United States to command respect throughout the world, supporters worried that the price of establishing that respect was to erode at home rules that established the accountability of people for their acts and the ability of people to live as they wanted.

The starting point for supporters of the investigation was the desire to protect their capacity for self-government against a growing tendency of powerful executives to manage and ultimately silence citizens. Eager to protect their personal relationships, supporters championed diversity of lifestyle and belief and protection for minority rights against intrusion by either majorities or strong governments. They turned their deep fear of unchecked power into a strong defense of the Constitution and its doctrine of checks and balances. The real threat was from zealots who were so eager to promote their own agendas that they had little respect for the rights of people who disagreed with them, and little understanding that government was created by and belonged to its citizens, not to those who temporarily held its offices. Supporters grounded their case in procedural defenses that placed means above ends, that held government accountable to citizens—the most common theme of the investigation's supporters, mentioned by 52 percent of all writers. In this vein, 24 percent believed that the rule of law was the issue at stake in the hearings (the sixth most common theme) and 37 percent thought it was about democracy (the fourth most common theme). The most fundamental of all defenses for supporters was the Constitution, the founding document that gave Americans both the ideology and the legal means to restrain those whose thirst for power would threaten their worlds. It was mentioned by 41 percent of supporters.

History was the story of how people had increasingly fought for and won the struggle against rulers who had wielded arbitrary and unlimited power and in their victory had secured the capacity to govern themselves:

> The real issue is whether one man, be it the President or the National Security Director, can privately determine the fate of America. Certainly the founding fathers had no intention of creating another king with no obligation to listen to others. The real problem that threatens us is the existence of a shadowy, non-elected government in which loyalty and truth, deniability and responsibility are hopelessly entangled. (Woman, Philadelphia)

> While listening to Admiral Poindexter and Colonel North testify these past few weeks, I have sometimes felt myself to be living in a world where the Magna Carta had never been signed, where Louis the Sixteenth had not lost his head to disprove forever the doctrine of absolute monarchy, where George Washington had accepted, rather than refused, the crown of the United States of America. (Woman, Sherman Oaks, Calif.)

> The United States is a unique historical experiment in large-scale democracy, and real patriotism necessitates a strong belief in our Constitution and the idea of checks and balances which insure that no one cadre of individuals can control national policy. (Woman, Seattle)

The Constitution loomed as large to supporters of the investigation—their second most frequent theme—as communism did to its critics. As critics feared threats from without that required strong governments to protect them, supporters feared threats from within that required constant vigilance against those whose abuses of power would erode their liberties at home.

Believing that North and Reagan could be held accountable when the Constitution could be made to work, they called on Congress to use its powers to investigate and withhold funds as the most effective means to protect their intimate worlds. If the Constitution could not be made to restrain North, then citizens lost the most basic bulwark of their liberties. By holding North accountable, Congress preserved constitutional government:

> Our basic law has been badly battered. We count on you to continue the work of trying to restore the Constitution to some semblance of health. (Woman, Mashpee, Mass.)

> Do not allow Constitution to be shredded because North telegenic. (Woman, Irvine, Calif.)

> The real way to celebrate the writing of the Constitution is to keep it from being trampled in the name of "heroism and patriotism." (Woman, Summertown, Tenn.)

> Checks and balances are a bore.
> They mess up Reagan's contra war.
> (Since commies pose an evil threat,
> Please don't mention fascists yet.)
> Why heed the rules when we know best?
> Democracy is just a pest.
> (Man, Norwalk, Conn.)

Looking inward, supporters of the investigation believed that the first priority for American will and resources was to ease the private burdens that Americans themselves faced at home. Fully 5.7 percent of supporters wrote that domestic priorities should be higher than international ones. Because aid to the contras was the topic of the hearings, they often stated this priority in the form of a contrast:

> When we think of our own U.S. problems—the disintegration in our cities—homeless people—hungry people—the problem of AIDS—pollution—congestion—so much could be done right here with the millions that are being squandered in financing the Contras. (Man, West Tisbury, Mass.)

> If those who worked so diligently to aid the Contras would throw their weight into helping the poor and the suffering in our own country, this would be a better country for us, but more importantly for our children and grandchildren. (Woman, Denver)

With the same fear of unchecked power that led them to embrace the Constitution, supporters identified with the struggles of people in other lands to gain control over their lives. They believed that people ought to have the right to think and act as they wanted. By intervening in the internal affairs of other countries the United States was meddling where it did not belong, in other people's business, precisely the threat writers felt most acutely to their own lives.

We have no right to be messing with people's lives in Nicaragua. It's their country, not ours. (Woman, San Rafael, Calif.)

I would like to see us stay home as a country and mind our own business for a change. Why are we meddling all around the world? (Woman, Fargo, N.Dak.)

I don't want to cram our form of government down the throats of other peoples. (Woman, Houston)

Our tax money should be used at home, not in Haiti, Israel, and God knows where else and we should mind our own house and stay out of other countries trying to tell them what to do. (Woman, Bradfordsville, Ky.)

Eager to protect the ability of people to control their own lives, to provide jobs, health, food, and shelter, convinced that the violence that threatened Americans took place not in some remote place but on the streets of American cities, many supporters constructed their own history of American empire. The noble crusade to help weaker nations resist subjugation by stronger ones had increasingly degenerated into propping up local dictators:

Historically this nation has supported right wing dictators throughout the world. (Husband and wife, Minneapolis)

I hope to look at our flag one day without being reminded of assassination plots and the mass slaughter of non-white peoples. Nothing brought me so low as to hear the best people in Congress—you, for example—smoothly nodding agreement that covert actions are necessary. . . . Afraid you'll be called a commie? Please, sir, gentility has its limits. Get us out of the killing business. (Man, New York)

Those of us who really care about freedom, self-determination and other ideals connected with democracy cannot help but wonder why our government was never worried about the spread of some of the most undemocratic and brutal dictatorships seen in recent history. Our government, in fact, installed some of them, supported others, and has advocated "constructive engagement" in still others; witness the histories of Guatemala, Chile, Iran, El Salvador, South Africa. (Woman, Somerville, Mass.)

By the late 1980s, many committee supporters believed, the United States had settled into the role of "self-appointed law enforcer and policeman of the world," in the words of a Seattle man. For a man in Ashland, Oregon, the behavior of the United States conjured up the picture of behavior he dreaded in intimate relationships: "We are really the great 'bully nation' at present, all over the world." The United States was "imperial policeman of the world" (Aptos, Calif.) and "self righteous giant of the world" (Hartford, Wisc.).

By assuming the role of world policeman the United States transformed local conflicts into pieces of a single ideological struggle with communism. That struggle subjected the diverse ways people lived around the world to a single test. It reduced economic, cultural, religious, and political diversity and conflicts to military challenges. In the same way that they condemned opinion management for reducing their rich range of experiences and perspectives to a single denominator, supporters of the investigation tried to persuade congressmen that local uprisings were just that. They were neither military challenges nor parts of a monolithic communist menace:

> We have become increasingly appalled by the ideological game that the U.S. government insists on perpetuating while the lives of innocent Americans and destitute Nicaraguans are threatened and cast into upheaval. (Nine people from around San Jose, Calif.)

> The colonel seems to believe for instance that the only two sovereign nations on "the planet earth," to employ one of his own favorite phrases, are the United States and the Soviet Union, all the rest being merely pawns in a superpower chess game. (Man, San Diego)

> Does Nicaragua exist solely as a possible base for a military confrontation between the United States and the Soviet Union? Is the attitude of the United States in world affairs to be continuously based on a paranoiac fear of communism and Marxism (however expressed), as it has been in our attitudes toward Korea, the Philippines, Vietnam and now Iran and Central America? (Man, San Diego)

The consequence of militarizing disputes abroad was to lose American ideals at home. Indeed, 6.7 percent of the committee's supporters advised Hamilton that the hearings revealed that the result of promoting democracy abroad was indeed to erode the ability of Americans to shape their own fates:

> At home our society has become militarized and secret. As it has become so, we the people are denied real participation in the decision-making process. (Woman, Carmel, Calif.)

> The most precious thing we have is our constitutional form of government. Those who sidestepped the provisions of the Constitution in their zeal to bring democracy to Nicaragua have imperiled democracy here at home. (Woman, San Francisco)

> When Congress enacted the National Security Act of 1947, it was the beginning of the end of our constitutional form of government. It was an admission that our system was unable to cope with world problems as a free and open society. (Man, Williamsburg, Mich.)

The militarization of policy had bestowed domestic power on the military. While many supporters had served in the military and many more admired individual military officers, writers drew on an American tradition of civilian control to express fears of too much power for the military at home. The mission and culture of a professional military corps, these writers believed, ran counter to those of democracy. "We want men responsible to the laws of the land, the will of the people—not a free-floating military," wrote a New Yorker.

The zeal and resourcefulness with which Admiral Poindexter and Colonel North had hidden their activities from Congress, their indifference to law and the Constitution, persuaded many Americans that they symbolized the domestic consequences of pursuing an ideological and militarized presence abroad. The United States was coming to resemble the military dictatorships that it was promoting and defending. Just as committee critics feared that Hamilton and Democratic congressmen were making over the United States to resemble the Soviet Union, supporters believed that North and Poindexter were making over the United States to resemble a military junta:

> Shades of the Junta and the Colonels of South America. He would destroy the very democracy he claims to love in his zeal to destroy the Sandinistas. (Woman, Newton Center, Mass.)
>
> Have we become a "Banana Republic" where the Col's take over whenever they feel like it? (Raynham, Mass.)
>
> Never in my long life (nearly 90) have I been so near to be frightened of a military coup! (Woman, Sanford, Fla.)
>
> With Poindexter's testimony I am more certain than ever that the Congress should legislate against having military men in high positions with executive discretionary power. I fear more flagrant Juntas in the future. These men are robots, trained to obey . . . they do not belong in high positions in this ostensibly Democratic government. They mean a Banana Republic. (Woman, San Diego)

For supporters more than critics, Nazi Germany offered the most haunting historical memory that framed their thinking about democracy, militarization, and diplomacy. The frightening story from Germany was that people in an "advanced" society had lacked the will and democratic capacity to resist a dictator's rise from within and then seemed to become a mass that would do whatever the dictator wanted, even when his desires threatened the most basic values that people tried to live by in their personal relationships. The challenge in the North case was whether a determined band of zealous officials could overturn American laws and traditions and seize power at home as Nazis had in Germany. And the frightening parallel was not that a strong nation was threatening a weaker neighbor but that a zealot was using the fear of communism to justify suspension of democratic procedures at home. From the example of the Nazis, committee supporters "fear[ed] FASCISM more than communism," wrote a woman from Palo Alto, California.

On the afternoon of July 9, 1987, North said something that encapsulated the deepest fears of those who were reminded of Nazi Germany. Senate attorney Arthur Liman asked North why he had not asked his boss, Admiral Poindexter, whether he had discussed the Iran-Contra matter with Reagan. North replied by passionately defending the obligation of a soldier not to question authority or to take personal responsibility for evil he could prevent:

> I'm not in the habit of questioning my superiors. If he deemed it not to be necessary to ask the President, I saluted smartly and charged up the hill. That's what lieutenant colonels are supposed to do. . . . And if the Commander in Chief tells this Lieutenant Colonel to go stand in the corner and sit on his head, I will do so. And if the Commander in Chief decides to dismiss me from the NSC staff, this Lieutenant Colonel will proudly salute and say, "Thank you for the opportunity to have served," and go.[6]

The democratic principle that soldiers had a responsibility to question a superior officer's unjust or immoral orders was the most important lesson supporters of the investigation had learned from the experience of Nazi Germany. German officers could have stopped the Holocaust if they had followed their consciences instead of their orders:

> North's partial excuse for his perjury and other crimes is "I was following orders." This rings hollow after the Nuremburg trials. Eichmann and Klaus Barbie also testified "I was following orders." (Man, Los Angeles)
>
> Mr. North thinks "my commander-in-chief right or wrong" is proof of American Idealism, but I think it is more consistent with Nazi patriotism than our own. (Man, Flushing, N.Y.)
>
> It is frightening that so many of our citizens feel "sincerity" is the highest virtue. Many of those tried at Nuremburg (if I may be so bold) were very "sincere." (Man, Plainville, Conn.)

Supporters of the investigation proposed three alternatives to military solutions that they hoped would wean the United States from habits of empire that were propelling American policy beyond the reach of standards that people used in their everyday lives. The first was to encourage indigenous movements by people to revolt against unrepresentative rulers. Inheritors of a revolution that threw off the British Crown, Americans should identify with—and support—insurgent and revolutionary movements abroad like Solidarity in Poland and indeed the Sandinistas in Nicaragua.

The second approach was to provide an example of democratic and constitutional ideals in action. By investigating and prosecuting those who acted as though patriotic motives entitled them to violate the law, the United States would prove the strength of its ideals. "I'd like to see us win over the peoples of other countries by good example—not by killing them," wrote a woman from San Jose. "The best thing Americans can do to fight communism is to conduct our own governmental affairs according to our own laws. . . . The worst thing . . . is to demonstrate that we have no respect for our laws and institutions if we happen to disagree with them," wrote a man from Franksville, Wisconsin.

Drawing on their everyday habits of dealing with conflicts, some writers proposed a third approach in which the United States should "encourage a foreign policy that tries to settle disagreements diplomatically instead of with guns," proposed a woman from Millbrae, California. "We cannot *kill* our way to peace—and peace is what we need," declared a woman from Atlanta. Calling for "negotiated solutions," a husband and wife from Santa Cruz, California, wanted to "remove war from our foreign policy agenda."

■■■ The debates over covert action and contra aid recapitulated the fundamental differences that divided Americans while also illustrating the different ways citizens and congressmen approached issues. While congressmen tried to narrow the issues of covert action and contra aid into limited debates over how much aid for the contras and what kind of supervision for covert actions, most writers saw these two policies not as practices to be compromised upon, but as manifestations of principles to be defended. They either favored or opposed covert action. They either favored or opposed aid to the contras. The debate over these two issues provided an opportunity for Americans to express the full range of their views on empire, to make choices, even while congressmen eagerly sought to rein in the debate and find low common denominators—"consensus." But common denominators were a fantastic invention of people who were simply not listening to Americans talk that summer.

Writers debated covert activities as a choice between security and accountability. "Secrecy and covert actions are absolutely necessary for any viable government to deal with allies and adversaries," declared a man from Morrow, Ohio. "War and conflicts must be planned and decisions must be made in secret and begun in secret. How else will the enemy and enemies not know our plans?" demanded a man from Odessa, Texas. The contras had blocked the Sandinistas from implementing their revolutionary program because of covert American aid. Without that aid the contras would have disbanded and the Sandinistas would have been unimpeded. To have revealed the aid to even a few congressional leaders was to risk opening a public discussion with consequences they might not be able to manage and control. "The fewer people that know the safer the secret," summed up a man from Gladstone, Missouri.

Supporters of the investigation replied that the real purpose of covert actions was to prevent Americans from participating in choices and interfering with decisions. "The price of protecting the secrecy of covert actions at home," explained a woman from Elysburg, Pennsylvania, was "the concentration of power in the hands of a tiny band of zealots, and that is the end

Table 9 Themes in Letters to House Select Committee: Nicaragua

Theme	Procommittee (%)	Anticommittee (%)
Aid contras so Americans won't have to fight	0.2	6.4
Contras kill innocent people	17.1	0
Contras run drugs to U.S.	2.8	0
Contras fight for Nicaraguans' freedom	0	0.9
Sandinistas threaten neighboring countries	0	1.8
U.S. destabilizes legitimate Nicaraguan government	8.0	0
Political/diplomatic solutions better than military ones	11.1	0.2
U.S. has no right to intervene in Nicaragua	15.3	0
$\mathcal{N}$ (letters)	660	546

of democracy." Believing that democracy was a process, not a victory or an institution, supporters believed that there would be no difference in people's everyday lives between an American and a Soviet empire if both were operated by unaccountable elites. "Time and time again," observed a man,

> Oliver North said that the United States must emulate the Soviet Union in the way that it deals with international events. I watched his eyes virtually glow when he described the means used by the Soviet Union to counteract terrorism. . . . It seems sad to me that the very people who most strongly profess to believe that the democratic system is the strongest and best are the very ones who seek to subvert that system by using the means championed by totalitarian regimes.

A woman in Seattle posed a stark question and answer: "Question: What's the difference between the secret government in the White House and in the U.S.S.R. Answer: Nothing. N.S.C. = K.G.B." The desire to proclaim the superiority of democratic or American values should lead the United States to renounce, not embrace, covert actions.

Nicaragua provided a second issue over which Americans spread their positions across a much wider spectrum than did congressmen. Although the question of whether to support the contras in hopes of defeating the Sandinista Revolution was a major ideological issue between Democrats and Republicans and between conservatives and pragmatists within the White House,[7] the debate in Washington occurred within a relatively narrow band, while the debate in bars, officers, and homes was sharp and ideological, pitting one worldview against another. The debate over contra aid recapitulated the terms of wider debate over whether the United States should police the world (see table 9).

The war between Sandinistas and contras for control of Nicaragua split writers into two camps. There was no middle ground. Many writers warmly supported the Sandinistas, something no congressman did. To the Right, the contras were fighting for the freedom of the Nicaraguan people, to keep communism out of the Western Hemisphere, and, in the view mentioned most often by procontra writers, to prevent Americans from ultimately having to go to war in Nicaragua. A husband and wife from Tyler, Texas, underscored how aid to the contras would protect their own children from an outside menace: "Money from Congress would support the contras to defend their own country, then my children's lives would not have to be put in jeopardy." Invoking the American struggle for freedom from British meddling in their internal affairs, however, a man from Los Angeles deeply resented Reagan's characterization of contras as freedom fighters like the revolutionaries of 1776 because he doubted whether the founding fathers of the United States "would have found a force led by members of Somoza's secret police to have much in common with them."

The writers disagreed passionately over the proper role for the United States. In a vivid image of how outsiders could destroy the health of people, a man from Provo, Utah, wanted the government to "enforce the Monroe Doctrine and rid our continent of the Ortega cancer." Others agreed with the man from San Francisco who could "think of no basis for the attitude of this country toward the Sandinista government other than a desire to bully a small, impoverished country into pledging fidelity to the programs of this country." "What legal right does the United States have to oust the government of Nicaragua when it is duly elected by the people?" demanded a man from Dayton, Ohio. "Let the Nicaraguans fight their own war," added a woman from Ardmore, Pennsylvania. "In view of our own history," asked a man from St. Helena, California, "would it not be prudent, and proper to allow the people of Nicaragua to make their own mistakes?" By intervening, including by mining Nicaragua's harbors in a move that brought censure from the World Court, the United States "must be considered an outlaw nation," concluded a man from Long Beach.

To many writers the Sandinistas "liberated the people of Nicaragua from the dictatorship of Somoza, just as the revolutionaries in colonial states liberated America from the oppressive king of England," in the words of a man from Omaha. Sandinismo was "one small country's attempt to take control of its own destiny, to move at the same time away from the brutal military dictatorships imposed upon it, and from the super power that in fact imposed those dictatorships," wrote a couple from Philadelphia. The Sandinistas were "a government that actively works to deliver health care, education and land to the poor" (Pasadena) and "a social-democrat regime" (San Mateo, Calif.) who brought "the vitality of democratic institutions and processes" to Nicaragua along with "the freedom of average people to disagree with the government without fear of reprisal" (Great Barrington, Mass.). To a man in Oceanside, California, on the other hand, "tens of thousands of innocent people whose only crime is to want freedom and self determination have been jailed, tortured, mutilated and murdered by Daniel Ortega's secret police and army."

Nicaragua exploded into a battleground between those who feared that the right to live as people wanted was threatened by unchecked power and those who believed that they would only be personally secure if outsiders respected American authority. The Reagan administration made the overthrow of the Sandinistas its top diplomatic goal. While Democratic legislators refused to defend the Sandinistas, they did determine that the contra army should not receive direct military aid for part of the decade. In Washington congressmen argued over the amount and form, not the objective, of American policy. But with those around them Americans debated the basic issue of whether the United States should intervene when people chose governments that offended American policymakers.

IV For many Americans the issue of whether Oliver North was a hero provided an opportunity to restate the basic ways they interpreted the world. Agreeing on what North thought he was doing, writers fought passionately over whether his actions and justifications were good or bad, heroic, pathetic, or treasonous. And that debate soon circled back to the reason Americans had written congressmen in the first place: to claim the right to proclaim their own heroes. The power to define and proclaim heroism was, after all, the power to define and proclaim the values the community would pass along to its children and expect its members to uphold in their daily lives. For this reason, as table 10 indicates, writers were more concerned with North's claims to heroism than his claims to patriotism, a claim they associated with vague and inclusive rhetoric. The debate over what Americans looked for in their heroes was simultaneously a debate over which American traditions to activate, a reprise of the debate over foreign policy, and the chance to reaffirm the supremacy of face-to-face values over those of selling and acting.

Table 10 reports the frequency with which the investigation's critics and supporters mentioned themes and personality traits in their discussions of Oliver North. Far from responding as an mass audience to a dramatic performance, viewers agreed on North's qualities but then valued those qualities very differently.[8] Most viewers found him charming, for example. A woman in Georgetown, South Carolina, believed North was "extremely intelligent, loyal, sensitive, warm, caring, affable and possesses a sense of humor" in calling him a "charismatic hero," but a man in Los Angeles warned Hamilton that "the devil is usually portrayed as a similarly charming and daring personality."

The debate over North's heroism was not over whether he had done extraordinary or superhuman things but over how to judge what he did. And

Table 10 Themes in Letters to House Select Committee: Oliver North

Theme	Procommittee (%)	Anticommittee (%)
"Heroism"	24.0	15.2
"Patriotism"	10.9	10.1
Military heroism	1.7	2.7
Positive personal qualities	3.3	4.2
Gets the job done (ends above means)	1.4	19.2
His beliefs and convictions	1.4	5.9
Dedicated, selfless, zealot	8.1	8.4
Lied and deceived (means above ends)	23.3	3.7
Told truth	0.8	3.7
Obeyed orders	3.5	2.7
Unaccountable	11.1	0
Prosecute him	4.4	0
Don't prosecute him	0	6.0
He protected, defended me	0	3.8
N(letters)	660	546

what shaped that judgment was how writers' own personal styles of relating to those around them reinforced their political commitments in the debate over whether the United States should police the world. Writers considered North heroic when he used personal traits they admired in others to advance goals they approved, and they were appalled at his claims to heroism when he used personal traits that offended them to advance goals they hated.

Viewers agreed that North was a dedicated advocate who promoted what he thought was his country's welfare. In a world of greedy interests and selfish politicians, critics of the investigation admired North's selfless commitment:

> . . . a true hero and role model—one who loves God, country, and family above all else and would sacrifice his all for each or all of them. (Husband and wife, Long Beach, Calif.)

> Look to the dedication and good things he has done for this country at his own self-denial. (Unidentified)

What looked like selfless dedication to some looked like dangerous fanaticism to others, however:

> I see North as a dangerous zealot whose mentality poses a real threat to democracy. (Woman, Bellmore, N.Y.)

> The Lt. Col . . . may have zeal . . . but he is a dangerous man who would do anything to achieve his goal (misguided). (Husband and wife)

Fired on by his singleminded devotion to country, North was remarkably successful at what he set out to do. The thing his supporters admired most about him—and nearly one in five mentioned it—was his ability to get things done. Taking pride in work and doing it well were qualities writers admired in those around them, and they believed that too many politicians no longer valued doing a job well. In a world of gridlocked interests, Oliver North successfully negotiated the sale of arms to Iran in order to secure the release of American hostages in Lebanon, recruited the resources to keep the contras in operation, and eloquently defended the need to resist communism. Particularly in contrast to what they saw as the inability of politicians to do anything, critics of the investigation marveled at North's achievements:

> Ollie North turned out to be a man of immense ability, capable of getting things done. A man who can get things done is worth taking a chance on. (Man, Mt. Sterling, Ky.)

> Lt. Col. North . . . has done his very best to stem the tide of communism on our shores. This is more than I can say for you folks. (Man, St. James City, Fla.)

> I resent it that politicians, most of whom couldn't do in a lifetime what he's capable of in one month, are permitted to put a man of his caliber at risk. (Woman, Cincinnati)

North's ability to get results was precisely what frightened and outraged his critics. He lied to and deceived others. He tried to escape accountability for his actions. His ability to accomplish results became not heroic but dangerous, even treasonous. By selling arms to Iran, North "demeaned his nation by making it a merchant of death," wrote a woman from Los Angeles. To those who "see Oliver North as a hero," a man from Los Angeles "want[ed] to let it be known that many of us see him as a killer of innocent men, women and children."

By far the most common criticism of North—and it was mentioned by nearly one in every four supporters of the investigation—was that he lied to Congress and the American people and broke laws to advance his aims. He hid his support for the contras. In his world the end justified the means. Democracy was a flag, a victory, not a process. And writers condemned him:

> Lying to superiors, Congress, shredding evidence, withholding vital information from the President are activities of criminals, not heroes! (Husband and wife, Ontario, Calif.)

> If he is prepared to die for his country and its form of government, he should also be prepared to live by its rules. I consider him no hero. (Woman, Santa Rosa, Calif.)

> Colonel North claims to be anti-communist, yet his actions show that he practices and believes in one tenet of Marxism which most Americans abhor:

145

Clearly he believes that the end justifies the means. In other words, Ollie North believes in taking *any* action, however illegal or immoral, in order to achieve an objective which he defines as good. When he ultimately goes to face his God, whom he invokes so freely and righteously, he'll have a lot of explaining to do. (Woman, Ontario, Calif.)

I am horrified, fearful, and angry—all at the same time—when I see, when I hear, someone like Oliver North openly and defiantly flaunt the laws, the Constitution, the Congress . . . and yet be held up like "heroes." . . . Do we now promote law-breaking in the name of patriotism? (Man, Forest Park, Ill.)

He lied, cheated and stole, he relates, but it was all for a good cause. As far as I know that excuse will not work for anyone breaking the law but the very retarded. (Woman, Lynn Center, Ill.)

Because North acknowledged that he had broken laws, his supporters developed two basic defenses that still entitled him to be called a hero. The first was that, as with many great leaders of the past, his principles were more important than legal technicalities. "The civil rights movement of the sixties prominently displayed the banner of civil disobedience, when a higher moral purpose was to be served" by lawbreaking, wrote a man from Ellenwood, Georgia, who believed that North was "heroically standing for moral principle" behind a "higher law than that of our congress, or even our Constitution." Paul Revere and "the Boston Teaparty men" broke the law, recalled a man from Jupiter Beach Colony, Florida. "He lied for a cause that was just," added a woman from San Carlos, Pennsylvania.

North struck an unmistakable vein of popular sympathy and an equally unmistakable vein of popular fury with a second defense: he was shielding superiors whose orders he was obeying. Many writers sympathized with him even when they disagreed with his actions because he was a "fall guy":

He was probably doing what he considered his job (which all of us do daily) and following orders (which all of us do daily) albeit very creatively (which not all of us are capable of). (Woman, Forest Park, Ill.)

I believe it is possible that he is taking the blame for superiors and that he sought approval and went through channels. I've seen the less powerful in the civilian workplace take the blame for what superiors did wrong and imagine this could happen to North. (Woman, Mass.)

He was only carrying out orders from his Superiors. They are the ones your sermon should have been directed to. (Woman, Santee, Calif.)

These defenses reminded North's critics of the most terrifying example of totalitarian power in the twentieth century. Believing that the United States had made a major contribution to international law by executing German military officers who obeyed immoral orders, they were outraged by this defense:

Oliver North claims he was "just following orders." We hung men at Nuremburg for "just following orders." We should not look the other way when *any* law is broken. (Man, Salinas, Calif.)

Orders from above are no defense for violating the Constitution, as the world learned at Nuremburg. (Man, Galveston, Tex.)

If North's commander in chief hadn't asked him to do something illegal he wouldn't have to be a fall guy. Blind loyalty leads to dictatorships and holocausts. North's no hero. (Woman, Danville, Ill.)

Americans wrote to congressmen in 1987 in order to widen the spectrum of opinion than was represented in Washington. Writers supported the Sandinistas without flinching, and they accused Democrats of treason with confidence. They did not hesitate to express ideas that were unspeakable in Washington. Far from clustering around a group of low common denominators, the people who wrote Hamilton spread their basic perspectives across a wide continuum.

Most writers brooded that politicians, activists, and journalists had come so fully to embrace the world of mass opinion management that they no longer listened to their constituents or talked with each other in the ways people participated and interpreted in everyday life. Writers worried that politicians had lost everyday standards of personal responsibility and mutual respect as guides to dealing with issues. Americans hoped that by writing letters, by creating a bond with someone they (in most cases) admired, they might show anew the power of face-to-face habits to shape politics.

Through the common concerns that all brought and the individual concerns that each brought, writers created a fundamental pattern grounded in the direction they saw their worlds facing. For writers who faced outward, concerned with respect and protection, politics was about victory in struggles with enemies. These writers had their eyes on results. Uneasy with structures or traditions that dispersed or divided power, they acted as though politics was the means to establish respect in the outside world. They wanted the United States to police the world. For writers who faced inward, politics was a process in which means were much more important than ends. They worried about unchecked power and wanted above all to preserve the private and autonomous space that permitted them to live as they wanted. Their foreign policy was to support the right of peoples to form their own governments, and their natural instincts were to try to keep the United States from intervening in the internal affairs of other nations.

The sad truth is that the imperatives of opinion management have excluded or distorted attempts to shape the forum around any of these patterns. During the Persian Gulf war of 1991, for example, the common denominators had become so low that "debate" added up to silence. An uncritical media presented the war as just another television show, blurring and obscuring the surrounding realities and issues. And while there was a brief debate over the desirability of American participation before the bombs fell, one that echoed some of the positions that divide Americans so deeply on the desirability of policing the world, that debate disappeared with the first bombs and has not yet resumed. Even the disappearance of the communist "threat" and a consensus for federal budget cutting have not forced a serious reappraisal of the asserted need for a massive American military presence as an international safeguard. Across the spectrum in politics and journalism policymakers have simply assumed without asking that the American people will only tolerate commitment of American ground troops abroad when a quick positive result is assured. Instead of soliciting Americans' perspectives and then adopting a new course in response to what they hear (withdrawing the United States from NATO or transferring a huge "peace dividend" from military to health care spending, for example) or of taking responsibility together with political rivals for solving a problem, politicians seem increasingly able only to pose in risk-free sound bites aimed at low common denominators. Reducing political debate to the pursuit of institutional agendas through sound bites, politicians neither listen to what people really want nor take risks to overcome the resulting gridlock that leaves no one capable of solving any real problems.

In the "new world order" that has unfolded since the days of the Iran-Contra affair and the collapse of the Soviet Union, Americans may well be carrying around deep convictions (and divisions and ambivalence) about policing the world and constitutional government, but politicians have created no space similar to the Iran-Contra hearings where Americans can present those convictions. Instead, serious conversation about policy options takes place where Americans talk with people around them, not where politicians speak to cameras.

Eight

Making Citizens Visible

TOWARD A SOCIAL HISTORY OF

TWENTIETH-CENTURY AMERICAN

POLITICS

The time has come to step back from the Iran-Contra case and ask how popular citizenship can be healthy while the practice of democratic government is sick. This book tells a story of declining democratic practice in which politicians and journalists have come to treat citizens and even themselves as abstractions to be aggregated, but it also tells a story of resurgent participatory democracy in which citizens project what healthy democratic practice looks like. To reconcile these stories, to imagine how healthy popular citizenship might reinvigorate democratic government, we need first to ask where opinion management came from, why journalists and politicians have created a political world that separates citizenship from government by seeing citizens where they do not exist and not looking for them where they do. In order to reshape the public forum so that opinion management no longer regulates and distorts conversation, we need to understand where and how that management acquired its central position in our culture and politics. We need, in short, to give opinion management a history in which developments in many arenas have contributed to making the management of opinion into a fundamental conflict in modern American life whose individual battlegrounds are hard to recognize. It was, after all, a particularly stunning case of opinion management that inspired so many Americans to write the letters that we have been examining.

In proposing elements for such a history, we begin by surveying how citizens have come to experience politics in places that have become increasingly invisible to politicians and other citizens over the twentieth century. We then trace the growing use of opinion management to make citizens reappear, though often in places that badly distorted the conversations of citizens with each other and with politicians. We conclude by exploring the places citizens have invented for themselves to take part in and make sense of their worlds. Only by looking for citizens where they are can we appreciate how they have kept alive democracy when the work of the opinion industries has threatened it and imagine new political practice in which citizens and politicians can actually talk and listen to each other.

▌ Few states were represented by more respected senators than Maine with Republican William Cohen and Democrat George Mitchell. No one was surprised, therefore, when the Senate's Republican and Democratic leaders selected both men to serve on the Iran-Contra Select Committee. Nor was it surprising that these thoughtful senators wrote a book together about their experiences on that Committee.

In that book Mitchell and Cohen recalled how "'Olliemania' swept the nation." From their vantagepoint "all America liked Ollie" and "the audience was . . . cheering for North." "The American people loved" his testimony. "Olliemania," they wrote, began with "North's conviction, emotion, and charisma" that proved "intensely compelling" to viewers because it was great "drama." In short, "with Oliver North television had a torrid love affair."

To document this affair Cohen and Mitchell pointed to evidence that illustrates how politicians go about discovering what Americans think. The first evidence that North "gained public attention and support" came not from viewers at all but from the media: "The July 9 edition of the *Washington Post* contained twenty-three pictures of North." Cohen and Mitchell were so impressed that they repeated the point: "Twenty-three pictures of one person in a single edition of a daily newspaper!" The second piece of evidence was what Mitchell called "overnight polls" that showed North to be a "national hero," something no poll actually showed but a statement commentators repeatedly made. The third piece of evidence was the "ever-larger stacks of telegrams on the table in front of North." Their memory of the telegrams to North overlapped with the memory that their offices in Washington and Maine had been "swamped," in Mitchell's words, with pro-North communications. The final evidence of a dreaded mass in motion was that "the members of the Committee were increasingly intimidated" by North and his attorney.[1]

Carefully watching how a story played in the *Post,* repeating what spin doctors said polls said instead of reading the polls, unsuspicious of orchestration when piles of telegrams arrived, excruciatingly sensitive when their colleagues appealed to the mass instead of talking in their everyday voices, Mitchell and Cohen overlooked the evidence that was arriving in their own offices when the phones rang, when the mail was delivered. For each letter or telegram to Cohen that supported North, another one criticized North and six praised Cohen's conduct. During the hearings themselves Mitchell had been a "designated hitter," assigned a full hour on camera to challenge North's story. "The response" to his opposition to North, he recalled, "was immediate and overwhelming. Before I finished speaking, every line in every one of my offices was busy. By the thousands they came in, first the telephone calls, then the telegrams, then the letters. Most were favorable." Indeed, 82 percent of the communications to Mitchell during the hearings were favorable to him and the committee, and a large number of those were also hostile to North.[2]

Two of our very best politicians overlooked what was right in front of them. They heard the phones and saw the letters. Yet when it came time to really listen, to make sense of what people were saying, they enthusiastically retold the story of Olliemania. When they had the time to reflect on the larger meanings of their experiences, they recalled the imagined movement of an imaginary mass, the story told by journalists, and forgot what real individuals told them. It was as though the real people who called and wrote their senators had been invisible.

From the perspective of George Mitchell, however, the problem was not that citizens had become invisible to him but that he had become invisible to them. He later told me that he was puzzled, even offended by the very idea that he could not hear the people who were calling his office. He was eager, he insisted, to talk with individual citizens. He held town meetings in Maine and opened his office in Portland where people could discuss anything they wanted. He read mail counts provided by his staff that summarized citizens' concerns. When it came time to frame public conversation about issues, however, he turned to the natural place where popular concerns were defined, to the press, not to individual citizens: "I can read the *Washington Post* in the morning. I can't read the five hundred letters I get everyday." While depending on the press to define public concerns, he said that he was struck "all the time" by differences in the ways citizens and journalists approached political issues. Citizens talked about a wide range of experience from their daily lives, but journalists reported as a pack, telling the same stories, magnifying "to an extraordinary degree" tiny controversies they thought would appeal to the broadest range of their viewers and readers. The result was that journalists were not interested in what Mitchell thought was important. He was proud of his work on the higher education reauthorization act of 1991, for example, which he considered "one of the most important laws of recent years." But when he raised the topic during a town meeting in Maine he discovered that no one had even heard of it. And the reason was that journalists had not reported it. The same journalists who framed public reaction to the Iran-Contra hearing so that actual citizens were invisible to Mitchell framed Mitchell's activities so that he was invisible to citizens.[3]

Citizens and politicians have become increasingly invisible to each other because the cultures and institutions where they used to meet have lost their authority and because the practice of opinion management and interpretation has transformed the ways citizens and legislators talk and listen to each other far beyond recognition as conversation between real people. In place of the things that matter to individual citizens and senators in their daily lives—experiences, achievements, needs, values, relationships—conversations narrow toward the denominators that can assemble masses that are then presented as Olliemania.

■ With the fading and blurring of the cultures where citizens and politicians once found each other, citizens have developed voices and politicians have developed practices that make it harder for them to see and hear each other where they actually are.

The best way to trace these developments is to look for changes and continuities in the places from which citizens have sought to be seen when they introduced themselves to politicians. In letters they wrote congressmen, Americans revealed where they wanted politicians to find them by the voices they chose to present to those politicians.

Table 11 compares the voices in which Americans wrote to legislators who opposed presidential initiatives that projected American military power abroad. It compares the voices they selected to write Lee Hamilton during the 1987 Iran-Contra hearings with the voices in which they wrote antiwar senators Robert M. La Follette (Wisconsin) and George Norris (Nebraska) during the 1917 debate over American participation in World War I, William E. Borah (Idaho) during a 1939 debate over the proper role for the United States in the war in Europe, and Birch Bayh (Indiana) during a 1970 debate over the Vietnam War. While citizens in each case typically thanked legislators for speaking out against what they saw as popular patriotic "hysteria" or "mania" manufactured by the media, they expressed themselves in very different voices. The table indicates the proportion of writers who associated their sentiments with no voice other than their own, with the intimate face-to-face worlds of family and friends, with their own larger cultural experiences, with political movements, and with huge categories that could be claimed by almost any American.

The changes and continuities in these popular voices help define how citizens and politicians have become increasingly invisible to each other. Over the past seventy years Americans have made claims far less frequently in the cultural identities through which citizens and politicians once recognized each other. Instead, they have written in voices that are both smaller and less visible.

Between 1917 and 1987 the proportion of writers using the smallest of all voices, that of the individual, more than doubled from 14.6 to 35.2 percent,

Table 11 Voices in Which Americans Wrote to Congressmen during Foreign Policy Debates of 1917, 1939, 1970, and 1987

Theme	Hamilton 1987 (%)	Bayh 1970 (%)	Borah 1939 (%)	La Follette/Norris 1917 (%)
I. Exclusively own voice	35.2	34.9	17.1	14.6
II. Voice of family and friends	31.0	39.6	35.1	33.5
III. Voices of unique cultural experiences	20.2	27.4	57.1	73.4
Gender/woman	0.8	1.6	8.2	3.2
Community	5.8	9.1	11.0	26.3
Political Party	4.4	2.8	5.7	5.9
Occupation	4.4	10.8	13.8	13.0
Ethnicity/race	2.0	0.6	12.4	13.1
Religion	2.8	2.5	6.0	12.0
IV. Political movement	1.6	12.9	2.8	5.2
V. Large national voices	27.5	13.9	30.5	26.4
Americans	12.8	1.9	16.0	4.9
"People" or "public"	9.4	1.6	6.4	7.7
Majority	2.2	0.9		5.6
Citizen	6.0	3.8	5.7	6.7
Taxpayer	1.8	0.6	1.1	0.2
Voter	0.4	5.0	1.4	1.3
N (letters)	500	318	282	594

Note: For category III (cultural identities) each writer was counted for as many categories as the writer mentioned in the letter. For categories II and V each writer was counted only once if the writer referred to any voice in that category. In the case of category V, I selected the term that was used most often and with most emphasis. To be included as identifying with an "occupation" a writer had to refer to that occupation in some way other than simply putting the letter on letterhead that indicated an occupation. For category IV, I included only references to social and political movements (e.g., antiwar or women's) but not to pressure groups. The sample was chosen from messages that included more than a perfunctory sentiment in a sample of 500 letters from my collection of the letters to Hamilton; from Boxes 91-53 (last names Hubbell to Johnson) and 91-56 (last names Kurowski to Lazarus) in Birch Bayh Papers for 1970; from all the letters to Borah in response to his neutrality radio address of March 25, 1939 (Boxes 661–62, Borah Papers); from letters by people whose last names began FIN to HAMI to La Follette (Boxes 25 and 26, La Follette Papers) and all to Norris (Box 47, Norris Papers) in response to their March and April 1917 speeches against American participation in the war. The Borah, La Follette, and Norris Papers are in the Manuscript Division, Library of Congress, Washington, D.C. The Bayh Papers are in the Lilly Library, Indiana University, Bloomington.

jumping from one in seven to more than one in three of all writers. There was little change in the proportion—roughly a third—of writers who embedded their voices in their personal relationships with family and friends, which also existed outside the view of politicians. There was also little change in the proportion of citizens–26 percent in 1917 and 28 percent in 1987—who wrote in the vaguely inclusive voices of citizenship and patriotism, voices that were also invisible to politicians and journalists because each individual meant different things by them.

By far the most important change between 1917 and 1987 was the striking decline in the number of people who projected their political conclusions out of the cultures of community, occupation, ethnicity, partisanship,
gender, and religion in which nineteenth-century Americans had forged
their political identities. These were the identities that had shaped modern
political practice, the places where politicians and journalists traditionally
expected to find citizens. By 1987 the proportion of writers claiming these
cultural allegiances was between a quarter and a third of the figure in 1917.
The proportion of writers to associate their conclusions with their occupa-
tions fell by two-thirds, with their communities and religions by four-fifths,
and with their ethnic backgrounds by more than five-sixths.

While Americans counted on family and friends as much in 1987 as in
1917 to help them make sense of politics, those primary arenas of interpretation have become dislodged from the larger cultures in which they were
once embedded. There has been no change in the dependence of Americans on conversation with those around them for interpreting the world; the
dramatic change has been that these face-to-face interactions are no longer
shaped so fully by cultures grounded in overlapping experiences of ethnicity,
community, class, religion, partisanship, and gender that once mediated between citizens and politics. At a time when parents raised children within
tight communities in which people spoke the same languages, read the same
newspaper, attended the same schools and churches, supported the same
political party, belonged to the same social groups, worked at the same kinds
of jobs, they faced outsiders from different cultures with a whole system of
beliefs and experiences that were easily recognizable to themselves and to
others. They drew on the particularities of their circumstances—the homelands their parents came from and the languages they spoke, the places
where they worked and lived and worshiped—to make cultures of identity
that shaped their lives, isolating groups of people in space and circumstance
into separate and distinctive spheres. While the spheres retained the capacity to shape their members' worlds—sometimes by what appeared to be
choice (such as religious commitment or partisan allegiance), sometimes by
what appeared to be necessity (such as racial segregation or sexist prejudice)—they also drew their power from their members' fear that people
with different values posed a real threat to their worlds. Newspapers interpreted the outside world in languages of political partisanship, local community, and ethnic group that reinforced the shared experiences of individual
members of the culture. When the collapse of the cultures threw the work
of interpretation and participation onto individuals in their primary relationships, they experienced the political challenge to their face-to-face relationships in new ways. When cultures were strong, the basic political challenge for those relationships came from the larger culture, to mobilize
households in battle against other cultures, and the most explosive issues

centered on processes like assimilation, intermarriage, and mobility by which individuals abandoned the culture. When those cultures fragmented, the basic political challenge for everyday relationships came from within, whether individual members would remain committed to the relationships, and the most explosive issues centered on divorce and "family values."

Because conflicts between these cultures shaped the basic content of political debate, participants a century ago actually faced a relatively easy task of ascertaining the opinions of others. Conversation in primary groups such as families, religious congregations, or neighborhood gatherings was embedded in larger cultures, so that insiders and outsiders alike assumed that what concerned one individual from the culture likely concerned the next. Behind an individual letter from a quarry worker in a South Milwaukee neighborhood was a culture in which most voters spoke Polish, attended Mass, sent their children to a parochial school, interpreted the world through a Polish-language newspaper, and voted Democratic. Behind an individual letter from a Republican partisan in a northern Indiana town was a culture which included memory of a relative's service in the Union Army, participation in a moderately evangelical Protestant church, and the reading of at least one Republican newspaper, which framed the latest events from the party's perspective and in the English language. Parties controlled what Americans learned about government by owning most newspapers and shaping their content. Parties controlled access to government itself through a patronage system by which government employees who touched the everyday lives of people—sheriffs, postmasters, policemen, tax assessors—reached their positions through loyal work for their parties and individual party leaders. Each culture had its rebels, of course, but clergymen, politicians, editors, and others who spoke for a culture knew how its members would approach an issue. And citizens expected politicians to be recruited from and literally to represent these cultures. Politicians and citizens knew where to find each other.

The practice of politics a century ago encouraged politicians and citizens to listen to each other as individuals, as well as members of cultures. Citizens and politicians did favors for each other. Individual politicians helped individual citizens get jobs, find food and housing, raise their children, stay (or get) out of trouble with the law, and more generally secure what they wanted from government. Individual citizens helped their patrons by promoting their candidacies with friends, contributing to their campaigns, voting themselves, and getting others to vote. This reciprocal exchange of favors created bonds of loyalty between individuals who knew and helped each other, politicians who could understand the concerns of their constituents and citizens who could interpret the behavior and needs of their representatives. Even when citizens reached out to a politician they did not know personally—as with the average of 137 people a month who wrote President Thomas

Jefferson in the early nineteenth century—they wrote for the most part to request a personal favor: money, a job, release from debtor's prison, help with education. Citizens expected—and received—a personal response in which Jefferson would give advice, largesse, or wisdom.[4] Out of personal exchanges grounded in the distinctive needs of individuals, political parties emerged as dense confederations of face-to-face networks, each led by lieutenants whose value was precisely their capacity to mobilize other individuals in their networks. Parties were based on the reality that someone knew someone else who could solve an individual's problems. Politicians knew what their constituents experienced and thought through the conversations that made up everyday life. And at a time when congressmen spent most of the year in their home communities, they knew what people around them were thinking when they went to Washington.

With the dramatic erosion of these cultures and political practices over the twentieth century, citizens and politicians approach the world of politics without traditional means for finding and conversing with each other. As primary groups have become dislodged from larger cultures, popular political interpretation takes place in smaller spaces than in the past.[5]

New collective voices have appeared, but none with the richness of the traditional cultural identities. Some of the new voices—"baby boomers" and "yuppies"—though they may seem so to market researchers and pundits, are barely cultures at all. In fact, not a single citizen approached Hamilton in these voices of taste or fashion, which seemed irrelevant to people who were looking for political voices in which to be recognized. The new and very vocal political voices that organizers have constructed out of what seem to be traditional allegiances—voices with names like the "New Christian Right," "Year of the Woman," or "Angry White Males"—differ from traditional cultures in that they represent only a small part of a person's experience and mobilize it toward a particular issue while they often fail to represent deeper feelings of empathy or proclaim wider experiences that religion and gender were capable of nurturing.

Even for those Americans who speak in collective voices that have become louder and more vivid than before—gays and lesbians or Moslem immigrants, for example—for cultures whose points of identity would appear on the surface to be sources of greater visibility, both the nature of these newer cultures and the political changes that have affected all Americans have eroded the ways their members are seen and heard. Like the voices constructed for a single issue, these new identities represent only part of a person's collective experience, not the kind of traditional cultural integration of many different experiences in which mass media reinforced pulpit and political parties extended what people talked about at work, neighborhood, and church. By splitting instead of integrating the different pieces of people's lives, the newer collective voices are a thinner reflection of individuals' experiences and exacerbate the changes that have made it increasingly difficult for individuals to speak fully and be heard in the public forum.

The emerging new collective identities also leave their members more invisible than more traditional cultures have because of the decline of political parties as links between daily experience and public policy. To the extent that Americans feel party allegiances, they or their parents or grandparents formed those allegiances in earlier times when traditional cultures, not the new ones, shaped the defining concerns and edges of political parties. Put another way, gays and Moslems are less likely to experience a political party as a natural extension of their voices than were Irish Catholics or evangelical Protestants a century earlier. And while race persists as a source of deep division, it does not shape political opinions in the same way that traditional cultures did. African Americans might vote overwhelmingly Democratic, but the Democratic Party is not the same central feature of their lives that it was for Irish Catholic immigrants or many Southern whites.

Parties have ceased to grow naturally out of and reinforce a full range of people's experiences. Most citizens no longer expect parties to advance their most fundamental faiths or to mobilize citizens to vote as they did in earlier times when citizens saw their votes as the first line of defense for their cultures. Parties no inspire the loyalty to command discipline at the ballot box or in legislative halls.

Many changes in this century—the ebbing of patronage and party loyalty, the rise of mass media and political merchandizing—have eroded the reciprocal bonds that once made individual citizens and politicians both visible to and dependent upon each other. The rise of television advertising as the means of communication between voters and candidates, for example, eroded the intensely personal networks of trust and information through which people shared concerns with others around them, probed commitments, exchanged favors, made pledges, cross-examined argument, and traded firsthand news and assessments of candidates. Even in Chicago, where personal bonds persisted longer than in most places to link voters and their cultures with larger political organizations, the change came. In that city's Cabrini-Green public housing project, for example, voters had long ignored television commercials by candidates and instead participated in politics when people they respected in their buildings personally vouched for a candidate and urged them to vote. By 1988, however, Joyce Johnson reported that "no one is interested enough in the elections to work the community." Estrella Tudella "used to work like mad" among Chicago's Hispanic voters, but the media orientation of modern campaigns meant that "politicians don't care about the people" any more.[6]

The gradual disappearance of individual citizens that accompanied the fading and blurring of larger cultures transformed the ways citizens and politicians conversed with each other, or failed to, in two sadly interconnected ways. As citizens disappeared from their traditional places, politicians increasingly placed their hopes for conversation on the opinion industries, which claimed the ability to rematerialize these citizens—albeit usually in places and talking in ways that had been distorted by the process, sometimes purposefully, often inadvertently. Politicians grew accustomed, however, to this seemingly new kind of citizen, who moved in masses, suddenly and decisively. They lost the capacity to see and hear individual citizens even when their voices were on the other ends of phone lines or in the pages of letters being answered in senators' offices. Americans cried out against both changes in the summer of 1987. They tried to make themselves visible once again to their legislators, to be heard as real individuals, not as a faceless wave of Olliemania.

■■■ Before we can once again find individual citizens we must explore the traditions, sources, and interests that the opinion industries have drawn on as they have compressed everyday conversations into units for manipulating opinion.

The modern opinion industries originated in an assortment of professions and industries that together practice the management of consent. These professions and industries brought a variety of perspectives, some with ancient roots, others with recent origins, to developing theories and technologies for observing and manipulating opinion. They invented the means for listening—market research, opinion polls, focus groups, civilian and military surveillance—and the means for speaking—advertising campaigns, public relations, spin doctors—that now distort politics. What made this way of listening so compelling was precisely that it came from so many directions, from the imperatives that drove commerce, entertainment, expertise, and bureaucracy, integrating and concentrating what it drew from each. The strands converged in the conception of individual buyers or viewers or voters as uniform components of audiences or markets, as submerged in masses whose voice existed only when it could be quantified by the techniques of opinion management. "Attitudinal research arises not out of any need of the holders of attitudes," James Beniger has written, "but rather from the needs of an audience interested in the potential exploitation of those attitudes." When collective voices were developed to allow these created masses to speak, means were also crafted to "manufacture consent" from indifferent, often hostile, people, as Walter Lippmann characterized their purpose in his pioneering 1922 exploration of modern "public opinion."[7]

The management of opinion originated in the ancient assumption that some people are by nature or right superior to others and therefore have the responsibility to control the behavior and beliefs of those they see as inferiors. Conservatives and aristocrats reaching back to Heraclitus and Plato anticipated one strand of modern opinion management by arguing that most people are vulgar and ignorant as individuals and become irrational and dangerous when they come together as a group. Since most people are intellectually insignificant, socially inferior, and morally offensive, leaders know what the masses need better than the masses themselves. Romans from Juvenal to Marcus Aurelius turned elitist belief to imperial practice by delivering cheap food and entertainment ("bread and circuses") to the masses in hopes of diverting the presumed brutality, stupidity, and sensuality of Roman plebeians into a state of passive self-absorption.[8]

The modern imperative to make people visible in new ways in order to manage them reaches back to paradoxes that accompanied the erosion of face-to-face authority in the late Middle Ages. When the Renaissance, the Reformation, and capitalism freed individuals from the rigid places they had been assigned by local princes, landowners, and priests who supervised them every day, it ultimately became possible for individuals to identify with ever larger "groups" of people who did the same thing (bought a product or voted for a candidate) or identified with the same thing (Methodism or "Germany") even though they did not personally know the other individuals who acted and thought as they did. Individuals were also exposed to a wider range of opinions and could associate with strangers (or at least their opinions) out of the view—and supervision—of leaders in ways that were inconceivable in the intensely local worlds of the Middle Ages. The increase in the number of people who could act in the same way brought with it both the centralization of authority over dispersed face-to-face worlds and the invention of new forms of surveillance to replace those that disappeared with face-to-face control. With the collapse of local, dispersed, self-governing estates, local landowners and local experience lost their authority to shape people's behavior to increasingly powerful national states (as typified by the rise of absolute monarchy in France) and to a new class of interpreters who claimed to be able to find universal laws for the physical universe and human conduct and to have the means to administer those laws (as typified by the philosophes in France, who aided Louis XIV in centralizing authority). In place of local experience, Enlightenment thinkers sought to enshrine abstractions that empowered them to make rules to govern their societies: universal reason and critical thinking. Uprooted and evicted from their dispersed and diverse local worlds, "'the people' stood first and foremost for an unfulfilled and urgent political task—the imposition of discipline over behavior, order over chaos," noted Zgymunt Bauman. Centralization, universality, and reason became agents that turned the "dense sociability" of the Middle Ages that pivoted around "mutual watching" and "the ability to make 'the other' familiar, to transform him or her into a fully defined person with a fixed station inside the familiar world," into the modern challenge in which "the activity of surveillance now split the affected group into two sharply and permanently separated subsections: the watchers and the watched. . . . The tendency of uni-directional surveillance is to erase individual differences between its objects, and to substitute a quantifiable uniformity for qualitative variety," Bauman continued. "As the scale of institutions has become larger and more centralized," observed C. Wright Mills, "so have the range and intensity of the opinion-maker's efforts. The means of opinion-making . . . have paralleled in range and efficiency the other institutions of greater scale that cradle the modern society of masses."[9]

Those in authority tried to expand or protect their prerogatives by making visible and thereby controllable invisible and potentially rebellious individuals. They feared challenges in forms that ranged from crime to revolution to unions. Using everything from essentially military forms of surveillance such as fingerprinting and electronic eavesdropping to commercial forms such as market surveys and television ratings to political forms such as polls and elections, their goal was above all to make the invisible become visible.

Employers, for example, wanted to establish their authority over workforces that were often fragmented both by the diverse backgrounds of the workers and the different bands of friends they split into. Believing that they could only expand production by wresting control of shopfloors from the face-to-face codes by which workers had traditionally disciplined production, managers developed elaborate means of surveillance—time-and-motion studies and time clocks, for example—to find out how workers thought and acted and then imposed incentives such as competitive bonuses for workers who accepted managerial authority and standardized orders. By the 1950s IBM boasted: "Our training makes our men interchangeable."[10] To get people from diverse cultural backgrounds to accept a single standard that exalted productivity and competition, the builders of American capitalism promoted public schools as the nursery for creating ambitious and deferential young people. Inventing discipline by teachers as the means to impose standardized habits—punctuality, obedience, sobriety— over individual and cultural diversity, the public schools imposed remarkable innovations in surveillance that ranged from truant officers to hall passes, psychological tests to school counselors, color-coded exams to holes through which to spy on children in bathrooms. By such means schools hoped to impose a single set of values over the knots of friends and different cultures from which many children tamed an institution that so often seemed alien.[11] Workplaces and schools have endlessly reenacted dramas of resistance to campaigns by employers and teachers to manage consent.

Because opinion management has its roots in such attempts to establish authority over possible rebels and build consent among strangers, it is interested in individuals only to the extent that they can become part of larger aggregations. Because what matters is not unique individuals but the number of individuals they resemble and associate with, the challenge is to discover what assembles them into a mass. The basic task is to turn real people into interchangeable abstractions that receive their identity and voice from outside.

The invention of the printing press in the sixteenth century assembled individuals into impersonal "audiences" with potentially nothing in common except their exposure to an opinion expressed by someone they had never met. It transformed the expression of opinion from an active conversation among individuals to a written text that readers encountered in isolation from the speaker and other readers. Unprecedented numbers of people encountered potentially subversive ideas outside the view of local authorities. It freed readers from dependence on intermediaries for interpretation of texts such as the Bible and enabled them to interpret for themselves, to find and create their authorities from among the infinitely more diverse ideas to which they could now be exposed. By turning the exchange of opinions from personal interactions into myriad isolated encounters between people and texts, the printing press and subsequent mass media turned opinion from a face-to-face interaction into an artificial assembly of invisible individuals. In doing so the mass media simultaneously caused diverse conversations to pause and center on the same text while they also sped opinions across space, expanding dramatically the audiences for both consent and rebellion. By the eighteenth century, when newspapers and pamphlets introduced voices that turned isolated rebellions into national revolutions in France and America, many would credit the new media with assembling the masses that overthrew the authority of the French and British kings.

By the eighteenth century the public expression of opinion had acquired the explosive capacity to recruit supporters and became a place for subversive conversation and action that, in turn, unleashed ferocious battles between people in motion and political leaders over where and how political opinion could be expressed. The outcome of those battles shaped the modern electoral and legislative arenas in which citizens and politicians talked with each other. By suddenly inventing places that ranged from coffeehouses to salons, from crowds to riots, from newspapers to elections to take their subversive conversations, eighteenth-century rebels realized that through their capacities, directions, and places for conversation, they had the ability to empower themselves. From conversations that started in salons, newspapers, and riots people developed ever more subversive ideas, ever wider support for that subversion, and ever greater confidence to challenge leaders. To stop this movement, leaders hoped to freeze dangerous talk and narrow it to acceptable limits and to identify possible allies among people who did not join crowds or gather in coffeehouses. Out of these struggles emerged representative government, the compromise that narrowed the range of debate and slowed the pace of popular empowerment but gave to the majority—not elites or activists—the final authority to stop conversations and decide among alternatives. The election of representatives to lawmaking parliaments blocked revolutionary alternatives, kept discussion within safe limits, and allowed leaders to hear from all voters, not just the noisy ones. Leaders embraced the principle of majority rule both to elect representatives to lawmaking bodies and then to decide what bills became law in those representative assemblies because it compelled losers to stop talking and acquiesce in laws and election results. Out of these conflicts, too, was born the modern faith that "public opinion" ought to prevail over social or political privilege or hierarchy.[12]

In justifying their declaration of independence by appealing to "a decent respect to the opinions of mankind," the founders of a new American nation in 1776 addressed a faceless audience that would encounter their declaration in the new mass media. Writing in the same year that Adam Smith imagined a new economic order in which an "invisible" and impersonal hand would replace the very visible regulations that had guided economic activity in the past, the American colonists envisioned public opinion in the same spirit, as composed of isolated individuals who moved in response to self-interest and individual reason.[13]

With the widening of conflict between consent and rebellion, builders of modern states in the dynamic eighteenth-century world of territorial expansion and political revolution wanted to be able to predict and control the behavior not of individuals but of masses. To this end governments began to classify individuals into groups, as in new censuses of population and trade, in order better to place individuals into places they could be seen, counted, and administered.

Statisticians made a crucial contribution to the capacity to imagine people as interchangeable pieces of a mass in the nineteenth century by refining procedures for studying social and natural phenomena in aggregate masses without first having to know about each individual that constituted the mass. By showing how large-scale order and regularity could emerge from patterns that lay hidden beneath individual differences, statisticians turned the point of observation from the individual to the mass. They turned the random into the orderly, the unique into the comparable, the distinctive individual into a piece of a single mass. And statistics proved "especially valuable for uncovering causal relationships where the individual events are either concealed from view or are highly variable and subject to a host of influences," explained Theodore Porter.[14] The point, after all, was to discover the invisible.

From the capacity to imagine and predict a mass the next step was to manufacture the appeals that the mass would form around, to define its voice. The modern arts and crafts of opinion management were inspired by selling a war and then took shape around selling consumer products.

Early in this century assembly lines began producing cars and radios that millions could afford if only they could be persuaded to need or want them. What would persuade them to buy the products? The challenge was real. There was no obvious message, such as patriotism in wartime, that would sell. By 1919 superficial wartime harmony had collapsed into bitter conflicts between workers and bosses, whites and blacks, Protestants and Catholics and Jews, young and old, women and men, farmers and city dwellers, immigrants and native born. Managers needed new denominators that could make people who hated each other not only want a car but also buy the same car. They needed to know which of an individual's thoughts were widely enough shared to be aggregated into appeals that would inspire people from different backgrounds and tastes to buy the same product. The invention of marketing research as a means to find the denominators that turned individuals into a mass began with questionnaires of newspaper and magazine readers in 1911 and house-to-house interviews in 1916.[15]

The key problem in listening to great numbers of people, for those with conservative biases, was how to permit inferior people to have views when they lacked the capacity to think seriously. This challenge deepened, as Donald Fleming has suggested, with the simultaneous spread of the Freudian belief that people were not even conscious of why they said what they did. By the 1920s researchers found a way to listen to marginal people by inventing the concept of "attitudes." Attitudes required minimal thought; they could be possessed by socially inferior people. Originating in some location between conscious and unconscious activity, the concept of attitudes allowed the survival of the ancient prejudice that the masses were composed of emotional beings incapable of real thought while acknowledging that they had *something* to say. So rapidly did attitude surveys spread that by 1928, less than two decades after W. I. Thomas had pioneered the use of "attitude" as a basic means for listening to "other" people such as women, peasants, and immigrants and for inspiring efforts to assist them with problems, Americans had conducted over 3,000 attitude and opinion surveys.[16]

New theoreticians and practitioners proclaimed in the early 1920s that the ability to make people who hated each other buy unwanted products was "a revolution . . . infinitely more significant than any shifting of economic power," as Walter Lippmann wrote in the pathbreaking *Public Opinion* (1922). They had perfected the capacity to imagine, measure, predict, and appeal to individuals in the mass. They built, of course, on earlier foundations. Gustave LeBon proclaimed in *The Psychology of Crowds* (1895) that individuals lost their identities when they became part of crowds that were, by nature, homogenous and irrational in their fixation on a single object. Crowds were easily manipulated by images and myths presented by leaders. Gabriel Tarde added that the most characteristic mass was not the physical assembly of people into crowds but their emotional assembly behind a single "opinion" presented in a mass medium. Because the opinions of this aggregate were invented by mass media and "adhered to blindly by individuals who cannot see one another," Tarde believed that the aggregate's "voices can only be counted and not weighed. Unconsciously the press thus worked to create the strength of numbers and to reduce that of character." In short, summarized Yale President Arthur Hadley, the press "organized emotion" in its readers.[17]

The next challenge for opinion management, as it emerged from World War I, was to persuade people not to form their beliefs on the basis of everyday experience with individuals but rather to trust minimal denominators and masses imposed from outside. In 1922 Lippmann argued that cognitive principles (the habit of people to think in "stereotypes") and psychological processes (making symbols out of conditioned responses) offered techniques for "overcoming subjectivity of human opinion based on the limitation of individual experience." The next year E. L. Bernays grounded his strategy for crystallizing public opinion in instinct psychology, fascination with unconscious motivation pioneered by his uncle Sigmund Freud, and behaviorism, together with a faith in "the tendency the group has to standardize the habits of individuals." In subconscious yearnings theoreticians identified potential common denominators that could replace particular loyalties. The quest among these discoverers of "public opinion" in the 1920s for ways of leading people to surrender their personal standards to common denominators imposed from outside took its most ominous direction in *Mein Kampf* (1925) by Adolf Hitler. Impressed by what he saw as the herd-loving incapacity of people to think and act for themselves, Hitler wrote that "our ordinary conception of public opinion depends only in very small measure on our personal experience or knowledge, but instead for the most part on so-called 'enlightenment' that is drummed into us by penetrating and persistent effort."[18]

Creators of the new arts of opinion management in the 1920s centered their attention on how advertising could invent popular demand. Since the challenge of selling was to focus and manage demand, advertising became "the art of creating a new want," of "making the luxuries of today the necessities of tomorrow." What moved the mass was fear of social disapproval. Gerald Lambert invented "halitosis" (bad breath), a social nightmare that could be overcome by purchasing (and perhaps using) Listerine mouthwash. By turning psychological principles into laws that motivated Americans, *Printer's Ink*, the advertising trade journal, headlined that "People Have Become 'Standardized' by Advertising."[19]

Advertising both inspired and epitomized the quest for common denominators that would offend no one, amuse everyone, and sell products. The places where audiences could be attracted by common denominators based on entertainment and escape were the new mass media, movies and radio. In the 1920s as the radio industry became less dependent on the sale of receivers and more on the numbers of listeners who might buy a sponsor's product, the success of a program came to be equated with its ability to attract the largest number of listeners. Comedy, music, drama, sports, variety, all helped to assemble common denominators that sold sponsors' products. The mass media became the place where entertaining reinforced selling, where common denominators formed the dominant voice.

Through mass marketing and mass communications Americans became visible only when many of them did the same thing—listened to the same program, bought the same product, or voted for the same candidate. The artificial denominators that shaped what marketers put into advertisements and radio programs aimed at the visible mass were very different from the needs of the invisible individuals who purchased soap or listened to radio programs. Those differences keep the story of the evolution of modern consumer culture from being a story of the successful conflation of individuals into a mass. Instead, it is a story of contests across a wide range of fronts in which consumers experienced goods and amusements, not in the mass, but as individuals whose taste in cars and movies grew—like the conclusions viewers sent Hamilton about what they were watching on television—out of relationships with people around them. The very diversity and resistance of consumers, however, has only heightened the pressure on opinion management to come up with theories and technologies to expand the sizes of markets and audiences.

While marketing and advertising provided opinion management with its characteristic ways of listening and speaking, ways that turned consumption into a place where real individuals sought to meet their needs even as hucksters tried to reduce them to marketing denominators, individuals found politics to be an arena where twentieth-century managers of consent could add stunning new coercive dimensions to the management of opinion. Of course, regimes have mobilized supporters to intimidate critics at least since the loyalist Church and Crown mobs of the eighteenth century. But managers of consent in the unpopular Great War transformed the older tradition of suppressing critics into one that inspired the modern pioneers of opinion management in the 1920s with whole new possibilities for turning individuals into a faceless and irrational mass that would do only what its creators wanted. Aided by espionage and sedition laws, vigilante terror, censorship, and 250,000 informers, the American opinion industries, orchestrated by the government, drove all but prowar messages out of public space.[20] Advertisements, pamphlets, and public speakers "proved" the barbarity of the

Germans and exhorted war supporters to report any critics of the war to the authorities for prosecution. The success in silencing critics through this totalitarian management of consent gave rulers unprecedented and ominous powers in the minds of supporters and enemies of the war alike. People who had once been individuals against or in favor of entry into the war had been successfully massed as traitors and informers. Political conversation was silenced, for conducting a war in silence was close enough to acquiescence.

The issue of how masses should be assembled and mobilized in politics became a central theme in the 1920s, World War II, and the Cold War. The Nazi, Fascist, and Soviet regimes created the defining nightmare of an obedient, visceral mass that would haunt North's critics half a century later. Totalitarian movements, wrote German refugee Hannah Arendt, aimed to control opinion by constructing "an atomized and individualized mass" composed of individuals whose "isolation and lack of normal social relationships" had "destroyed the very capacity for experience" they could use to resist propaganda.[21] Nazi totalitarianism, with its prominent use of opinion management techniques, in concert with brute force, raised the specter of whether citizens could retain the autonomy to resist mass emotional appeals to visceral instincts without the support of their fellow citizens. Would individuals do *anything* their leaders asked? Hitler and Josef Goebbels regimented consent (and awed many American advertising agents) by orchestrating and dominating public space with a single message and then, in the name of the mass—and with help from the secret police—brutally driving all other voices into silence, and then worse. In Russia Stalin made the suppression (and worse) of critics the centerpiece of his political domination. And even in the United States political leaders like Franklin Roosevelt and Father Charles Coughlin used radio, as Hitler had, to frighten critics with their personal popularity.

Dreading the mobilized masses and brutal regimes of Europe but eager to manage opinion in the insurgent decade of the 1930s when people were demanding far-reaching redistribution of power, Americans invented pressure groups and opinion polling as basic tools for managing political opinion. Workers, farmers, and the elderly organized to make political claims on a New Deal that seemed to respond to any group that could deliver large numbers of voters. Copying public relations techniques pioneered by war champions and corporations in the 1910s and 1920s, these groups mounted publicity campaigns in the new mass media to seek public support. With these new groups widening political debate amid international fears of propaganda and mobilized masses, orchestrators of opinion in the United States wanted to arbitrate competing political claims on the same basis as commercial competition. Victory should go to the claim that sold the most products—in this case, attracted the largest following—without changing the rules of the game. But how would consumers decide which product to buy—which pressure group to support—at a time when FDR wanted to please the largest number of voters without fundamentally redistributing power?

To find out what Americans were thinking, managers turned not to traditions of popular organizing or political debate but to a technology developed by market researchers to sell products and used by journalists to sell newspapers. Market researchers refined sampling procedures to measure opinion in order to forecast buying habits. Newspapers introduced and sponsored public opinion polling for the first time in the presidential preference poll of 1936. Opinion polls provided choices not available in Germany or Russia. But in the best tradition of market research they limited the topics and alternatives to those that mattered to those who paid for the polls. Victory at the polls was not followed by any mobilization or change. It sold newspapers. Calling the technique not "the pulse of democracy," as polling pioneer George Gallup had, but rather "its baby talk," Lindsay Rogers argued in *The Pollsters* (1949) that the new technology distorted both everyday conversation and democratic traditions by freezing conversation that in democratic tradition was the way to resolve conflict, by failing to ask people to say what they meant and instead limiting the topics of conversation to alternatives imposed from outside, by overturning the traditional right of people not to report their opinions to strangers (a right that seemed nearly sacred at a time when people in other countries were afraid to say what they thought in public), and by ignoring the intensity and priority of people's perspectives.[22] Polling came with the sounds of newsboys and hucksters, not those of marching jackboots, with the invitation to make a choice, not the threat of the police if one associated with people who made the wrong choice. In a culture that valued commerce above politics, polling provided a harmless way to identify and manipulate denominators while saturating politics with the vision of competition that prevailed in the market.

The invention of the mobilized mass has distorted everyday conversations by making large numbers of people reluctant to reveal what they really think. War has provided the best opportunity for American regimes to mobilize masses in unprecedented ways to promote their agendas and silence their critics. Beginning with the modern mobilizations of opinion that regimes refined in World War I, wars were won as much by managing consent at home as troops and weapons abroad. This was the lesson in victory, as in World Wars I and II, and of defeat, as in Vietnam, where both supporters and critics of the war perceived lack of unity as the reason for not winning. Wars have justified unprecedented surveillance and control of citizens at home and vicious low-denominator portrayals of enemies as brutal Huns and Evil Empires. In short, wars have provided the cover that leaders have used to coerce a silence they hope will be seen as consent. In the face of obvious evidence that people opposed his policy—unfavorable polls, unprecedented popular demonstrations, election defeat of politicians who agreed with him—Richard Nixon gave the classic formulation to this attempt to use fear of a mobilized mass when he boldly invented a "silent majority" of Americans that he insisted agreed with him. He set that faith into motion by unleashing massive and paranoid surveillance of his critics, which led ultimately to Watergate and to his own resignation. But throughout the Cold War Republican conservatives from Joseph McCarthy and Nixon through Ronald Reagan and Oliver North have repeatedly tried to intimidate their critics by presenting the "majority" of Americans as supporters of expansive foreign policy. And a deep fear of a mobilized mass has led Democrats and other critics of empire not so much to change their positions as simply to shut up. Indeed, for fifty years Republicans stifled criticism with the fear that they could mobilize masses to punish critics. Like McCarthyism and Nixon's silent majority, Olliemania was the most recent construction of the conservative faith that masses supported regimes, this time given an entertainment twist. Like them, it was, in fact, less a description of what Americans thought than an excuse for would-be critics to blame others for their own failure to speak.[23] And while politicians might retreat before an imagined mass, individuals draw on the rich range of their experiences and relationships to resist attempts to reduce them to a single denominator. From within their primary relationships they strike out to contest with managers and speak for themselves—as, for example, when writing to a congressman.

In addition to making some people afraid to say what they think, the invention of the mass has eroded the confidence many citizens have felt in each other. Because people buy products, enjoy escapist entertainment, and acquiesce in dictatorships, citizens have been haunted over the last half-century by a basic question at the core of the invention of masses: To what extent and in what ways are individuals responsible for Listerine's sales (or indeed its very existence), for escapist dramas, or brutal dictators? Because individuals lack the ability to find out for themselves what strangers are thinking, they simply do not know the answers. And, as the writers to Hamilton made clear, their dependence on the opinion industries to tell them what their fellow citizens were thinking eroded their confidence in democracy at its core.

The invention and manipulation of the mass has become a process in which personal relationships can reinforce cultural expectations or ideological convictions as the opinion industries have created a self-contained forum. At work and at play those who report and interpret opinion see and hear only people like themselves. Elaborating his observation that these makers of images "have given themselves a name, the Insiders, and a language," Michael Kelly recently explained:

> They go to the same parties, send their children to the same schools, live in the same neighborhoods. They interview each other, argue with each others, sleep with each other, marry each other, live and die by each other's judgment. . . . They tend to believe the same things at the same time.[24]

When I asked David Gergen how and where these insiders listen to public opinion, he answered "by word of mouth" at dinner parties in Washington and New York, where politicians and journalists turned into "the chattering classes," talking among themselves to decide what is important and how to spin it. If a person hears (or repeats) the same thing at three or four dinner parties, soon it becomes the "conventional wisdom" in a process that Gergen likened to "conversation in an echo chamber." James Carville used a different metaphor to evoke the same enclosed world: "We live in this Washington cauldron every day." In fact, Gergen observed, there is "a tendency among elites" in the United States to "know the streets of London and Paris better than they know the streets of Chicago and Detroit." Whether they are on a beat or in a newsroom, journalists feel enormous pressure to talk among colleagues and agree on a story before they file it. Worse, Carville explained, "they can't stop themselves once a story gets going, gains a momentum. There's no braking mechanism. . . . We're not going to criticize ourselves, [reporters] say." They welcome neither questions nor criticisms from outsiders. When I asked him whether he had observed how journalists formulate their stories, Carville sighed: "Oh, man. Go in the back of the [campaign] plane and they all agree. The people who don't go along are ostracized, vilified by their colleagues." Michael Schudson has concluded that reporters and pundits misremember polls about Ronald Reagan's popularity because they trust what people tell them by word of mouth in the "oral culture" of Washington more than they trust the actual numbers in poll results.[25]

By talking mainly with others like themselves, those who report and interpret opinion establish the boundaries of their own self-referential world by inventing and believing in an incompetent mass of outsiders, unworthy of being heeded or respected, urgently in need of guidance from the insiders. Both Carville and Gergen believed that opinion managers view what Gergen called "all the people outside the gates" with contempt and condescension. Most Americans are ignorant (defined by Gergen to mean that they did not know whether the Soviet Union was in NATO), intolerant (toward immigrants and blacks), emotional and dangerous and even hysterical (which Gergen defined by the fear that "they're going to get carried away," something that apparently does not happen to elites). Both Carville and Gergen observed that elites convey their deepest fears of the menace outside the gates by wildly exaggerating the popularity of Rush Limbaugh—with his unmannerly and incessant personal attacks on established political leaders and journalists—and by emphasizing many differences that seem to define qualities that set outsiders apart from them: experiencing life in rural communities and urban poverty, worshipping in fundamentalist churches, and hunting with guns. Washington leaders believe that the direction of popular intelligence is toward "the dumbing of America," Carville reported: "If you went to the National Press Club and said voters are less informed than they were in the 1950s they would all say yes."

Opinion management has led naturally to the creation of a self-referring group of insiders who see it as their mission to keep public conversation among individuals within the limits they have so expertly crafted. When they do their jobs of measuring an imaginary mass or giving it voice, they adopt the professional standards of objectivity and mass marketing that teach them to ignore the needs and perspectives of any real person. While real individuals feel free to express a vast range of experiences and relationships in their everyday conversation, professionals jettison their diverse experiences and curiosities. The ultimate creation of opinion management is a class of people trapped within their narrowed world, trapped into promoting and perpetuating that world and the tiny corner of their rich personalities that it permits them to express.

Commercial pressures have reinforced personal relationships and ideology in encouraging opinion managers not to listen to people on their own terms. The costs of measuring opinion and marketing denominators has limited who gets a chance to be heard and determined whether, how, and where people will engage opinions for what by the late 1980s had become the $2.5 billion a year opinion industries. Television has deepened a pattern that originated with the printing press of dividing the few with the wealth of sponsors or the power of public officials to command access, on the one hand, from the many who consume or ratify opinions already offered, on the other. In fact, Cohen and Mitchell were themselves invisible to many citizens for much of the hearings because the commercial television networks abandoned live coverage in order to preserve revenues from game shows and soap operas. More viewers wanted to see the hearings than the soaps, but the networks broadcast the soaps. "Ollie's doing very well" in ratings, explained a CBS executive during live coverage of North's testimony: "Unfortunately, he's not sponsored." Each day the networks replaced commercial broadcasts with the unsponsored hearings NBC lost $600,000, ABC $800,000, and CBS $1,000,000 in advertising revenues. Cohen and Mitchell could be seen and heard not on networks that assembled viewers through low denominators into huge masses, but on specialized networks and stations that respected the real range and diversity of individual viewers.[26] The high costs of finding and assembling individuals into masses have taken an even more ominous direction when the political action committees that pay the costs of measuring and manipulating opinion have told politicians what they can talk about and vote into law and what they cannot.[27]

Commercial pressures likewise encourage reporters to ignore the real concerns of individuals and to listen only for low common denominators that they then report as serious experience. Gergen complained that news organizations no longer send reporters to spend a month in Iowa or New Hampshire, listening to individuals talk as they go about their lives and then reporting what they hear, but instead do the far cheaper thing of commissioning a poll. The same commercial pressures that inspire news gatherers to listen to citizens in the mass and not as individuals lead reporters to present visual images they hope will entertain viewers with common denominators instead of letting them hear what an individual newsmaker really thinks. As the quest for television ratings blurs traditional distinctions between entertainment and news, producers and reporters do not document events, but present "a rapid succession of visually arresting images" that they hope "will capture the audience eye."[28]

The opinion industries have thus created a self-contained world in which individuals cannot talk about what matters. The invention of the mass has been both cause and consequence of habits of thought that keep experts from hearing the wide range of ways real people meet needs. "What happens in the political world is divorced from the real world," Michael Kelly wrote.[29] By denying the voice and authority of everyday experience—of home remedies, folk wisdom, word of mouth, and firsthand experience, by which people have long made sense of life—experts have concluded that everyday talk is ignorant. By narrowing the range of experience worth learning from, experts have simultaneously made only a tiny fraction of life visible and eroded the confidence people bring from their intimate worlds to public conversations.

Struck by the "remoteness from the actual life of the country" of recent presidential elections, Joan Didion observed that

> people inside the process, constituting as they do a self-created and self-referring class . . . tend to speak of the world not necessarily as it is but as they want people out there to believe it is. They tend to prefer the theoretical to the observable . . . a mechanism seen as so specialized that access to it is correctly limited to its own professionals, to those who manage policy and those who report on it, to those who run the polls and those who quote them, to those who ask and those who answer the questions on the Sunday shows, to the media consultants, to the columnists, to the issues advisers, to those who give the off-the-record breakfasts and to those who attend them; to that handful of insiders who invent, year in and year out, the narrative of public life.[30]

Or, in Goethe's words:

> All theory is gray,
> And green the radiant tree of life.[31]

For in the end the struggle is between life as Americans live it and theory as it is invented.

The opinion industries are left to construct and then possess drab public spaces where life's blacks and whites blur into grays, where data stand in for people and statistics for voices. Overlooked are the radiant trees all around where people live and talk. These trees are as near at hand as our talk with people around us, and to turn theory into life we need only turn from pundits toward friends to see how to approach life differently. For in primary relationships Americans have developed their own experiences into values to challenge the powerful and into conversations to supplant the management of opinion. These are the places where Americans in the twentieth century have increasingly lived their lives, made sense of the world, and ultimately shaped the fate of issues that insiders only deluded each other into thinking they were resolving.

IV Americans have come increasingly to make sense of the world in intimate relationships with other people. The emergence of face-to-face relationships as autonomous centers of interpretation to replace crumbling traditional cultures has reshaped the social history of modern American politics. These primary relationships are the places from which Americans made themselves visible by calling Senator Mitchell and writing Congressman Hamilton. Why have these intimate places become such important features of modern American life? What distinctive ways of conversing have citizens developed in these places?

To answer these questions we enter the world of "everyday life" where things are so obvious, or at least near at hand, that scholars often overlook them or dress them in incomprehensible jargon, where practice is so rich that theory presently lacks the tools to describe it. "Our own immersion in this talk as an ordinary activity is surely part of the reason it has proved so resistant to specification, so hard to pin down, as a subject for study," Samuel Schrager observed.[32] But if people are to become visible to each other we need to explore how and why Americans have come to talk differently since their primary relationships have come loose from the larger cultures in which they were once embedded. We need at least to outline how these places have come into being, and how and why they have nurtured alternatives to opinion management.

We will look first at historical developments such as immigration, mass production, and consumer culture that provided the contexts in which Americans for the first time made themselves visible through primary relationships. It was these large changes in the twentieth century that created primary groups to fill a void left by the fading and blurring of traditional cultures. Next we will step back and try to identify common features that seem to characterize primary relationships wherever they take place. We need to find out what primary groups share as their members think and act for themselves beyond the reach of opinion management. Finally we will explore how individuals apply experiences and values learned in their primary relationships to imagine and create forums for citizenship and even political programs for restoring popular control over large institutions in the age of television.

Primary groups and relationships have emerged to meet needs that individuals remembered had once been met by all-embracing cultures. As traditional cultures came under attack from overlapping, massive changes—individualism, capitalism, evangelical religion, secularization, industrialization, democracy, mobility—they lost the capacity to provide individuals the clear identities and interpretive authorities that had shaped life in their cultures. As their cultures lost their grip on members, Americans began to look for new places to find out who they were, new places to belong.

Individuals contributed to the erosion of traditional cultures by doing things that both loosened the authority of cultures over individuals and blurred the lines between cultures. By literally moving away from their cultures, individuals escaped from and eroded the authority of those cultures. For personal attractions of love, opportunity, adventure, education, even weather, Americans left places that had shaped what they could aspire to, whom they could marry, where they could live. With mobility rates twice those of other industrial societies, Americans have defined themselves—and struck others—as people on the move, slow to root themselves in geographic places, which have defined traditional cultures in other parts of the world.[33]

Individuals contributed even more dramatically to the fading of cultures when they formed families with people from other backgrounds. For example, among Americans of Italian ancestry born before World War I, only 6 percent had any non-Italian ancestors, while for Americans of Italian ancestry born after 1965, 80 percent had a non-Italian ancestor. By 1940 many scholars believed that the United States had become a "triple melting pot" in which Catholics, Protestants, and Jews married across ethnic lines but within the same religion. By 1980, however, 40 percent of Catholics and Jews married outside their faiths.[34] The lament that churches and political parties have over the twentieth century lost the capacity to shape their members' interpretations of events and to guide their members' conduct has echoed through modern American political and religious history.

The desire for acceptance by "Americans" inspired some individuals to abandon their cultures and traditions, at least in public. Employers, school administrators, and public officials have promoted "Americanization" over the past century under various names to compel individuals to forsake their distinctive cultures in favor of a single allegiance to standard or official "American" values. During World War II the army assembled individuals from different communities, social classes, religions, ethnic backgrounds, and party loyalties to die for a single flag and, since then, has lowered barriers of race, gender, and perhaps sexual preference that have kept Americans in separate spheres.

Mass marketing and mass media have likewise blurred the lines between cultures, inventing and marketing tastes and attitudes that all Americans might share as common denominators when they wanted to talk with people from other cultures. These inventions have over the twentieth century entered homes of people from all backgrounds. In the case of electronic media, for example, the average American listened to three or four hours of radio a day by the 1940s, and the average television set was on for six hours a day in the early 1960s at a time when 90 percent of homes had television sets. Beginning with the merger of many independent radio stations into the National Broadcasting Corporation in 1926, major commercial networks standardized the content that entered homes. Promoters of electronic media such as radio and television and movies turned to comedy, sports, variety, romance, and adventure to define common denominators that people from different backgrounds could talk easily about when they met at work or on the streets.[35]

The fading and blurring of cultures transformed Americans' expectations of where to look for and how to engage strangers in ways that ultimately turned political encounters from wars between cultures into conversations among individuals. As a place for simultaneously presenting basic needs while encountering people different from themselves, political encounters had long required participants to reconcile the familiar with the strange. A century ago, when Americans moved beyond their families and friends and looked to politics to help them meet their deepest needs—to educate their children, to defend their languages and churches—they mostly encountered people very much like themselves. Popular politics had grown up in the nineteenth century as a place for cultures to aggregate and mobilize their individual members—Yankees, Irish, Southerners, Democrats—for war against strangers from different cultures. With the erosion of cultures, however, citizens could no longer immediately recognize another individual's political beliefs by knowing that person's background, and as a result, they could no longer determine at first encounter whether that person was friend or foe. Instead of being a place where Americans felt surrounded by people like themselves or mobilized for war against different cultures, Americans found when they moved beyond their immediate families and friends that there were only vast and diverse primary groups, knots of individuals bound to each other in tiny worlds. The only way to find out what those strangers were thinking, whether they were friends or enemies, was to talk with them. Instead of a war between large cultures that made individual members instantly recognizable, political space became a place for conversations, for presenting needs and developing bonds, for deciding whether to include or exclude a stranger from everyday relationships.

As Americans tried to turn these conversations into organizations that could mobilize participants and programs to address twentieth-century problems, they developed a faith in government. This faith held for a generation or two before its collapse at the end of the twentieth century—reinforcing the fading of the familiar—thrust the reality of political interpretation and participation onto primary groups. Over the first half of the twentieth century many Americans hoped to replace traditional cultures as mobilizing and defining agents by concentrating people and resources into institutions such as labor unions and farm groups and corporations and behind public policies that promoted organization and growth. The thrust toward bigness and growth formed a trajectory of economic and political life that, guided by federal regulation, would deliver prosperity, national self-respect, and justice. Government would provide the security, and experts would provide the authority that traditional cultures had delivered. Beginning in the 1960s, first from the Left and then the Right, large numbers of Americans lost faith in the capacity and then the legitimacy of large institutions, including corporations and government, to meet their needs and represent them. They complained that the promotion of growth and bigness failed to deliver justice (as blacks and women insisted), prosperity (as workers insisted amid unemployment, declining real wages, and layoffs), meaningful lives and work (as students and workers complained), victory in or disengagement from foreign wars (as Left and Right complained about Vietnam). Government failed to solve the worsening problems of health, crime, environment, transportation, and drugs while officeholders and experts alienated many Americans by professing a paternalistic confidence that they knew what was best for others. Pollsters measured this declining confidence: In the late 1950s, 28 percent of Americans expressed lack of confidence in government; by the late 1970s, 67 percent expressed no confidence in government. In 1964, 29 percent of Americans believed that a few big interests ran the government, but by 1992, fully 80 percent held that view. While their distrust in large institutions deepened, their confidence in their own intimate worlds remained strong, even grew. In 1992, Gallup found 24 percent of Americans satisfied with the way things were going in the country but 73 percent satisfied with their own lives.[36] Losing faith in large organizations that had once promised a consensus around economic growth and empire, Americans retreated to their more intimate relationships.

Feeling the declining capacity of traditional cultures or large institutions or government to shape and explain life, Americans at the same time faced a profusion of materials from many different sources that told them who they were, what they should think and feel, what they should eat and wear. Appeals from salesmen, entertainers, and experts, from popular movements and interest groups, mingled with materials people brought from fading folk traditions. When an individual's connection with another country survived mainly as snatches—the memory of a cooking aroma, stories of a grandparent, a phrase in a forgotten language—folk traditions survived mainly as vague personal pride or embarrassment triggered by some everyday encounter, not as the "separate spheres" that had shaped lives for their members in nineteenth-century America. Everyone—entertainers and advertisers, experts and activists, family and friends—presented things to meet an individual's needs and wants.

To help screen these appeals, individual Americans sought to strengthen the capacity of their face-to-face relationships to do on their own what they had once accomplished through their embedding in surrounding cultures. Remembered as complete systems of belief and conduct, those cultures had given members a secure sense of who they were and where they belonged. With the erosion of these cultures the challenge of belonging—where, how, with whom—became much harder for individuals. To face the terrors of illness and death and eternity, of the apparent indifference of nature and society to their fates, Americans felt urgent needs to belong—needs for love, for family, for food and shelter, for appreciation and acceptance, for assistance in telling what was real and mattered. They needed others. They sought to make relationships where they could belong and then discover an identity, learn whom they could trust, tell what was authentic. Increasingly dependent on other individuals more than their cultures, they worried in desperate moments how easily or suddenly their ties to other people might snap, feared with Albert Camus that "it is only our will that keeps these people attached to us." The challenge of life was to find permanence or impose order over lives that were threatened by dangerous and unpredictable intrusions.[37]

Americans worried how they could know and be themselves. By frequently changing jobs, residences, and partners over the twentieth century, Americans faced constant challenges to create new identities. With everyday contacts obscuring the divisions that had once created separate spheres, individuals could choose from among many potential identities—of place, of religion, of class, of ethnicity, of gender, of party, of sexual preference, even of "American." When they looked for identities through which to feel a sense of belonging in the present, what they sought proved elusive: Identities were no longer inherent, automatic, physical things that came fully formed; they were now objects of choice and negotiation with others who claimed the same allegiances. Instead of being inherited from parents or triggered automatically by circumstances, Irishness or Republicanness or secretaryness or

Alabamaness, were increasingly experienced and interpreted differently by different people as the cultures named by those identities blurred and receded. Small wonder, then, that the crisis of identity emerged as the most talked-about challenge of mid-twentieth-century American life.

As they developed intimacy with others, Americans found their way back to larger identities, though not the traditional ones they had outgrown. The recognition of the true self within a person, the reaching out to others to share it, and the feeling of empowerment, even transformation, that came with proclaiming that identity to the world blended the desire for acceptance by individuals with the desire to be recognized by a wider world. What gave power to the proclaiming of that identity was precisely the ways individuals combined personal experiences with larger group circumstances or traditions, the ways they projected their personal voices as they embraced world-ordering perspectives of religion or political ideology, the ways individuals met their own needs by becoming part of something larger.

With salesmen, entertainers, and experts claiming to meet people's needs, the most basic interpretive challenge was to discover what was real and authentic. The old authorities no longer existed to answer these questions, and since the 1960s, many Americans had lost whatever faith they had in experts, large institutions, and government to frame, let alone answer, important questions. Indeed, by the 1980s and 1990s, many American scholars concluded that there were no answers to social and political issues, only perspectives on those issues.

Needing stable relationships in which to define who they were and discover what was real, Americans developed primary groups as autonomous units at two points in twentieth-century American life. Primary groups came into being, or at least became visible to scholars at the points, first, where individuals felt torn between traditional cultures and the lures of individualism and Americanization and, second, where opinion management sought to assemble them into masses in ways that violated traditional values.

The struggle of immigrants from traditional European cultures to adapt to life in the United States provided the context in which American scholars discovered for the first time in the early twentieth century that families forged an autonomous and "primary" existence between cultures and individuals. For the new immigrants from southern and eastern European Catholic and Orthodox Jewish cultures who made 1900–1910 a peak decade for immigration in American history, the twin challenges of leaving their rooted cultures and making lives in a strange new environment compounded problems of everyday survival with threats and opportunities created by individualism and Americanization. Families became the principal places where individuals tried to resolve the resulting conflicts. Torn between culture and environment, often with the younger generation pleading with the older to abandon old ways so as not to embarrass or hinder their

acceptance in the New World, immigrant families became such obvious arenas of interpretive authority that native-born reformers and scholars alike
had to redefine longstanding dualisms that had depicted society as a conflict
between individual and society in order to assign primary and autonomous
importance to families. Reformers such as Jane Addams concluded from
living in an Italian neighborhood in Chicago that families were the building
blocks of society and that social order depended on keeping them strong,
autonomous places for creating and passing on values. The disorganizing
strains that migration from settled European cultures placed on individual
immigrants provided the social circumstance from which pioneering scholars W. I. Thomas and Florian Znanecki (in *The Polish Peasant in Europe and
America* [1918–20]) developed the concept of primary groups to explain
where people made sense of their worlds and met their needs for identity
and belonging.[38]

Families have over this century become ever more crucial interpretive
centers of American culture. By 1987 they formed by far the most frequent
identity that writers presented to Hamilton. As sites where people connected
individual choice and cultural authority, they (and their close relative
"households") have continued to reflect and project conflicts in the political
arena. Consumer culture and mass media encouraged young people to develop different tastes and imagine lives outside the surveillance of extended
families. Youthful rebellion divided families from within, but those conflicts
also caused and reflected larger cultural conflicts over whether movies and
mass media taught offending sexual expressions, violence, language, tastes,
and costumes. Battles in the larger culture originated in and were ultimately
answered in families. The women's movement and economic pressures on
households projected into everyday conversation and negotiation issues
ranging from birth control and abortion to day care and apportionment of
family responsibilities and then projected them back to the center of political debate. The power of "family values" as the final arbiter of larger political conflict became clear in the 1980s and 1990s as Americans of all ideological perspectives tried to persuade others that their family values (that is,
their resolutions of their conflicts) were the real ones.

Primary groups came into being, or visibility, a second time at the places
where managers of consent tried to impose standardized controls over
different individuals and cultures. In response individuals have formed or
strengthened face-to-face groups to defend a local tradition or prerogative
against managerial innovations. Since the late 1920s scholars have discovered primary groups as central interpretive components of mass production,
mass consumption, and mass media.

Because mass production in the huge new assembly plants of the early
twentieth century epitomized the drive to turn individuals into masses, that
arena was one of the first places where scholars discovered the existence of

autonomous primary groups. Beginning with Elton Mayo's *The Human Problems of an Industrial Civilization* (1933), an exploration of the Western Electric plant in Hawthorne, Illinois, scholars discovered that workers turned shop-floors into welters of small, informal, stable groups whose members felt primary loyalty to each other and whose productivity depended on whether their primary group felt autonomy to shape work. Further studies in the 1930s and 1940s concluded that these groups, not managers, made the interpretations that shaped a plant's productivity. Neither wages nor working conditions were nearly as important to workers as participation in these groups of workmates who, among the repertoire of their behaviors, could slow the pace of work, ostracize a boss or coworker, form unions, or strike.[39]

The most remarkable place where scholars discovered that what seemed to be a faceless mass was actually a collection of distinctive primary groups was the military. Surveying troops following World War II, sociologists found that American armies had defeated the Nazi vision of a fused, visceral mass, not by fighting to uphold the American flag or values like freedom and democracy, but by fighting to defend intimate groups of loved ones at home or buddies with whom they had bonded in the army. Indeed, sociologists found that American soldiers were five times more likely to have fought to defend their primary groups than they were to defend values or flag.[40] American military leaders equated this tight bonding with military success. They resisted demands for full acceptance into the military by blacks, women, and homosexuals because they feared their participation would erode the power of the primary group.

In the space between mass communications and their audiences scholars discovered that readers and viewers created another use for primary groups as they developed their own standards for evaluating messages. Since the mid–1930s scholars have investigated whether the mass media shape popular tastes, purchasing decisions, behaviors, and values. They have increasingly concluded that the experience of watching a movie or buying a product is much more about what viewers and consumers do with each other around the activity and is, to quote Paul Cressey in 1938, "only incidentally associated with film content." In their studies of radio listeners Paul Lazarsfeld and Robert Merton established the tradition of observing how readers, listeners, and viewers interacted with people around them when they encountered media texts and thereby incidentally provided a model for this book. Lazarsfeld and Elihu Katz summarized this perspective in *Personal Influence* (1955): "Interpersonal relationships seem to be 'anchorage' points for individual opinions, attitudes, habits and values," the places where consumers scrutinized messages by comparing experiences and needs with people they knew and trusted. Summarizing research on advertising in 1984, Michael Schudson reported that people trusted their friends and relatives much more than advertising or mass media when buying products. By the

1990s communications scholars emphasized the ways viewers ignore, argue with, make fun of, evaluate, and incorporate pieces of media texts. Advertising and entertainment provide materials that Americans bring into their lives as they meet everyday needs with people around them.[41] Instead of assuming that a text has a single meaning intended by its author and perhaps created by interest groups, postmodern scholars emphasize how "readers" make their own meanings as they talk about texts with people around them.[42]

Americans have developed autonomous primary groups in this century to fill cracks and voids caused by crumbling traditional cultures and institutions. For this reason primary groups have come into view for scholars where they do things—where a family mediates between Italian and American cultures, where a platoon wins a battle, where a group of watchers makes fun of a television commercial or discusses a congressional hearing. They are usually an incidental part of the story of immigration, urbanization, labor relations, mass communications, a part of the larger forces they mediate, not a subject in their own right. At an earlier time when scholars discovered and recognized primary groups as basic social units, they often envisioned them as the true centers of responsibility within those larger institutions and cultures, assigning them the capacity to control production on a shopfloor or win wars on the battlefield, to shape church congregations or local unions. As academics have come to see primary groups in larger aggregates like race, class, and gender, opinion management to blur them into a mass, and institutions to subordinate them to profit and institutional legitimacy, they have removed from actual human beings the capacity to converse and take responsibility for each other or for the welfare of the institution. In the process they have paradoxically contributed to the massive decline in popular confidence in institutions. That confidence had emerged from the faith that platoons would fight wars, work groups would shape production, and friends and neighbors would choose political candidates and consumer products, that the institution would be guided by the primary groups that gave it meaning. Because in both reality and visibility primary groups came into existence, not as abstractions in nature, but as places for connecting individuals to larger activities, we lose some of their substance by trying to extract common elements from their different functions. And yet in order to explore what makes them such resilient and persistent sites of thinking and acting in this culture, in order to imagine how political conversation and policy might be remade to incorporate the places where citizens revealed to Hamilton how they wanted to think and act in politics, we need to identify common features that primary groups share. As they mediate between Puerto Rican and U.S. cultures, between television and its viewers, between sellers and buyers, when their members think for themselves. To understand the worlds from which writers approached Hamilton, we pick up clues from a wide, if eccentric, range of perspectives that taken together help to make visible how people think and act very differently in primary relationships than in the arenas imagined by opinion management.

The common experiences of primary groups can provide an alternative perspective from which people once again become as visible to strangers as they are to their fellow group members precisely because those experiences have taken place in such a wide range of circumstances that have been observed in very different realms of theory and practice. Those realms are indeed different. Progressive sociologists have looked at immigrant families, urban gangs, soldiers, voters, consumers, radio listeners, children at play. From the 1930s to the 1950s students of group dynamics looked at primary groups as they functioned in factories, schools, and neighborhoods. In business and economics the recent emphases on participatory management and small-is-beautiful economics provide clues. Since the 1960s movements to transform society and empower individuals have provided a rich arena for analysis, often by former participants. By emphasizing relationships as sources of values feminist scholars since the 1970s have established that the most primary thing about face-to-face associations is the relationships between members, not the durability of groups, that primary groups might better be called primary relationships. The postmodern turn in all scholarship—cognitive psychology, folklore, anthropology, literary criticism, the new pragmatism, oral history—has emphasized how people have actively and creatively constructed meanings, identities, recollections. From such diverse topics and disciplines scholars have rediscovered primary groups as the places where Americans built the relationships that mattered to them and made themselves visible to others.

Charles H. Cooley invented the concept of "primary groups" in *Social Organization* (1909) and assigned them the function of "forming the social nature and ideals of the individual." Eager to refute such theories as Herbert Spencer's that reduced life to isolated individuals and uniform masses, Cooley concluded that in families, play groups of children, and gatherings of neighbors "human nature comes into existence: Man does not have it at birth; he cannot acquire it except through fellowship, and it decays in isolation. What else can human nature be than a trait of primary groups?" As the places where members met basic needs, primary groups were informal face-to-face gatherings where daily interaction with the same people over a long period "fills our minds with the imaginations of the thought and feeling of other members of the group" so as to build "the sort of sympathy and mutual identification for which 'we' is the natural expression," so that "we identify our self-feeling with them" as we evolve moral principles. In meeting everyday needs with others, members learned the experiences and processes that they wanted to be the values that governed the larger society. Dismissing those who argued that people learned values from "abstract philosophy," Cooley argued, for example, that "kindness is aroused by sympathy, and can have little life except as our imaginations are opened to the lives of others and they are made part of ourselves." The point was obvious: "No doubt every one remembers how the idea of justice is developed in children's games."[43]

From Cooley onward, the feature of primary groups that has impressed the widest range of observers has been their size. They are small, intimate groups in which members have come over time to know each other well. "There is something deep within human nature which pulls toward settled relationships," and "vital and thorough attachments are bred only in the intimacy of an intercourse which is of necessity restricted in range" to face-to-face relationships, assumed John Dewey.[44] With the fading of traditional cultures, Americans have developed strong needs to find intimacy with others in order to escape isolation and loneliness. As part of the quest for intimacy, Americans have severed relationships (by divorce, for example) that cease to meet these needs. Americans may depend on primary relationships more than people in other parts of the world, as Richard Flacks has argued, because of distinctive American traditions that have defined control over life in terms of economic independence, capacity for self-defense, freedom from intervention and regulation, and enough privacy for members to do as they like. The small size of primary groups reinforces personal control over time and space.[45]

Primary groups have also struck observers as informal places where members present a full range of their needs. Because members know and trust each other, primary groups are places where members can be candid in stating their needs, blunt in their disagreements, and, at the same time, loving in their support for each other. Primary relationships are deep and complex, Freud believed, in contrast to the simple and shallow emotion of escape that he believed was elicited by mass appeals.[46] Primary groups adapt quickly and flexibly, moving subtly from addressing one member's need to another's, from one mood to another as new needs arise. Spontaneity and immediacy shape their informality.

Primary groups are places where people engage each other as they come to understand what they think and why they act. In these relationships participants test reality with others they trust as they discover and confirm who they are and what is authentic for them. Bombarded by salesmen, entertainers, bosses, and experts, people have needed others they could trust in order to "come to know one's authentic experience," as Mary Daly observed. Individuals test their impressions against observations of others and turn the impressions that survive this test into their convictions, Kurt Lewin believed. Family and friends can, of course, reinforce self-destructive or self-deceptive tendencies, but there is at least the opportunity for people to test reality with others who care for them. In sharp contrast to the experience of watching television, members control the direction and pace of interpretation. They interrupt and cross-examine witnesses until they are satisfied of the relevance or veracity of an experience the witnesses are describing. Members know how much to trust the firsthand experiences and information of others because they know how to evaluate the people who provide that information. With a unique capacity to help members know and evaluate sources and stories, primary groups are places where individuals explore what matters and what does not.[47]

In primary groups members reformulate experiences and texts to define who they want to be. New spouses form identities for their new families, as Maurice Halbwachs has observed, through "a great mutual effort full of surprises, difficulty, conflict, and sacrifice" by which they identify memories from their earlier separate families that they want to make the defining features of their new identity. By starting at her relationship with her mother, Kim Chernin has brilliantly traced how a daughter, mother, and grandmother developed a shared identity across three generations. Beginning as individuals who felt mostly embarrassed by their shared Chernin genes, femaleness, and Russian Jewish ancestry, they talked with each other in conversations that combined revelation, argument, evasion, confrontation, embarrassment, pride, and love until they discovered a we-feeling that united them.[48]

The evaluation of experience is the most common way people use primary relationships to form opinions. Members change opinions as they encounter new testimony from people they trust. The real challenge is to evaluate experience and turn it into reliable information or guides to conduct. Jonathan Schell has evocatively traced how a husband and wife in suburban Milwaukee developed from their everyday experiences social and political views that differed both from their parents' and from each other's as they decided who they would vote for in 1984. In the presidential election of 1980, fewer than half the voters "knew all along" who they would vote for, and 21 percent changed their minds in the last four days in response to conversations with the people around them.[49] Their opinions of the moment interested pollsters and pundits, of course, but the uses of experience were what interested Americans such as the family Schell described.

Because Americans turn to primary groups to escape isolation and loneliness, preservation of the relationship and group is a very high priority that differs dramatically from the concerns that animate opinion management. The passion of primary groups such as families to keep themselves together, as they change in composition, fortune, and direction, to insure their continuity, is one of their defining features. Feminists insist that primary relationships are alternative sources of experience and values to what they see as a male preference for understanding reality through hierarchies and winning. Women form face-to-face "networks" as bonds among particular women that can subvert "old boy" networks by which men marginalize women and make them invisible. Likewise, viewers of the Iran-Contra hearings turned themselves into active citizens by formulating with people around them messages for Hamilton. Placing relationships ahead of results shaped face-to-face participatory democracies such as the communes of the 1960s and 1970s, Jane Mansbridge found. While valuing relationships "allows debate, empathy, listening, learning, changing opinions, and a burst of solidarity when a decision is reached" that "can bring real joy," it also left members reluctant to raise unpleasant topics because disagreements sometimes sounded like personal criticisms that hurt relationships.[50]

Primary relationships are fundamentally places where individuals learn and explore responsibility. Through the punishments, praise, and blame of those around them, individuals learn that they will be held responsible for some things they do or that happen to some people and not for others. They come to assume varying measures of responsibility depending on the criteria by which they weigh an action—the consequences of their actions, how much their actions could reasonably alter a situation, where an action fits on a scale of wrongdoing from unexpected accidents to premeditated malicious choices, and a hierarchy of a community's values.[51]

Because their purpose is to meet needs of members while maintaining the group, primary groups have developed many ways to bring closure to a topic. They insist that each member contribute. They adopt a superficial consensus that offends the fewest members. They defer to the person who cares most deeply about the topic. They take a formal vote. They "agree to disagree" without resolution. Decisions are less important than preserving the relationship.

For all their functions, primary groups persist because they resolve a crucial paradox: each is a unique unit that responds with exquisite sensitivity to the most personal needs of each individual member at each moment, but all serve needs that are "primary" for human existence. Their styles and conclusions are unique, spreading across a tremendously diverse range. The challenges they face vary from moment to moment, reflecting changes and conflicts their members face in the world. The changes in circumstances they respond to range from the historical—wars or depressions—to the intimate. In adapting to the particular, however, they always seek the universal. Indeed, this sensitivity to particular needs permits members to meet primary needs for survival and answer timeless questions with eternal truths. As they each develop unique ways of experiencing universal yearnings for fairness and responsibility, primary groups illustrate, perhaps even shape, the larger pattern in which "thought is spectacularly multiple as product and wondrously singular as process," as Clifford Geertz has observed.[52]

How primary groups find the universal in the unique is illustrated by the most characteristic form of communication in primary relationships, gossip, as Patricia Meyer Spacks has argued. Emphasizing what people have in common, dwelling on the frailties of the person gossiped about as a means to deepen an alliance among gossipers, seeking the hidden rather than the obvious, subjecting private details to public scrutiny in an attempt to decide what is at stake in those private details, gossip is used both to mock and uphold the strong. By gossiping about others both inside and outside the primary group, people define the moral values that the group expects its members to live by.[53]

From the participatory cores of their primary relationships Americans have both guarded their groups' autonomy as safe havens against outside intrusions and drawn into the group materials from the outside world, used and reshaped them, and sought to remake the outside world to better meet their needs. As relationships among people who know each other well, primary relationships face inward and outward at the same time. Within, they are deeply interactive places where individuals can present a full range of feelings and needs that they can meet in incredibly diverse ways—in contrast to the range of needs and resolutions that cultures or parties can present. Offering opportunities to argue with, love, and ignore people around them, primary groups are places for individuals to imagine how they want to relate to strangers. Facing outward from primary relationships, members can relate to strange people and ideas across an equally wide range of needs. Primary relationships have come increasingly over this century to nurture challenges to the powerful and alternative conversations to those framed by managed opinion, to be the site where conflicts and ideas in the larger society are ultimately resolved. They have enabled Americans to be effective participants in the larger society because they face both inward and outward, turning easily from the safe autonomy of their primary cores to the exciting differentness of the outside world. By moving back and forth between safety and challenge, familiar and strange, primary relationships encourage participants to imagine large social changes while protecting their cores against distortions that accompanies contact with outsiders.

Members of primary groups reach outward, as Charles Cooley observed, by projecting the processes and experiences that guide their intimate worlds into values such as accountability and fairness that writers to Hamilton insisted that they wanted to shape the larger society. When group members choose to make themselves visible to outsiders, it is often for the purpose of presenting needs they hope others will meet. As primary groups came adrift from larger cultures, they wanted more than ever to make themselves visible to strangers. In the nineteenth century Americans had projected issues out of the concerns of their cultures: religion, race, ethnicity, geographic region, occupation. But over the twentieth century they have increasingly generated issues out of concerns experienced within primary groups: health care, crime, pollution, education, taxes. They adopt familiar ways of making needs known to strangers, making phone calls and writing letters to friends, in order to make their experiences with these needs visible to congressmen.

From the spirit and substance of primary relationships they imagine values to govern the larger society. They extend reciprocal bonds between brothers and sisters and parents and children into movements whose members relate to each other "like a family" or with "familylike warmth," who call each other "brother" or "sister," or who embrace a paternalistic ideal that the strong should care for the weak. From their experiences as brothers and sisters Americans have imagined labor unions founded on brotherhood, feminist groups on sisterhood, or causes like racial equality and world peace grounded in the experience of brothers and sisters.

From experience with primary relationships many Americans have imagined new values to transform both public policies and relationships between groups. The forces of immigration, urbanization, and industrialization deposited the privileged native-born Jane Addams in a different late-nineteenth-century world from the apprentice dressmaker and Irish immigrant Mary Kenny O'Sullivan. There were few meeting places in the Chicago of the 1880s for rich and poor, Italians, Irish, and "Americans." Feeling that she and other educated young people of her generation lived "unnourished, over-sensitive lives" while they "eagerly long to give tangible expression to the democratic ideal," Addams in 1889 moved into a rundown mansion in the Italian community in the hope that sharing neighborhood life with people from different backgrounds might make her own life more meaningful and generate new ways to connect the separated worlds. Joining the life of the neighborhood, learning about and respecting the needs of other neighbors from all backgrounds, native-born reformers like Addams and immigrants like Kenny began to relate to each other in new ways that would reshape society. "It was that word 'with' from Jane Addams that took the bitterness out of my life," reported Kenny: "For if she wanted to work with me and I could work with her it gave my life new meaning and hope." From their primary experience as neighbors they began to abandon conventional assumptions that one group's lifestyle was superior to another's and instead to project the more equal and reciprocal sense of social justice in which both groups had needs the other could complement with programs like day care, factory inspection, housing regulation, and organization of working women.[54]

Many Americans began to imagine how primary relationships might prefigure a new form of society in which they would feel more empowered, their voices heard more clearly—a society guided by different rules. Instead of idealizing an abstract future, they turned the ways they related to others into a shape toward which they wanted to move the larger society. In illustrating how Americans have created larger social movements out of primary relationships, participants in such movements also illustrated how the public forum might be recreated better to resemble and incorporate people in their primary relationships.

By claiming possession of a particular machine in a factory during a sit-down strike in the late 1930s or refusing to leave a lunchroom stool during a sit-in of the early 1960s, trusting individuals around them to stand their ground however vicious those who tried to remove them, workers and blacks created the trust and determination with others that became the cracks through which they imagined they might achieve acceptance for their union or equality for their race. They claimed the right to be heard, to be visible, as equal partners in conversations, by acting as though they were entitled to it. By personally challenging individuals with power while acting as equals with others who shared their determination, they widened debate, developed confidence to challenge segregation and employers (and their armed enforcers), and in everyday life prefigured an egalitarian society.

Coming into visibility within the huge new institutions that increasingly dominated economic life over the twentieth century, primary groups inspired values and expectations many social thinkers drew on as they sought to evaluate and regulate large-scale institutional life. In the pathbreaking *Sin and Society* (1907), Edward A. Ross argued that as corporate activities grew in size and impersonality, corporations grew in their capacity to harm society, "to become soulless and lawless" and thereby to escape accountability for their acts. Through its spectacular growth, commercial activity was removed from the control of face-to-face transactions. But Ross believed that the moral standards by which individuals had traditionally judged each other in their intimate relationships provided the surest way of evaluating modern impersonal activity. "The sinful heart is ever the same," he began the book with an affirmation of the timelessness of primary relationships, "but sin changes its quality as society develops. . . . Today the villain most in need of curbing is the respectable, exemplary, trusted personage who, strategically placed at the focus of a spider-web of fiduciary relations, is able from his office-chair to pick a thousand pockets, poison a thousand sick, pollute a thousand minds, or imperil a thousand lives." Unfortunately, it was hard to see the underlying reality that by traditional primary standards those corporations were picking pockets and poisoning consumers. "There is nothing like distance to disinfect dividends," because the corporation "transmits the greed of investors, but not their conscience; that returns them profits, but not unpopularity. . . . The hurt passes into the vague mass, the 'public,' and is there lost to view." To Ross the challenge was to develop both criteria and means that enabled people to judge corporate activities that harmed people as if the poisoning or pickpocketing had been perpetrated face to face. "To-day the distinction between righteous and sinners is *the main thing,* for upon a lively consciousness of that distinction rests the hope of transmitting our institutions undecayed, of preserving our democratic ideals, of avoiding stratification and class rancor" that emerge when activities are judged by other criteria than the unique and universal ones of primary groups. Ross advocated public exposure and legal restraints that would hold officers accountable for their corporations' deeds. By reinvigorating the traditional responsibility individuals felt toward each other in primary relationships, Ross hoped to establish popular control in an increasingly institutionalized society.[55]

Primary groups even subverted and transformed foreign policy for their members. In the case of the central controversy in this book, the war by the United States government on the Sandinistas in Nicaragua, groups of activists in more than forty American cities had formed close connections with similar groups of (primarily) Sandinistas in sister Nicaraguan cities. Those connections carried everything from love to material aid. Personal relations among people in the two communities who knew each other as members of two extended families, grieving over deaths and rejoicing in births and marriages, exchanging photographs and gifts, staying in each other's homes, became places for listening to each other's needs that for Americans meant supporting a movement that the U.S. government was seeking to obliterate. In the partnership between Bloomington, Indiana, and Posoltega, Nicaragua, for example, Barbara, Jack, Tony, Patti, Dan, Janice, and John got from Orbelina, Juan, Rolando, and Veronica both personal friendship and a conviction that human beings together could control their lives and create far-reaching changes. They felt the same sense of empowering possibility and usefulness that Jane Addams had described and that seemed otherwise beyond reach in the mass and imperial cultures of their own country. When Bloomingtonians provided health care manuals in Spanish so that fifty brigadistas could provide primary health care to the 20,000 residents of Posoltega, they not only met friends' needs but also developed confidence that it was possible somewhere in the world to deliver universal, preventive, low-cost health care even if American professionals and interest groups seemed incapable of doing it within the United States.

By reaching outward, primary groups have widened debate, have introduced life and reality to debates shaped by privileges, winning, and abstractions, and have with identities, commitments, and imagination empowered people to make claims and challenge privileges. By shaping in their intimate worlds the general changes they sought in the larger society, the most successful and creative movements for social change over the twentieth century—by workers, African-Americans, women, homosexuals, to find voices and then claim equality—have drawn direction and inspiration and nurturing from primary relationships.

As they have reached outward, however, members of primary groups have discovered that enlarging the scale and extending the reach of primary groups has often distorted the experiences and values they were projecting.

To enable others to better see them and hear their needs, Americans have embraced strangers who shared their circumstances (as workers, blacks, women, elderly, veterans) or beliefs (for peace, environmental protection, equality). By swelling their numbers and concentrating their resources they hoped to be seen and heard. But expansion of numbers often opened a chasm between members and the organizations they developed to speak in their names. The more they sought visibility and voice within worlds shaped by opinion management, the more the new organizations and their spokesmen neither resembled their members nor reflected their intimate spirit. By widening their scale the new organizations came to value institutional survival over relationships among people, numbers over individuals, winning over authenticity or responsibility, conclusions over experience, frozen positions over conversation or participation, common denominators over meeting people's needs, outside over personal control of agenda and choices, predictability and hierarchy over spontaneity and responsiveness, passivity over making needs known, abstraction over particularity or universality, respectability over militancy or conviction.

On primary groups has fallen a choice: Reclaim organizations for the spirit of primary relationships or let them move into the arenas of opinion management, beyond intimate reach. Less than a decade after autoworkers and steelworkers formed militant local unions, managers of their international unions seemed more interested in making members conform to the wishes of employers and the federal government than in listening to members. During World War II union leaders dampened grassroots militancy, usurped local autonomy, suppressed rebellious locals, accepted no-strike pledges that infuriated members in many communities. And local civil rights groups likewise chafed under leaders who cautioned restraint and limited goals as they sought respectability in the larger world of opinion managing.[56] Each election year activists in both parties have used the shells of local political parties to widen political debate, and each year party officials have resisted them in order to preserve low common denominators that keep the party "respectable."

Originating as places where individuals could find and become the real person within themselves, primary relationships encourage a search for authenticity and a spirit of inclusiveness. But as relationships widen into larger groups, as members grow concerned with how others see them, as they worry that strangers claim the same identity that has empowered them, some members begin to draw boundaries for their groups, to define the "true" lesbian or Republican or Marxist. Communities grounded in intimacy become communities grounded in exclusion.[57] Some begin searching for an ideological vision that will explain all reality or a law that will right things for all time. While members of Students for a Democratic Society (SDS) early in the 1960s invented participatory practices that outlined the

more democratic society they were aiming toward, many came by the mid–
1960s to seek an all-inclusive ideology that would define their larger purposes. As this quest led members into ideological battle over which totalizing
ideology to favor, SDS lost its participatory spirit. At Santa Barbara in the
early 1970s, likewise, the demand for a total commitment to a single understanding of revolution disaffected people from the diverse primary groups
that earlier had found in a common heterogeneous student movement
enough space for a wide range of different members to feel included.[58]

Torn between the goals they formed in their face-to-face worlds and the
imperatives of opinion management that define how they will be heard,
many members fight to defend their original voices against distortions introduced by the mass media. While they gather to define injustices, demand
changes, widen agendas, and empower themselves, participants feel compelled to decide how to respond to the media's exclusive interest in their
numbers, the respectability of their appearance, their ability to silence "ex-
tremists," and the "reasonableness" of their demands.[59]

Whereas organizations have become battlegrounds in which members
have tried to preserve their participatory cores while they reach outward to
prefigure a new world, the larger historical outcome of the struggle between
opinion management and primary relationships is clear and paradoxical.
Movements grounded in primary experiences have successfully challenged
the powerful. But they have failed over the long run to halt the growing
power of the opinion industries to shape where Americans become visible
or how they carry on political conversations in public. A world of press con-
ferences and punditry now exists where "opinion" is assembled to support
particular interests. But instead of responding by bringing their conversations into these arenas, politicians and citizens alike have increasingly abandoned the forum. Returning to their participatory cores, Americans have
shaped their identities and formulated their values in ever smaller and more
dispersed places. In fact, over the course of the past generation, movements
for change have increasingly blossomed in primary groups scattered across
the continent, where people have reshaped their relationships with other
particular individuals and developed local communities to support those
changes. As drives to turn intimate values and bonds into larger ideologies
and institutions have distorted their prefiguring instincts and failed to transform society, people have increasingly defined empowerment and social
change within small face-to-face groups.

Grounded in the conversations and experiences of meeting needs in face-
to-face relationships, Americans have simply acted to demonstrate that arguments over values will be resolved not by pundits or public policy but in
relationships where primary processes work as sources of change, empowerment, and participation, in short of autonomy. Primary relationships have

themselves remained the places where many ideas originate and where they are finally settled. The proposal for an Equal Rights Amendment grew from intimate experiences of women, passed through two decades of public conversation, and failed to secure ratification by enough legislatures to become a constitutional amendment. But the original push toward equal rights also entered everyday conversations where it profoundly transformed relations between individual men and women. When failure to bring about revolution shattered the student movement in Santa Barbara in the early 1970s, activists retained powerful commitments to live their lives by moral and empowering lines of personal development that they had developed in their earlier political activities.[60]

Because reaching outward has the simultaneous capacity to effect a new world and to erode the participatory core from which people reach outward, members of primary relationships have developed a remarkable ability to make their needs known and move toward a new society while also nurturing their relationships as safe havens. The opinion industries suggest that only they can make people become visible, but in truth primary relationships have strengthened over the twentieth century even as opinion management has shaped public arenas. Primary groups remain the active places where Americans reveal their experiences and needs, where they decide what is real and desirable. These are also the places where they decide how and where to make themselves visible to strangers. And they have become more significant over the twentieth century because they keep alive relationships and experiences, as they seek the human in the particular, the eternal in the immediate, as they work to meet personal needs in their simultaneous screening of new material and prefiguring of a more responsive and just society.

In 1987 unprecedented numbers of Americans wrote letters and made phone calls to transform the public forum from a place shaped by the values of opinion management to one shaped by their experiences with primary relationships. In doing so, they illustrated how the fading and blurring of traditional cultures as sites where Americans recognized each other opened a struggle to define the new ways in which citizens would be seen and heard. Because politicians and journalists were also citizens who often preferred political conversation in which individuals could present a full range of their needs, the conflict was more between two visions (and the experiences and training that informed them) of what the forum would look like than between individuals or pressure groups. Even master campaign managers and spin doctors like David Gergen and James Carville believe that the way to listen to people is not to poll them but to listen to them in their everyday worlds. No writer to Hamilton put the case for primary relationships more eloquently than the man who pioneered the modern forms of political spin in the Reagan administration, David Gergen, when he told me the most basic lesson that he wanted to convey to his students at Duke University in 1995:

> A lot of these questions that are constructed in big highfalutin terms have a lot more to do with personal responsibility and trust and human relationships. It's like having a relationship with somebody down the street or in your school or in your family. It's who you build up with, what kind of relationship you build up, trust over time.[61]

Because the ways to make people become visible again, after larger cultures have faded, have evolved amid basic conflicts such as those illustrated in this book over Olliemania, we need to see the evolution of the forum not as an inevitable or irreversible process but as one that people can shape in different ways. Television, for example, provided both the excuse and the place for the creation of Olliemania, with all its consequent distortions. It was also, however, an arena where viewers could watch evidence and testimony unfold at public hearings and listen to serious argument among politicians; taking these materials, viewers could evaluate them on their own terms in their primary relationships and draw their own conclusions.

In the letters written to Hamilton, citizens spoke in the voices and of the values that they wanted to hear in public conversation. We turn at the end to the challenge of imagining what kind of public forum might result from this transformation. What will politics and government look like when they better reflect the primary relationships of citizens?

Drawing Politics Closer to Everyday Life

The commercial management and professional interpretation of "opinion" are driving further apart the worlds citizens inhabit in their everyday lives and the worlds politicians inhabit as they govern. By their intervention between citizens and politicians the opinion industries have distorted both worlds and eroded traditional connections between them. Indeed, they have created a land of make-believe in which people converse in polls, sound bites, photo ops, attack ads, and spin doctoring in a system whose massive irresponsibility they blame on the victims, the voters, in stories like Olliemania. They have left citizens and politicians feeling invisible to each other, cut off from hopes, traditions, and skills each had brought to politics.

As opinion industries have come to define where and how citizens and politicians will find and engage each other, they have driven both voters and legislators out of the political arena. Indeed, they possess these arenas by dispossessing citizens and politicians. "Our leverage in the election quite candidly goes up as the voting population goes down," explained master conservative political strategist Paul Weyrich. But what was good for opinion management, even Weyrich lamented, brought the country "perilously close to not having democracy. . . . Nonvoters are voting against the system, and if we get a bit more of that, the system won't work."[1] Citizens and politicians know where they are not wanted. By 1992 five out of every six eligible voters deserted the political arena in the most dramatic way: they did not vote in the presidential primary elections. And in 1992 politicians also fled the arena: "Hating to go to work every morning," Senator Tim Wirth of Colorado declined to run for reelection to a body where the "money chase," public "posturing," and negative campaigning were making him into "someone I didn't like."² A record number of ninety-one members of the House of Representatives decided not to run for reelection in 1992.

As the 1996 elections approached and the numbers of incumbents abandoning Congress headed toward new records, senators and representatives blamed the spread of opinion management for sapping the rewards and fun and pride from their work. In announcing his retirement after twenty-one years in Washington, Senator Paul Simon explained: "I enjoy policymaking. I even enjoy campaigning. . . . But I do not enjoy asking for money" to finance campaign advertisements, polling, and other opinion management. "We are excessively responsive to the polls and to campaign contributors," Simon lamented. As opinion management reduced debate and lawmaking to wedge issues that could move common denominators, Representative Pat Schroeder (D-Colo.) described the resulting toll that convinced her to retire after twenty-four years in Congress: "We're in kill-or-be-killed politics now. People take every issue and think, what kind of 30-second ad would that make? It's gotten so surly and so mean."³

Meanwhile, the opinion industries are booming. Their fees for managing opinion soar beyond reach of all but the wealthiest candidates and the special interests whose business is to bypass the forum entirely, pursuing their clients' interest without debate. These interests finance opinion management for candidates and harvest their rewards when laws and administrative regulations benefit their clients, not voters or politicians. In explaining why the United States uniquely among industrialized nations left 41 million of its citizens without health insurance, Senator Simon blamed the policymaking distortions introduced by the opinion industries: "Those who benefit financially from the present system make large campaign contributions; the 41 million who are harmed do not."⁴

I Over the decade since citizens wrote Hamilton to challenge the story of Olliemania, opinion management has continued to shape the public forum. During the 1992 presidential campaign, the familiar distortions of conversations between voters and candidates worsened. In 1992 the average sound bite through which candidates spoke uninterrupted on the nightly network news continued to shrink from 42.3 seconds in 1968 to a new low of 8.4 seconds. Journalists interceded more than ever between candidates and voters as they consumed 71 percent of campaign coverage on evening newscasts and left only 12 percent for candidates. The hunt for common denominators went berserk with at least four daily sets of tracking polls identifying themes to frame coverage. The proportion of total election news devoted to issues continued to decline (from 40 percent in 1988 to 32 percent in 1992), while the proportion dedicated to "horse race" coverage of who was ahead rose from 25 percent in 1988 to 35 percent in 1992. Small wonder, then, that scurrilous rumors that would have gone unreported in the past became scandals and then "feeding frenzies" at the expense of issues that interested candidates and voters.[5]

Three years later the "hot button" issue of 1995, affirmative action, illustrated how opinion management inspired politicians to talk in irresponsible ways that made it harder for individuals to turn principle into everyday reality. By expressing "opinions" that they thought would both activate partisans and interest groups and appeal to the lowest of common denominators, politicians and partisan pundits framed realities in language and choices that neither employers nor workers could experience as anything but a hindrance to greater workplace diversity. Bill Clinton proclaimed that he supported "affirmative action" while he opposed its British synonym "reverse discrimination" because, many observers believed, he wanted to persuade Jesse Jackson and others not to challenge his bid for reelection, without taking substantive steps to reverse encrusted patterns of discrimination. Later that year California Governor Pete Wilson directed his appointees on the University of California governing board to end race-biased admission to that institution because, many observers believed, he wanted support from conservatives in his run for the Republican presidential nomination. Meanwhile, at the Ryerson Coil Processing steel company outside Chicago, where company officials and workers were trying to make affirmative action a workplace reality, three *Chicago Tribune* reporters concluded from interviewing hundreds of people that "their stories provide an intricate human rebuttal to the media tendency to present affirmative action in terms of polar extremes." By filling the mass media with appeals to low common denominators in order to mobilize troops and win electoral wars, politicians like Clinton and Wilson made it harder for real workers such as Ryerson's four-and-a-half year old machine operating team of Hispanic Lorenzo Orona, Turkish-born Michael Erkan, and black Lance Ermon to build the individual respect for each other they had developed as colleagues. "Affirmative action may be under fire in Washington," declared president Sandy Nelson, "but we are going to stay on track" in continuing to hire more women and minorities in a traditionally white, male workplace. Affirmative action was not an abstraction, but the sum of individual shopfloor interactions among workers from all backgrounds. By reducing experience to abstraction, the hard work of everyday relationships to demagogic sound bites and partisan punditry, the self-contained world of opinion management seemed to be growing ever more remote from the lives of steelworkers Orona, Erkan, and Ermon and their boss, Nelson.[6]

The public forum thus has taken visible shape as the place where conversation amounts to manipulation of a mass: Pollsters measure the denominators that turn individuals into a mass. Campaign consultants and advertisers craft sound bites and ads that they hope will move the mass or persuade others that the mass is moving. Spin doctors turn news into stories that explain why an officeholder or candidate is saying or doing what the mass wants. Special interests raise and contribute the money to finance these industries. And pundits keep the pieces together by endlessly commenting on what individual Americans are thinking as if they existed as interchangeable pieces of a mass.

Beside the managed surface of politics, however, voters have reached out to create their own arenas where they can be seen and heard as individuals and thereby remake political conversations. Americans have turned the means they use to talk with people around them—letters and phone calls—into arenas where they can seize control of conversation from managers. "Scream TV" and "talk radio" fill the airwaves as ordinary citizens replace actors in telling stories to audiences and as ordinary citizens replace journalists in questioning politicians. By 1992 the questions that citizens telephoned to presidential candidates turned "Larry King Live" into what *People* called a nightly "national town meeting." "The public switched places with the campaign press," wrote King: "This time around, voters interviewed the candidates while the journalists watched."[7] Between 1988 and 1990 two hundred radio stations accommodated this popular desire to talk and listen to strangers by converting their formats into talk shows, and by the fall of 1994 the talk/news format became for the first time the most popular kind of radio programming, edging out the older favorites of adult contemporary, country, and Top 40 programs. Explaining the popularity of his new radio talk show in 1995, Chicago's powerful politician "Fast Eddie" Vrdolyak explained that on talk radio callers "don't feel conned or hustled. . . . We're the kitchen table, the corner bar." Talk shows, observed a *Chicago Tribune* writer, provided "the kind of interaction that many citizens feel has been lost in their relationship with government and politicians."[8]

Although public talk about politics has taken new commercial forms in response to popular demands to be seen and heard, those innovations do not foster the kind of political engagement that citizens called for when they repudiated Olliemania by writing Hamilton. While the mass media has provided places where people can talk and listen to each other outside the mainstream and its common denominators—entertainment for those who spoke Spanish or loved rock music, punditry for evangelical or conservative or academic viewers, stories of personal experiences through which viewers might ponder mysteries in their own families, workplaces, or sexual tastes—these responses create separate spheres with their own specialized participants. Because these innovations leave intact the values and rhythms that shape the self-contained core of political conversation, that conversation continues to be distorted. Writers to Hamilton knew that they could not become truly visible to and engaged with each other until the conversations of everyday life replaced those of opinion management.

▐▐ The real public forum originates not on television or in Congress, but in us. It is embedded in the primary relationships of our everyday lives. This reality—the fundamental message that writers explained to Hamilton—is sometimes hard to see because professionals have defined politics as an independent arena shaped not by our everyday needs, but by opinion management. We comfortably talk with friends about our experiences with doctors, explore with them why so many Americans have problems finding health care and how such care might be made more responsive, but we have been taught that these conversations are not part of the political forum. The forum, we are told, exists in high-level meetings with Hillary Clinton and Newt Gingrich and health industry lobbyists and receives its outward appearance in Harry and Louise television ads.

We decide when and where and how we want to make our everyday conversations into a wider and more visible forum, to force the actors we see on television to pay attention to us where we actually are, not where they imagine or wish that we would be. This book tells the story of how the televised Iran-Contra hearings presented an extraordinary threat and opportunity that inspired individuals to reach out to other citizens and congressmen to make visible the experiences that they ordinarily shared only with family and friends. Faced with the story of Olliemania—and particularly the discovery that they could not recognize what seemed to be moving their fellow Americans—citizens felt compelled (as they did during crises in their intimate relationships) to seek out and strengthen their bonds with others, citizens and congressmen alike. Olliemania drove citizens back to the places where they formed and nurtured their core values, to their primary relationships, to strengthen and then make clear to others both the values and needs of those relationships. In the summer of 1987 large numbers of Americans needed their everyday conversation to be visible to others so they could reaffirm its values and authority, could gather up what they needed to assume responsibility for shaping things outside their daily lives. They had to make the forum visible in order to draw what they saw on television back toward what they valued. In so doing they became citizens.

Journalists, politicians, and pundits could see that something unusual was moving Americans in the summer of 1987, and—in keeping with the mission of their crafts—they wanted to understand that movement. Some even wanted to take part in the forum that citizens were initiating. Lee Hamilton and Daniel Inouye wanted to know what Americans were saying to them. Legislators retained many staff members whose sole responsibility was to listen to constituents and to answer their letters. Pollsters wanted to know what people were thinking. Spin doctors wanted to know how popular winds were blowing in order to best position their messages. Some even thought they could see the forum best by reading individual letters and talking with individual citizens. David Gergen and James Carville said that they learned more by talking with people than by reading polls. David Broder turned what his neighbors told him during his summer vacation on Beaver Island, Michigan, into his picture of the forum.

And yet, as this story make painfully clear, many of the best-intentioned professionals were so used to looking for the forum in the wrong places that they could neither see nor take part in it. Under pressure to narrow diversity to minimal denominators, pressure to find the mass that must somehow exist among all the eccentricities of individuals, many people who use the tools of opinion management—by profession or by choice—feel powerful limitations that keep them from meeting and talking with individuals where they really are. Politicians, journalists, and pundits really do want to see and hear and take part in the forum, but they are so accustomed to thinking in terms of aggregation and typicality and objectivity, to looking for averages and denominators, that their vision of themselves as professional facilitators and interpreters becomes the means that transforms them into spectators and manipulators. It is precisely when they start listening and speaking *as* journalists, *as* politicians, *as* pundits, when they leave the realm of their own personal experience, their conversations with family and friends, that they also leave the forum. They are trained to distance themselves from individuals, to regard the individual merely as a source of human interest anecdote, and in so doing they trap and blinker themselves within the make-believe world of opinion management. In this world, they cut themselves off from both their unique individualities and their basic humanity, from their ambitions and competencies and dreams, from their capacities for empathy, growth, learning and unlearning, for taking and shirking responsibility for others—in short, from learning with others how to do things differently to make better lives and a better world.

Since speaking and listening are the major activities of a forum, the basic challenges center on the media through which interchanges occur, on how those interchanges are framed by participants, and on how individuals make the forum visible to others. Before citizens and politicians and journalists can see and hear each other in the same forum, we need to overcome the suspicions that have arisen between those who approach the forum from the experience of personal relationships and those who approach it from the perspective of opinion management—elites' suspicions of the passions and capacities of the people, the people's suspicions of the arrogance and manipulations of elites. This distrust has stripped from both groups any sense of common responsibility for either the forum's conversation or its outcome because it has denied the basic individuality and humanity they all share.

Because they find the notion that individuals are uniform enough to be treated as pieces of a mass to be simply nonsense, citizens see measurements of the mass as listening devices that keep them from entering the forum on their own terms. In polls, for example, individuals are asked suddenly on the telephone to choose among options presented by a stranger at a particular moment on a topic that may or may not interest them. Turning them into faceless averages of aggregates, polls also make them isolated individuals. They are isolated from the problems they are being asked about, isolated from other participants in the forum, and isolated from the stranger who crashes into their lives at the other end of a phone call. Encouraging passivity and isolation, polls create a forum that is the opposite of the active, noisy exchange of experience, the making and unmaking of opinion, among people who care for each other. Because polls are the most congenial way for managers to listen to people they would prefer to dismiss as poor, evangelical, unlettered, and emotional, many interpreters can see only ignorance when people cannot recall some fact that matters to a pollster or when polls produce results defined to be contradictory. Instead of deepening mutual understanding, polls deepen mutual suspicions.

For citizens and politicians alike, it is hard to converse and build solutions to real problems when managers try to shape the forum around advertisements and sound bites. Since conversation cannot center on problems as people experience them, it is not surprising that 60 percent of voters told exit pollsters in 1994 that the country was losing ground on the serious problems before it. Reflecting suspicions citizens brought to the forum, a cross section of eligible voters in 1994 agreed by a 65–22 percent margin that "public officials don't care much what people like me think" and that instead—this time by a 75–19 percent margin—"government is pretty much run by a few big interests looking out for themselves" and not "for the benefit of all the people."[9]

The mutual suspicions that keep managers and citizens from recognizing what they have in common have deepened in recent years because Americans have fewer occasions to get to know each other. In recent years, David Gergen believes, governing elites have felt greater condescension toward ordinary citizens because the spaces in American culture where once people from different backgrounds learned to respect the capacities and intentions of people unlike themselves—the military and the public schools—are no longer meeting places for all. After going to Yale and Harvard Law School, it was in the Navy, Gergen recalled, working with fifty enlisted men, that he came to respect people different from himself. "They knew a hell of a lot more about things than I did." Lamenting that there are few things "we do together as a people," Gergen worried particularly that elites attend the same schools, achieve similar things in the same arenas, talk with each other in an "echo chamber," while at the same time they are "less and less experienced in life" than leaders of an earlier generation. "Understanding the country comes through life experiences," Gergen asserted, experiences that people "can only get through your own firsthand contact and personal background," experiences in which failure might offer more valuable lessons than success to those with great privileges. Lacking those contacts, elites lack a range of experiences or empathy or curiosity about others and thus find it easier to ignore and condescend to different people by listening to them in polls. Politics, of course, has always been a place for people to encounter people who are different from themselves, but the absence of places when they are growing up to engage different kinds of people cuts them off from experiences and conversations in which they could see through a person's background and circumstances and explore the uniqueness and humanity of that person. Finally, the tremendous emphasis that opinion management places on winning makes the forum "so much more . . . partisan and poisonous" than it had been earlier, in Gergen's words, that citizens suspect that managers are just not interested in listening to people, building common narratives, or addressing problems. Instead, politics has become nothing but an arena of staged appeals. When the ferocity of partisan Senate appeals during debate on the 1994 crime bill hit what the *Los Angeles Times* called a "tragicomic low" and Arkansas Senator Dale Bumpers called "a living tragedy," media student Larry Sabato explained why politicians placed histrionic partisanship ahead of serious debate: "It has everything to do with the television cameras."[10]

In the letters to Lee Hamilton, Americans imagined a forum that would not only be free of suspicions introduced by opinion management but would also draw politics closer to everyday life, because in both form and content, in what they wanted the letters to do as well as what they said, writers created the letters for that very purpose. Abandoning the managed arenas of voting and policymaking, citizens created their own participatory arena by writing and calling politicians directly. In these letters Americans grafted a familiar way of expressing their deepest concerns onto the democratic tradition that called on citizens to "write your congressman" when they had concerns. By reaching out to a congressman to establish a relationship in which they would be heard, they pointed toward new kinds of political conversations. They wanted to show that opinion could be heard without being managed—that political conversations could resemble primary relationships.

To remake politics into a place where people liked themselves when they participated, writers challenged politicians to stop managing their talk by the rules of the opinion industries and to start talking as people did around them. Wanting to draw a congressman into their circles of family and friends, citizens assumed that primary relationships would provide common ground for people to approach and recognize each other. From the responsibility they felt for maintaining those relationships, writers acquired both the capacity to find common bonds with other people and yardsticks for measuring how far opinion management carried the forum away from everyday talk, how it narrowed and abstracted conversation and demobilized participants. Because primary groups nurtured continuing relationships, moving to address ever more needs with ever more depth while sustaining and deepening their bonds, they were natural places for taking and learning responsibility. Writers judged what they watched on television against everyday talk. They liked to hear experiences discussed at first hand as people argued about how to interpret those experiences. They liked give-and-take between people instead of sound bites. They liked the everyday air of genuine inquiry in which they, like legislators, faced the challenge of figuring out what was at stake in the whole topic—whether traditions were threatened, crimes committed, bad policies adopted, or good policies misapplied—and through that inquiry the challenge of identifying and affirming the values they wanted to govern the nation. They liked the empowering sense of responsibility that came when journalists and politicians trusted viewers to decide the outcome. Conversely, they condemned politicians who propelled the hearings beyond the reach of everyday talk. Feeling excluded when others told secrets behind their backs, writers bristled when legislators denied them the chance to hear important parts of the story either by taking those subjects into secret session or by ruling them beyond the scope of the investigation. They disliked staged appeals. They particularly disliked pandering to low common denominators. Because common denominators were hollow fabrications, not the voices of real people, they could not be engaged responsibly as one would another person to find an outcome that met real needs. They wanted legislators to say what they believed and meant. They disliked partisan posing and wrangling that diverted attention from the inquiry and recapitulated how politicians evaded responsibility for governing by appealing to imagined masses. They disliked pundits telling them what to think.

For politics to be more responsive and politicians to become more responsible, political conversations need to adopt the informal and adaptable spirit of everyday life. In real talk, of course, people change their minds as they hear new voices and needs. Because interpretations (as opposed to convictions) are flexible, rising and falling in confidence and changing in emphasis and even direction, writers wanted politicians to be quicker to change their minds, to open themselves to new voices (such as their own), new perspectives, new experiences. By freeing politicians to say what they mean with the same varying degrees of conviction and doubt that people express in everyday life, to change their minds freely, they hoped politicians would be more receptive to others. By imagining the conversations themselves—the hearings, for example—as evolving and informal, able to change direction, to stop and explore a new discovery, not places to recruit people to frozen "opinions," they imagined an arena in which participants would take responsibility for addressing problems and nurturing relationships. By replying to writers in some way congressmen acknowledged that writers expected at least a response that would show that they had started a relationship or at some level that they were being represented in other conversations.

Writers envisioned a forum where conversation is not so much a means for conveying opinions to be counted as it is an ongoing commitment to a relationship. Conversation in which people listen to each other and present a full range of needs as they try to solve problems *is* community, *is* the forum, *is* the end, not the means, of political participation. The forum opens up by the act of reaching out, of making a connection and engaging others, not by the making of choices and counting of votes. Citizens become policymakers when they take responsibility for sustaining a relationship that addresses the changing needs of individuals. What makes them good policymakers is that they know how to be good friends and family members, not that their positions of the moment prevail at the ballot box or legislative hall.

Because engagement is the objective of the forum, for the writers experience became more valuable than conclusion. Experience can be infinitely interpreted and adapted to meet a wide range of needs. The stories that people tell on his television show occupy a vast middle ground between what host Geraldo has called the conversation of anyone's "neighbors" and a "freak show." The appeal for viewers is precisely the chance to evaluate that experience for themselves instead of having it filtered and interpreted by professionals, to judge whether what they see on television is authentic or phony. In a world of hustlers and entertainers they want above all to listen to and talk with others about what makes an experience authentic. Trying to recognize and make sense of experiences provides a starting place for people from different social worlds to understand why something is important to a participant. Since conversation begins with what people recognize and share, experience can at least stimulate empathy.

The surest way to sustain engagement in the forum, Manfred Stanley has observed, is to begin with a problem.[11] For conversation to become substance in a democracy, the basic challenge becomes to uncover how the world works, to listen to how different people connect ideas, behavior, and emotions, and to negotiate a shared, cumulative narrative that explains how a problem has developed and how participants want its course to be altered and a new course charted and maintained. As different writers tried to figure out how a problem came about, they came to see that what was a problem for some—the sale of weapons, the secrecy of an illegal policy—was a solution for others and then to explore the interests, values, and ideologies, the practices and myths, that people brought to the ways they defined a problem. Because the objective was fuller understanding of how the problem was experienced by different people, participants explored different interventions or "solutions." Many viewers liked the Iran-Contra hearings because they first could hear from the people who created the problems—

spies, contras, soldiers, arms merchants, policymakers—and explore how the problem appeared differently to each. Then they could listen to congressmen argue about how to diagnose the problem. Finally, they could decide for themselves what, if anything, had gone wrong. After hearing different perspectives they then considered how to weigh and apply different values and codes—such as the oath at military academies not to lie, cheat, or steal or tolerate those who did or Oliver North's conviction that it was his responsibility to do as he was ordered. In a forum shaped by ongoing engagement the world became not a place to aggregate opinions or to solve problems for all time, but a place, as Stanley wrote, whose movement through time was marked by "sufferings and remissions, victories and defeats, chapters open and closed, ambiguities unending, and intimacies achieved."[12]

If common narratives that address real problems are to be possible, people must take responsibility for guiding conversation in this direction. Such taking of responsibility—whether in families or in Congress—accompanies, even requires, the development of trust. David Gergen believed that the key to governing is to build relationships in which people come to trust one another as they come to share experiences and risks and gain confidence in each other. Power within the House of Representatives, declared Congressman John Dingell (D-Mich.), "depends upon the trust of your colleagues. Their trust allows you to lead. Members will follow you. That gives you immense power, but it is also very fragile." Sound bites aimed through the mass media at faceless denominators were irresponsible ploys that made it harder to build personal relationships and solve problems. Saying "I couldn't bring myself to cater to the media," longtime House Ways and Means Committee Chairman Dan Rostenkowski worried by 1994 that opinion management had changed Congress: "Nobody wants to do the hard things, to solve problems. . . . They want to go to Washington to complain about Washington," declared the lawmaker who preferred to assemble majorities for bills than to grandstand to the media.[13] The challenge of figuring out what individuals are responsible for, and to what extent, and to whom, provides the means for individuals to discover, clarify, and deepen what they share as they talk of the moral problems of individual action, the political problems of common action, and the cultural problems of mutual understanding without requiring participants to accept a single philosophy or to share the same social worlds. By focusing on the challenge of fixing personal responsibility, individuals can turn differences over principle into recognizable and reconcilable formulations of fundamental issues. Writers could acknowledge that what was honor in one world was betrayal in another, what was hard work and dedication in one ideology was lawbreaking irresponsibility in another, while still finding a common problem to be explained. People from all ideologies and cultures recognized that assessing what individuals would be responsible for was central to maintaining personal relationships, cultures, and government.[14]

The challenge of fixing and assuming responsibility transcends all others because principles and laws and actions do not matter if no one accepts personal responsibility or is held personally responsible for what they do. This challenge was the starting point in the hearings: Who was responsible for murders and drug running by the contras? For breaking the law and violating the Constitution? For failing to advance larger agendas like restraining communism? Were these actions justifiable? How should Congress treat those who had acted or failed to act in these ways?

And the issues of responsibility simply reinforced the basic challenge for participants: Would they take responsibility for maintaining engagement in the forum, for widening the voices and deepening the content, for trying to find a process or outcome that seemed to get to the core of matters instead of ending in low common denominators and popularity contests? While managers and other elites have often assumed that they should define the proper initiatives for taking responsibility, the writers to Hamilton clearly illustrate that citizens can often transcend the constraints and temptations that divert professionals and are, therefore, more capable of defining and taking responsibility for solving real problems. The forum, after all, originates not in managerial manipulations, but in everyday talk.

Over the past decade the fixing of personal responsibility has been the theme underlying the critical events that have opened forums where Americans have brought materials from television to discuss in their everyday worlds. Some of the deepest and broadest engagements between politicians and citizens over the past half-century have begun with televised hearings—and televised trials may extend this phenomenon in the future—that have featured wider evidence, witnesses, and perspectives than ordinarily occur in political conversation. Triggering conversation wherever Americans gather, traveling between citizens and legislators through every medium from letters to polls, televised congressional hearings such as those on the Iran-Contra scandal (1987) or the nomination of Clarence Thomas (1991) or televised trials such as that of O. J. Simpson (1994–95) have engaged citizens to assess individual responsibility for behavior among people who inhabited different social and ideological and institutional worlds, where members viewed the contexts very differently. The mystery to be solved in each case was less what individuals had done than how they should be judged. But running through personal issues of responsibility were the largest social divisions in society, between gender and race, and the most profound issues of justice. With the unique actions of individuals to be judged and the universal accountability of all in the background, viewers explored common language as they weighed the social and ideological conflicts that divided them and how those conflicts generated different materials for understanding justice and responsibility and for defining narratives of experience across time.

To make the responsibility of others a central theme in the forum participants must themselves take responsibility for sustaining an inquiry that will fix responsibility. Failure to agree on criteria and then to hold individuals responsible reinforces the view of the forum as a scene of mass appeals, not a place where participants try to solve problems. In the case of the Iran-Contra hearings, the processes aimed at fixing responsibility ended in questions and arguments more often than closure. In granting Oliver North and John Poindexter immunity from prosecution in order to obtain their testimony at the 1987 hearings, congressmen argued that it was more important to have their testimony than to hold them legally responsible for their crimes. The congressional grants of immunity provided the basis for federal courts in 1991 to overturn North's 1989 and Poindexter's 1990 convictions by trial juries. When on Christmas Eve in 1992 George Bush pardoned all six individuals indicted for Iran-Contra crimes because "their motivation . . . was patriotism" and they did not "seek to profit from their conduct," Independent Counsel Lawrence Walsh charged that the pardons proved that "powerful people with powerful allies can commit serious crimes in high office—deliberately abusing the public trust—without consequence."[15] With Bush's pardon all actors escaped legal responsibility for their actions. Bush's 1992 justification and Walsh's rejoinder reprised precisely the 1987 popular forum that pivoted a debate over foreign policy and constitutional government around issues of personal responsibility. Because what had interested Americans most about North in 1987 was the response he generated among citizens, it was probably fitting that the most recent chapter in the Oliver North story was written not by Congress or the courts, but by the voters of Virginia in 1994 when they bucked a national Republican trend and defeated his bid on the Republican ticket to become a United States senator. In that election, too, the issue of personal responsibility—whether North deserved to go to jail or the Senate—overlapped a battle between the Christian and patriotic Right and organized liberals. From 1987 to 1994 through all the debates over policy the basic issue was how to evaluate North's responsibility.

III The public forum will come to more fully engage the experience and rhythms of everyday life, not because someone has a complete blueprint of its ideal form, but because someone identifies and adapts promising features of present practice. Instead of looking for new ideas, we need to value what we have already—what we already do around the dinner table and at the watercooler—so that we can be more aware of our own power, so that these places can spread ideas and experiences and in the process help us to converse and move toward making common narratives. Once we are in motion, connecting everyday conversation to a larger forum, we might, like many writers to Hamilton, consider how changes in structures could sustain that motion.

The most obvious place to start is with the arena described in this book: televised congressional hearings on critical incidents that bring underlying doubts and interests into view and then into conflict with each other. When hearings summon many different witnesses to testify, to answer questions from legislators with varied perspectives, they encourage viewers to probe deeper layers and look through different perspectives as they talk with people around them. As they sort through whom they want to hold responsible for what, they assess the stakes, priorities, and diagnoses of larger social conflicts and political issues.

We might build outward from an ancient institution that citizens have trusted to resolve conflicts and render a community's judgments: a jury of peers. The epitome of republican citizenship and primary relationships, juries bring to their deliberations diverse perspectives from the larger society as they assess testimony by others according to their own firsthand experiences. With members chosen by lot, not by income or ambition, juries are charged to talk until they agree how to apply the community's values to a person and circumstance. Rules of evidence give both sides equal chances to present their "cases." Requiring twelve strangers to find in their everyday experiences common and relevant principles for the case at hand, juries must extract the universal principle through the dynamics of primary relationships. Although members of the 1995 Chicago jury that weighed charges of sexual misconduct against Congressman Mel Reynolds "could very much sympathize with him," in the words of one, and believed that "it was a terrible thing to have to do it," in the words of another, the six black and six white jurors took pride in the "fact that we were capable of it, you know, that mere people like us were in judgment" and agreed that they could only fulfill their civic responsibility by convicting him on all counts.[16]

Juries could be models for forums where citizens discuss and recommend plans for health care or education or law enforcement that might widen debate on those topics. Panels could rank spending priorities or choose sources of taxation. Journalists might report the "trials," and a jury's "verdict" for a particular health care or transportation policy might encourage citizens to discuss the outcome, as happens now with trials. Freed from special interests and common denominators, equally open to any citizen and all perspectives, actively engaging policy choices against their own experiences and needs, forced to converse until they reach a fair conclusion, such bodies prefigure a more democratic forum grounded in primary relationships.

The letters to congressmen written during the Iran-Contra hearings provide another natural place for turning a current listening post into an arena of ongoing engagement. Because relationships cannot meet needs unless people respond to each other, writers wanted legislators to read and respond to the letters. While legislators had long believed in "the mail," particularly from constituents, they had confined their "listening" and "reading" to tabulations and prompt form responses. But in these spontaneous letters, writers wanted to start real conversations. To build on this start, toward a richer forum, staff members could try to identify common themes that run through different individual voices as well as a range of definitions of problems and proposed solutions to them. They could then write back to citizens and solicit their further engagement, asking, for example, whether their summaries actually fit the experience of individual writers. Through such exchanges politicians could talk with citizens about needs and experiences and try out diagnoses or solutions they had been considering.

Judging from their enclosures to Hamilton, many writers saw their local newspapers as another accessible forum, one in which they already participated. Although mergers and closings by mid–1995 concentrated ownership of 193 newspapers in six large syndicates with the result that they looked to a *New York Times* reporter "more and more alike, as though stamped from some giant corporate cookie cutter," many readers still engaged different parts of their local newspapers to find out what friends and neighbors and strangers were doing, to find out who considered what to be a problem or a solution.[17] Because they sometimes fulfill their potential for stepping out from the mass, it is easy to envision a forum in which local newspapers translate local concerns to Washington, holding representatives as accountable to their constituents as lobbyists hold them to the special interests.

While individuals could better see and hear each other by drawing on their primary relationships when they approached the public forum, they also brought rich traditions in their capacities as citizens, journalists, and politicians that, when activated, could drive out the worst distortions of opinion management. These traditions were enshrined in American civic culture because they reminded individuals of the dreams and hopes that had originally attracted politicians and journalists to these roles, rekindling their feelings of responsibility for representing fellow citizens and for defining and addressing common problems.

Journalists, for example, could draw on their rich traditions in order to avoid practices that narrow rather than widen debate. "The press all but missed the Iran-contra story, in three separate ways," concluded Mark Hertsgaard, "by coming to it too late, leaving it too soon and failing to convey its full significance along the way." Individual reporters picked up and reported pieces of the story, but major news agencies were unwilling to pursue these leads because they were afraid to step beyond common denominators of practice. "As usual, we all travelled in a pack," *Washington Post* reporter Howard Kurtz observed in explaining how the media missed the savings and loan story, "no one daring to suggest that the problem might be more than a few billion dollars worse than everyone else was saying."[18] Reducing both sources and readers to common denominators, journalists were easily steered away from the truth by the Reagan administration's spin doctors. Inventing or believing in Olliemania, journalists muted criticism of the powerful and failed to investigate larger patterns of abuse.

By the time a Lebanese periodical and the attorney general of the United States scooped the free American press by announcing the details of the Iran-Contra scandal to reporters at a managed press conference in 1987, the story of how the media had become part of the opinion managing industries, marginalizing voices that could widen debate, had become a cliche— and alibi—of American politics that required journalists to blame their victims, the readers.[19]

But everyday conversations point reporters toward an alternative to pack journalism, one that their craft rewards by bestowing its most prestigious prizes on those who ignore the pack, pursue conversations with unconventional sources, give voice to people the managers wanted to silence. With investigative traditions of discomfiting the comfortable, reporters could easily avoid repetitions of their own Olliemania by asking whether their stories report real experiences or rather insider gossip and propaganda, whether they widen and deepen debate or rather solidify a managed line and exclude challenges. Prodded by readers or competitors, journalists could keep conversation building across time as they follow leads and uncover new people or practices to hold responsible for making problems worse. Or, armed with their traditions of "fairness" and "balance," journalists could view partisan allegations of opponents' character failures as "dirty politics," requiring just as strenuous investigation of accusers and their motives as of the accused, and then could explore how the charges of scandal distracted attention from larger issues of public debate.[20]

Journalists could better report public opinion by listening to people in the ways that reporters themselves talk with their friends and families. Indeed, they become less capable of seeing the forum unfold before them when they shed the full range of their own needs and experiences and dismiss such needs and experiences in others in an attempt to squeeze individuals into special categories dictated by "objectivity" and "typicality." Even if they want to maintain professional ways of listening, journalists might adapt new ethnographic perspectives that scholars have developed over the past generation for watching people interpret their worlds as they go about their everyday activities. Because "reader response" and ethnographic methods have changed the modern study of popular culture it is astonishing that polling continues to shape reports of "public opinion" and that many journalists trust the results to the extent that they report as fact such stories as Ollie-mania.

Politicians, too, abandon their best traditions when they let stories like Olliemania divert them from engaging people as individuals, exploring a range of troubling issues, and discussing real policy choices. At one time politicians were rewarded for saying and doing what they believed was right, for listening to and trying to meet the wishes of a majority of their constituents (instead of powerful campaign contributors), and for taking responsibility for lawmaking that incorporated all views. The dreams that attract politicians to their craft, the experiences and skills honored by that craft, provide materials for rebuilding a political arena based on everyday life. Congressmen have, in fact, long depended on building trust in relationships with other congressmen. And their craft encourages them to continue the conversations citizens are trying to strike up with them.[21]

By striking up conversations with congressmen in their letters, writers activated traditions of citizenship that not only deepened and widened talk between voters and politicians but also inspired journalists and politicians to draw on their own traditions and skills in ways that have produced the most creative lawmaking in this century. Muckraking journalists pointed toward abuses and widened political debate in 1903–1909, 1931–38, 1962–73. Voters in their capacities as viewers and readers selected from among journalists' issues the ones they wanted to turn into policy and supported journalists for digging ever deeper into the sources and culprits responsible for those problems. When politicians have acted as though they were listening to citizens and wanted to address real problems, as Franklin Roosevelt did in 1933–35 or John Kennedy and Lyndon Johnson did in 1962–66, citizens responded by demanding great change and with help from journalists forcing agendas wider to include ideas once dismissed as "unthinkable." Voters mobilized popular movements that made it hard for politicians to ignore them. Citizens encouraged, even forced, responsible politicians to explore and enact creative answers to these new needs and voices—of the elderly, of unorganized workers, and of the unemployed in the 1930s or of African Americans and consumers in the 1960s, for example. The most creative policymaking—the Second New Deal, or the Great Society—grew from conversations whose agendas widened through often noisy confrontations between hopeful citizens, crusading journalists, and responsible politicians each taking the other seriously.

The creative, evolving engagement with problems by citizens, journalists, and politicians that took place in the Progressive Era or mid–1930s or mid–1960s required a forum where participants could see each other, define problems to be addressed, take responsibility for collecting evidence and testimony and for exploring common narratives and proposals. The key was for individuals to take responsibility for finding common ground where they could express their individuality but also feel part of and indeed make a larger community.

If individuals are to take responsibility for engaging others in making common narratives and finding common solutions, they must face the problem that opinion management claims to have solved with the development of polls: how to find out what strangers are thinking and to create or identify the solution that has the widest support. Real solutions to this problem have eluded many contemporary theoreticians. While postmodernists have empowered individuals to think for themselves, even depicted a viewer's encounter with a television program as a "conversation," they have been less successful at imagining what happens when individuals carry on—and, with more difficulty, bring to a close—real conversations with other real individuals. How can individuals who are strangers discover, create, and agree on what they will share when they are not obviously members of a visible larger culture or "interpretive community"? Reluctant to impose ideal futures or to give one group a privileged right to define and lead people to that future, postmodernists have retreated from proposing democratic ways for finding and assembling what people share. This retreat has made it more urgent for citizens to mobilize their own experiences to answer the challenge of how individuals can aggregate their experiences and conclusions, can make them add up in ways beyond the control of opinion management.

Writers to Hamilton approached the challenge of resolving controversies by insisting first that no single course would define or "solve" a problem for all time but that the process of moving toward common framing and temporary resolutions should incorporate elements that seemed too often missing from the present forum. For politics to be capable of addressing different people's needs, people have to say what they need and think. Participants have to express their deepest concerns. Each voice will be unique. As a result, political debate will spread across a wide spectrum that will give other citizens a real choice of places to enter the debate. Candor and diversity insure that people can hear a wide range of perspectives as they begin the search for common narratives and aim toward some kind of resolution. Because politics has become a place for people to find out what they share with strangers, diversity is an imperative, not a matter of fashion, toleration, or appeasement.

Closure requires a second feature of primary groups. As places for teaching timeless principles for meeting basic human needs, primary groups teach participants to seek human standards that transcend individuals and circumstances. Reflecting on the ways they themselves wanted to be treated, writers to Hamilton agreed that politics should be judged by universal standards of fairness and accountability.[22] Even more important, the quest for common ground requires individuals to take the same responsibility for deepening a relationship when they frame a problem and seek a solution as they feel when they talk with those around them.

Because the political arena is a place to make policy, it is a place to make choices. Writers wanted their positions to prevail in debates over Nicaraguan policy, covert actions, and, more broadly, the desirability of American empire. They wanted debate over decisions on policy alternatives, not fuzzy compromises and evasions in pretty packages. The opinion industries might value stability, but writers preferred to make, unmake, and remake decisions as experience and conversations unfolded rather than to evade them. They believed that majorities were not fixed or frozen things to be discovered, but momentary stopping places—shared understandings—in dynamic, changing conversations. Writers to Hamilton believed that people formed their own temporary majorities as they talked and listened to each other, but that they might just as quickly discover worse problems or better solutions and thus needed to be prepared to change course.

Before the forum can become a place where participants take responsibility for assembling common narratives, to persuade others of their views and abide by that majority's decisions at least for a moment, we need to measure a remarkable and tragic change over the course of this century that reflects how the opinion industries have come to depict rule by a majority. The prevalent construction of a majority has changed in ways that strip that majority of both the responsibility of its individual members and commitment to their collective judgment. Lincoln Steffens, the leading political journalist of the Progressive Era, stated the majoritarian faith that once guided journalism. Agreeing with Euripides that "the world's wise are not wise," Steffens believed that because it drew on the wisdom of many individuals, the majority had a power that was denied to people who brought mere expertise to the forum, that reflection on everyday experience provided the best starting place for democracies to reach decisions:

> Juries are juster than judges; they feel through the facts for the human story and through the letter of the law for the spirit thereof. The public is fairer than the press; the readers allow for the bias of the newspaper. And the audience is more open-minded than the critics. "Have I had a good time?" the playgoer asks and the question is more fundamental than the critics' criterion of art. And all the world knows that the world has welcomed, since Euripides, not only other artists (Wagner, for example), but prophets (Jesus, for example), and scientific discoverers (Darwin, for example), who were opposed by the authorities in art, church, state, and science.
>
> Uninformed and misinformed; pauperized or over-worked; misled or betrayed by their leaders—financial, industrial, political and ecclesiastical, the people are suspicious, weary, and very, very busy, but they are, none the less, the first, last, and best appeal in all great human cases. Certainly the first rule

for the political reformer is: Go to the voters. And the reason seems to be, not that the people are better than their betters, but that they are more disinterested; they are not possessed by possessions; they have not so many "things" and "friends." They can afford, they are free to be fair. And, though each individual in the great crowd lacks some virtues, they all together have what no individual has, a combination of all the virtues.[23]

Although individual voices, universal values, policy choices, majority rule, and taking responsibility may appear to be contradictory bases for reconnecting politics with everyday life, all were basic features of the primary relationships that writers to Hamilton believed were distorted by the opinion industries. By committing themselves to maintaining their relationships with each other instead of winning victories, citizens could see decisions not as choices and ends but as interventions that addressed a problem. With a view of the forum not as a scene of choice and combat but as a place for exploring common understanding of problems, citizens could answer the pandering, lying, evading, and denying ways the opinion industries twisted conversations of everyday life by their own alternatives of encouraging diversity, universality, choice, and responsibility for meeting needs and sustaining relationships. By writing letters in which they took responsibility for building a relationship, expressing needs, reporting experiences that helped meet those needs, defining their own positions, the writers approached a better form of carrying on conversations and settling differences in the political arena.

While Steffens's view of the majority as "a combination of all the virtues" might appall most modern pundits, we must share with him at least a starting point before our conversation can end in common understandings: Citizens are not interchangeable pieces of a monolithic whole. The fantasy that citizens—or "audiences" of any kind—are an escapist or narcotized mass of spectators at an entertainment spectacle or sports event, the story of Olliemania, has served managers and pundits by giving them a vision of how people act collectively that justifies, even requires, them to manage the stupid, dangerous, emotional mass. That fantasy permits them to make the absurd assumption that viewers "read" texts by the same rules that managers create them or lieutenant colonels enact them on television. That fantasy is an inaccurate description both of what spectators do most of the time at ballgames and of what people do when they watch television or interpret politics. The first step in remaking politics to resemble everyday conversation is for people to stop measuring, interpreting, and worrying about a "mass" and what it allegedly wants, thinks, and needs. It simply does not exist in the real world.

Politicians must recognize that the common denominators fabricated by pollsters are an instrumental convenience and a fiction of the moment. Citizens choose neither the questions nor the answers when they are polled.

Even though only one of the five thousand writers to Hamilton mentioned whether Oliver North would be a good son-in-law, *Time* magazine made his desirability as a son-in-law a matter of "public opinion," of implied controversy, by asking about it in a poll.[24] Common denominators do not reflect what people think about, what they think, or how they think.

If the majority could, however, become something real that individuals took responsibility for assembling through conversation, instead of a denominator discovered by market researchers, that majority could assume responsibility for governing its society. If we wanted that majority to govern more responsibly, Americans might consider a form of representative government that most nations have preferred to the American eighteenth-century practice of checking power in one place with power in another. American policy debates are narrower and American voters have less direct influence over policy than is true in nations with parliamentary forms of representation. In those countries political parties proclaim their principles in platforms, and the party (or coalition of parties) that wins the election simply enacts its platform. Parliamentary government shrinks the spaces where special interests and opinion managers intervene between voters and policymakers. Parties are expected to enact what they presented to voters as a definition of the nation's problems in processes shaped by the party's members and representatives.

From the vision of "participatory democracy" in the 1960s through attacks on government and bureaucracy from Left and Right, many people have suggested changes that would empower citizens with greater ability to widen debate, set priorities, define and choose alternatives, and resolve issues directly without intervention by elected officials. Since the 1890s initiative and referendum elections have appealed to majorities of Americans because they enable voters to raise issues and propose a wider range of choices than the representative process usually permits. In the late 1970s Americans by a three-to-one margin wanted to amend the Constitution to permit national initiative elections in which voters would supplement congressional lawmaking by introducing and voting directly on issues in the manner now authorized by the constitutions of twenty states. By together signing a petition on any topic, citizens can force a popular vote on that measure, and the outcome of that vote decides whether the idea becomes law. By empowering voters to make the choices, initiative elections encourage voters to take responsibility for governing. As the constitutional vision of an empowered majority that accompanied Steffens's faith in the Progressive Era, initiative and referendum elections continue to encourage individual voters to discuss and resolve issues on their own. As organizers of initiatives have battled wealthy special interests in election campaigns they have often brought into the open a conflict between two very different experiences of conversation in the forum. Some see it as a place for slick ads aimed at low common denominators and others as a place for face-to-face conversation in supermarket parking lots and on street corners. Whatever obstacles initiative elections have presented to turning popular proposals into laws, citizen organizers have found direct appeal to voters to be an increasingly attractive alternative to the obstacles of the legislative process. In the 1994 election, voters faced seventy ballot initiatives, the largest number since 1932.[25]

Instead of aggregating individuals through market research traditions of finding common denominators, we could learn from community organizers about how individuals find common bonds. Successful organizers have long known that active engagement among unique individuals, not manipulation of mass denominators, is the source of both democracy and empowerment. When journalists asked President Bernice Cortez how Communities Organized for Public Service in San Antonio had turned out ten thousand people to a 1980 rally, she answered with the truth: "One person at a time."[26] What opinion management framed as a huge and faceless audience was actually a diverse assortment of individuals each of whom brought unique concerns to the rally. In the same vein, what looked like a faceless revolution on the streets of Santa Barbara in 1970 was in fact a temporary assembly of different primary groups whose members brought different needs and understood problems in different ways as they stood together.[27]

Americans have developed many creative ways to remain individuals while also taking responsibility for assembling a collective voice. Friends of individual AIDS victims, for example, made personal tributes to their friends on pieces of cloth that they then stitched together with other patches to form the "AIDS quilt," a powerful expression of how individuals and their culture have faced a plague that by killing individuals threatens their shared culture. By 1992 the quilt contained twenty-two thousand patches, and by 1995 that number had doubled, as many thousands of individuals conveyed their love for people who mattered most in their lives by taking responsibility for presenting to the larger society a collective depiction of their shared experience.

Even experiences and circumstances that individuals believe to be common can become bonds when a new threat or opportunity leads them to recognize strangers as people with whom they share something important. As they listen to others tell stories that remind them of their own experiences, individuals immediately recognize a shared experience. From this recognition of a common identity they take common actions without needing agents or organizers to formulate programs.

Anita Hill's October 1991 testimony of how Clarence Thomas had harassed her—and the Senate's indifference to that testimony—provided such a spark. "After I saw the Anita Hill hearings I knew we needed more women in the U.S. Senate," declared Barbara Streisand, explaining why she committed herself to Barbara Boxer's Senate candidacy. "Women began to realize that Anita Hill's discussion of sexual harassment in the most public of forums was giving them the room to speak the truth about their own lives and in that collective truth lay their own 'empowerment,'" Boxer wrote in explaining why in 1992 female candidates for the first time began their races with an advantage over male opponents. Without even talking in public, women suddenly and dramatically rebuked pundits, punished the powerful, and placed firsthand experience ahead of managed opinion.

The Thomas hearings encouraged viewers to proclaim firsthand experience more valuable than performance. While pundits declared that the issue was whether Americans "believed" Anita Hill's charge that Thomas had sexually harassed her or instead were moved by Thomas's denial, viewers actually compared Thomas's and Hill's testimony against their own experiences, most frequently their experiences with sexual harassment. In a sample of 260 letters to Judiciary Committee member Paul Simon, Anita Hill's credibility was only the sixth most frequent theme raised by both supporters and opponents of Thomas's nomination. Nearly three times as many writers of all persuasions told Simon that they had been harassed sexually than told him whether they believed Thomas or not. Some writers had been afraid to report harassers to superiors. They empathized with Hill's silence. Others had paid high personal prices for blowing the whistle on harassers. They condemned Hill for waiting so long to report her story.[28] Viewers assembled their own solutions at the ballot box in 1992 by nominating and electing senators—Carol Moseley Braun in Illinois, Barbara Boxer and Diane Feinstein in California, Patty Murray in Washington—who insisted that the insensitivity of senators to the most intimate kind of harassment was reason enough to elect new faces, female faces, to the Senate.

As Americans reached out to connect with strangers in expanding their sense of community, they joined a general call for the decentralization of public power, for moving the responsibility for addressing problems from remote federal institutions to state, local, and neighborhood levels. The movement to transfer power over urban schools from centralized administrators to councils of parents and teachers in each school or neighborhood provides one example. Local watch programs have similarly recruited individuals to keep their eyes open to protect their neighbors against intruders and to try to prevent crimes as they take common action to defend their neighbors and community.

Before everyday conversations can fill the forum, we must confront political legacies that have over the past half-century threatened to shade the management of opinion into the coercive management of consent. As government has come to embrace corporate habits of surveillance in order to manage the thoughts and behavior of possible enemies at home and abroad, it has promoted values of spying and secrecy. And in an age of imperial rivalry leaders have defined differences with others in military terms— whether people in Waco whose religious views offend or people in Chile whose political views offend—that call forth military solutions. With the end of the Cold War "national security" can no longer justify the kind of militarized surveillance and secrecy behind which Nixon hid Watergate and North hid the Iran-Contra deals. Citizens told Hamilton that they could not trust a government that did not trust them, that hid things from them and treated them as an enemy to be monitored and lied to. Spying and secrecy must end. Government must no longer be able to hide what it is doing with our money and in our name. Secrecy, spying, and force destroy the trust upon which citizenship depends.

Since opinion management is an expensive habit that is fed by people with a special interest in controlling government, we can free elections from domination by managerial values of advertising and marketing by taking the profit out of managing opinion and limiting the supply of money. With the costs of election campaigns skyrocketing—almost seven times between 1975 and 1992 for a seat in the Kentucky House of Representatives, for example[29]—to pay for listening with polls and talking with television ads, a good first step in remaking politics is to make it no longer profitable to intervene between citizens and politicians.

The solutions are unlimited. Public financing of elections is one. Corporations and their political action committees could be denied unlimited access to media. Media could be required to provide access to those who cannot afford it. Media could be required to hold and air debates to which all parties have equal access or to provide other forums where people engage candidates in the spirit of everyday conversation. Government could limit or regulate campaign spending or limit the proportion of a candidate's expenses that could be paid by political action committees. Whatever the method, we must at least remove the incentives for inventing newer ways of turning elections into marketing and advertising campaigns. We must take the policymaking profit out of opinion management.

But structures in the end are only structures. They are remote and abstract. They can help us clarify problems, suggest directions we might take, and reassure us that change is possible. They can ease or hasten our journey. But they are not the journey itself. They have no spirit or movement or life. To remake politics we must do something at once simple and profound: we must speak. Rather than waiting to be polled and massed, waiting to massed and pandered to, we must do as the authors of these letters did. We must dismiss the figments and jargon of opinion management. We must think and act politically as we do with the people around us. The hard part is not to imagine a future but to develop confidence, as the people who wrote to

Hamilton expressed, that what we do every day provides a sure foundation for remaking politics. We, politicians and citizens alike, will know we are succeeding when we can see and hear each other. We will have remade politics when the pundits talk and act as we do, and we will know that we have failed to remake politics when we talk and act as they do.

Note on Sources and Method

This book is grounded in the letters, postcards, telegrams, and other communications that Americans sent to Representative Lee Hamilton from April to August 1987 in his capacity as chairman of the House Select Committee to Investigate Covert Arms Transactions with Iran. When the communications arrived, committee staffers removed letters from Indiana and sorted the remaining ones into boxes they labeled "procommittee" and "anticommittee" in the manner described in chapter 7. When I first examined the letters in September 1987, less than two months after the public hearings ended, they were in thirteen "procommittee" and ten "anticommittee" boxes in the committee's office on the fourth floor of the Capitol. When I examined them the second time in November around the time the committee issued its report, they had been moved to a basement locker in one of the House Office Buildings. On both occasions Congressman Hamilton's staff arranged for me to examine them in the La Follette Reading Room at the Library of Congress.

I looked at some communications in each of the twenty-three boxes and sampled them in roughly the same proportion as the overall volume in which 57 percent of the boxes contained communications that supported the committee and 43 percent criticized it. Altogether in Washington I analyzed a total of some five thousand cards, letters, and telegrams and photocopied almost three thousand for closer analysis in Bloomington. Many letters to Hamilton were actually copies of letters that writers were sending to other legislators and participants, including Oliver North, that they sometimes explained with cover letters to Hamilton and sometimes simply sent without explanation.

Because I was interested in how the communications to Hamilton compared with letters to other legislators who served on the investigating committees, I asked staffers for senators and congressman across an ideological spectrum to report the volume and breakdowns of incoming communications. I interviewed staff members who answered phones in order to learn their experiences. The best numerical map of the overall volume and gross direction of over 100,000 phone calls, letters, and cards was the daily numerical log of communications prepared by the staff of the Senate Select Committee on Secret Military Assistance to Iran and the Nicaraguan Opposition. Christopher Mellon showed me the records kept by Maine Republican Senator William Cohen's staff of the names and address and the content of each of 8,200 form letters that they sent to reply to people who had written Cohen. From the different form letters I got a good indication of the distribution of concerns that Cohen's staffers identified in letters that came into his office. I received statistics and impressions of mail and phone calls to other legislators from K. Brett Wesner (Senator David Boren, D-Okla.), Fred Millheiser (Senator Paul Sarbanes, D-Md.), Mary Catherine Toker (Senator George Mitchell, D-Maine), D. Sharon Matts (Representative Jack Brooks, D-Tex.), Joyce Larkin (Representative Louis Stokes, D-Ohio), and David Muha (Representative Jim Courter, R-N.J.). Matts and Larkin showed me samples of mail received by Brooks and Stokes. Representatives William Broomfield (R-Mich.) and Peter Rodino (D-N.J.) answered my inquiries by letter. I interviewed Congressman Hamilton on two occasions about his experience, showed and discussed my framing for chapter 8 with Senator Mitchell during two long phone calls that helped me to modify that frame, and talked at length with staffers from the House Select Committee, Casey Miller and Ellen Rainer. Laura Ison reported experiences of the Senate Select Committee.

While I am very critical of the limitations of opinion polling, I found that polls were often good sources for answering questions about the representativeness of particular opinions that were expressed in letters. I have cited them at many points in the book.

In order to evaluate the letters to Hamilton in response to the televised Iran-Contra hearings of 1987 I wanted to know how they were like and unlike letters to congressmen on similar issues at other times and on other issues around the same time. In November 1991 I examined hundreds of letters received by Senator Paul Simon (D-Ill.) as a member of the Judiciary Committee in response to televised testimony by Anita Hill on the proposed nomination of Clarence Thomas to the Supreme Court. One of the major problems with the study of constituent mail is that major manuscript depositories such as the Library of Congress are for understandable reasons of space no longer willing to preserve constituent mail for scholars. I also wanted to compare the letters to Hamilton in 1987 with earlier letters to congressmen on similar issues. After looking through dozens of manuscript collections of senators and congressmen over issues of American foreign policy going back to 1898, I finally settled on the collections of mail to Senators Robert La Follette (R-Wisc.) and George Norris (R-Nebr.) during debate on American entry into World War I and William Borah (R-Idaho) over American entry into World War II—all at the Library of Congress—and to Senator Birch Bayh (D-Ind.) during debate on the Vietnam War—housed at the Lilly Library, Indiana University. These collections contained a large enough volume for statistical comparison and in which writers were reaching out to someone who like Hamilton in 1987 seemed to be opposing a president's policy interventions abroad that the mass media referred to as "popular" even to the extent sometimes of "war hysteria" like "Olliemania."

My methods of analysis were standard historical methods of analyzing documents, but I experimented with methods for counting the frequency with which themes appeared in the letters. Because I was not interested in performing sophisticated statistical correlations and relationships among the themes I was counting, I saw this counting as closer to the historian's method of accumulating examples than the more precise social scientist's method of using several coders to identify and count themes. In most cases—counting the number of people who mentioned Nicaragua or used the word "anger"—it seemed unlikely that the results would have been much different if several people had coded the results. I was simply counting and recording frequencies that a word or phrase occurred.

Notes

❖ ❖ ❖ ❖ ❖ ❖ ❖ ❖ ❖ ❖ ❖

INTRODUCTION

1. *New York Times*, 16 October 1992; *Washington Post*, 16 October 1992; Jack W. Germond and Jules Witcover, *Whose Broad Stripes and Bright Stars? The Trivial Pursuit of the Presidency, 1988* (New York, 1989).

2. *Chicago Tribune*, 30 June 1995.

3. *Chicago Tribune*, 29 June 1995.

4. Kevin Phillips, *Arrogant Capital: Washington, Wall Street, and the Frustration of American Politics* (Boston, 1994), 7; Steven J. Rosenstone et al., American National Election Study (1994, computer file; in possession of Indiana University Political Science Laboratory).

5. *Chicago Tribune*, 26 May 1995.

6. Newt Gingrich, speech to Washington Research Group, 11 November 1994, distributed on the Internet; *Washington Post*, 12 November 1994.

7. Norfolk *Virginian-Pilot*, 20 May 1995; Joe Davis, "The Scoop That Never Was," *Amicus Journal* 17 (Summer 1995): esp. 18.

8. *Congressional Quarterly Weekly Report* 52 (10 December 1994): 3517–18.

9. *New York Times*, 26 March 1995.

10. I am indebted to Paul Simon for making his correspondence available for me to examine in November 1991.

11. Ien Ang, *Watching Dallas* (London, 1985); Janice Radway, *Reading the Romance: Women, Patriarchy, and Popular Literature* (Chapel Hill, 1984); Doris A. Graber, *Processing the News: How People Tame the Information Tide* (New York, 1984).

12. Overviews of the literature include Richard A. Brody, "The Puzzle of Political Participation in America," in *The New American Political System*, ed. Anthony King (Washington, D.C., 1978), 287–324; Sidney Verba, Norman H. Nie, and Jae-On Kim, *The Modes of Democratic Participation: A Cross-National Comparison* (Beverly Hills,

Calif., 1971); Malcolm E. Jewell and Samuel C. Patterson, *The Legislative Process in the United States* (1966; New York, 1977 ed.), 306–10; Bernard Barber, "'Mass Apathy' and Voluntary Social Participation in the United States" (Ph.D. diss., 1948; repr., New York, 1980), esp. 57–58, 84–98; David Horton Smith, Jacqueline MacAulay and Associates, "Political Activities," in *Participation in Social and Political Activities* (San Francisco, 1980), pt. 2; Lewis Anthony Dexter, "What Do Congressmen Hear?" *Public Opinion Quarterly* 20 (Spring 1956): 16–27; Stephen E. Fratzich, *Write Your Congressman: Constituent Communications and Representation* (New York, 1986); Lester Milbrath and M. L. Goel, *Political Participation: How and Why Do People Get Involved in Politics*, 2d ed. (Chicago, 1977). There are many good studies of how and why voters have chosen to leave a political system they find increasingly alien or to develop different ways of influencing politics: Frances Fox Piven and Richard A. Cloward, *Why Americans Don't Vote* (New York, 1988); Benjamin Ginsberg and Martin Shefter, *Politics by Other Means: The Declining Importance of Elections in America* (New York, 1990); W. Lance Bennett, *The Governing Crisis: Media, Money, and Marketing in American Elections* (New York, 1992). Two journalists, Jack W. Germond and Jules Witcover, told the story in the subtitle of their account of the 1988 election: *Whose Broad Stripes and Bright Stars? The Trivial Pursuit of the Presidency.* For alternatives, see Harry C. Boyte, *CommonWealth: A Return to Citizen Politics* (New York, 1989); William Greider, *Who Will Tell the People: The Betrayal of American Democracy* (New York, 1992).

CHAPTER ONE

1. *Broadcasting*, 11 May 1987, 31.
2. The best account of the arms deals and their contexts is by Theodore Draper, *A Very Thin Line: The Iran-Contra Affairs* (New York, 1991). Jane Mayer and Doyle McManus in *Landslide: The Unmaking of the President, 1984–1988* (Boston, 1988) and Frances FitzGerald in "Iran-Contra" (*New Yorker*, 16 October 1989, 51–84) provide insightful context for these details. A concise summary of the events, chronology, characters, and committee reports can be found in Joel Brinkley and Stephen Engelberg, eds., *Report of the Congressional Committees Investigating the Iran-Contra Affair* (New York, 1988). William S. Cohen and George J. Mitchell, *Men of Zeal: A Candid Inside Story of the Iran-Contra Hearings* (New York, 1988), xix—xxxi, contains a chronology. Oliver North testified (*Taking the Stand: The Testimony of Lieutenant Colonel Oliver L. North* [New York, 1987], 21, 27) that CIA Director William Casey agreed with him that the downing of Hasenfus would unravel their policies. *New York Times*, 2 December 1986, reports the poll result.
3. *Iran-Contra Investigation: Joint Hearings before the Senate Select Committee on Secret Military Assistance to Iran and the Nicaraguan Opposition and the House Select Committee to Investigate Covert Arms Transactions with Iran*, 100th Cong., 1st sess. (Washington, D.C., 1987), 1:4, 29; John Tower, Edmund Muskie, and Brent Scowcroft, *The Tower Commission Report: The Full Text of the President's Special Review Board* (New York, 1987), 96.
4. *USA Today*, 22 June 1987; 9 July 1987; *Broadcasting*, 11 May 1987, 32; *TV Guide*, 25–31 July 1987, A1; *New York Times*, 11 July 1987.
5. *USA Today*, 22 June 1987.
6. Interviews in late September and early October 1987 with congressional staff members K. Brett Wesner (Boren), Christopher Mellon (Cohen), Fred Millheiser

(Sarbanes), Mary Catherine Toker (Mitchell), D. Sharon Matts (Brooks), Joyce Larkin (Stokes), and David Muha (Courter). Laura Ison provided access to the Senate Select Committee logs, and Casey Miller and Ellen Rainer provided access to the letters to the House Select Committee. Provision for their use was arranged by Sara Binder (Hamilton). William Broomfield (20 October 1987) and Peter Rodino (23 November 1987) sent letters that described their experiences.

7. Louis Stokes, press release, 27 July 1987, courtesy of Louis Stokes's office; *National Review*, 14 August 1987, 40.

8. Louis Stokes, press release, 27 July 1987, courtesy of Louis Stokes's office; memos from Daniel Inouye, Ed Jenkins, and Mervyn Dymally to Louis Stokes, 14 July 1987. North in *Taking the Stand* (696) reports Stokes's speech a little differently.

9. *New York Times*, 18 March 1951; 20 March 1951; 21 March 1951; 25 March 1951; G. D. Wiebe, "Merchandising Commodities and Citizenship on Television," *Public Opinion Quarterly* 15 (Winter 1951/52): 689; G. D. Wiebe, "Responses to the Televised Kefauver Hearings: Some Social Psychological Implications," *Public Opinion Quarterly* 16 (Summer 1952): 184; Robert Lewis Shayon, "An Open Letter to the Television Industry," *Saturday Review of Literature* 34 (7 April 1951): 31.

10. *Newsweek*, 3 May 1954, 27. See also G. D. Wiebe, "The Army-McCarthy Hearings and the Public Conscience," *Public Opinion Quarterly* 22 (Winter 1958/59): 490–502; John M. Fenton, *In Your Opinion* . . . (Boston, 1960), 137–38.

11. For quantities of congressional mail, see Leila A. Sussmann, ed., *Dear FDR: A Study of Political Letter-Writing* (Totowa, N.J., 1963), 9, 13, 15; Stephen E. Frantzich, *Write Your Congressman: Constituent Communications and Representation* (New York, 1986), 9–12; Jewell and Patterson, *Legislative Process*, 306–7; Brody, "Puzzle of Political Participation," 317–18; Piven and Cloward, *Why Americans Don't Vote*, 161. Jacqueline Dowd Hall, James Leloudis, et al., *Like a Family: The Making of a Southern Cotton Mill World* (Chapel Hill, 1987), chap. 6, traces the spread of political letter writing to Southern working-class women in the 1930s. *New York Times*, 28 November 1987, notes a similar outpouring of telegrams that accompanied the investigations of Watergate and of the assassination of John F. Kennedy.

12. *U.S. News and World Report*, 27 July 1987, 22.

13. Wiebe, "Responses to the Televised Kefauver Hearings," 184.

CHAPTER TWO

1. *New York Times*, 7 December 1986; 8 March 1987. For a brilliant analysis of how Reagan connected his film roles to his political appeal, see Michael Paul Rogin, *Ronald Reagan, The Movie* (Berkeley and Los Angeles, 1987), esp. chap. 1.

2. *Newsweek*, 15 December 1986, 40; Sidney Blumenthal, *Our Long National Daydream: A Political Pageant of the Reagan Era* (New York, 1988), xvi; Donald T. Regan, *For the Record* (1988; New York, 1989 ed.), 6; *New York Times*, 3 December 1986.

3. *New York Times*, 2 December 1986; 7 December 1986.

4. *New Republic*, 22 December 1986, 9.

5. *Harper's*, February 1987, 8; Nancy Reagan with William Novak, *My Turn: The Memoirs of Nancy Reagan* (New York, 1989), 317–20; *Harper's*, February 1987, 10; *Newsweek*, 15 December 1986, 38.

6. *New York Times,* 13 December 1986; 19 December 1986; *USA Today,* 8 December 1986; *Washington Post,* 5 August 1987.

7. *New York Times,* 8 March 1987; *New Republic,* 6 April 1987, 9.

8. *New York Times,* 27 January 1987.

9. *Newsweek,* 15 December 1986, 38.

10. *Newsweek,* 1 December 1986, cover; *New York Times,* 26 November 1986; *Newsweek,* 2 February 1987, 22; 2 March 1987, 20, 21, 23–26.

11. *New York Times,* 3 December 1986; 7 December 1986; *Washington Post,* 5 March 1987; *Newsweek,* 16 March 1987, 19–20; *USA Today,* 5 March 1987.

12. *Washington Post,* 4 March 1987; *USA Today,* 4 March 1987.

13. *New York Times,* 5 March 1987; *Washington Post,* 5 March 1987.

14. *Washington Post,* 5 March 1987; *USA Today,* 5 March 1987; *Newsweek,* 16 March 1987; *New York Times,* 5 March 1987.

15. *USA Today,* 5 March 1987; *New York Times,* 6 March 1987.

16. *New York Times,* 9 February 1987; 6 March 1987; *Newsweek,* 16 March 1987, 19, 20.

17. *Newsweek,* 11 May 1987, 23.

18. *New York Times,* 12 May 1987; 10 July 1987; 17 June 1987; 8 July 1987; 9 June 1987; *Washington Post,* 28 June 1987; 17 June 1987; *Broadcasting,* 11 May 1987, 31.

19. *New York Times,* 24 May 1987; 26 May 1987.

20. *New York Times,* 15 July 1987; North, *Taking the Stand,* 751; interview with D. Sharon Matts, 30 September 1987.

21. *USA Today,* 9 July 1987; 10–12 July 1987.

22. *New York Times,* 11 July 1987; 20 July 1987; *People,* 27 July 1987, 33; *National Enquirer,* 18 August 1987, 6; Cohen and Mitchell, *Men of Zeal,* 157; *Time,* 20 July 1987, 27.

23. *Time,* 20 July 1987, 12–15; *Bloomington Herald-Telephone,* 14 July 1987; *USA Today,* 10–12 July 1987; *New Republic,* 3 August 1987, 7; *U.S. News and World Report,* 20 July 1987, 18.

24. *People,* 27 July 1987, 33; *New York Times,* 15 July 1987; *USA Today,* 13 July 1987; *New York Times,* 14 July 1987.

25. *Washington Post,* 21 July 1987; *Time,* 20 July 1987, 12; *Christian Century,* 15–22 July 1987, 611; *Newsweek,* 20 July 1987, cover.

26. *Bloomington Herald-Telephone,* 14 July 1987; *MacLean's,* 20 July 1987, 14; *U.S. News and World Report,* 20 July 1987, 18.

27. *New Republic,* 3 August 1987, 8; *New York Times,* 17 July 1987.

28. *Bloomington Herald-Telephone,* 14 July 1987; *U.S. News and World Report,* 27 July 1987, 18; *Time,* 20 July 1987, 13; *Newsweek,* 20 July 1987, 19.

29. *Time,* 20 July 1987, 15; *National Enquirer,* 28 July 1987, 2.

30. *Newsweek,* 20 July 1987, 18; Jefferson Morley, "The Paradox of North's Popularity," *Nation,* 15–22 August 1987, 122; *People,* 27 July 1987, 33.

31. *People,* 27 July 1987, 33, 35; *Harper's,* September 1987, 7; *Washington Post,* 19 July 1987; *Esquire,* December 1987, 14; *Christianity Today,* 4 September 1987, 8; *U.S. News and World Report,* 10 August 1987, 14; *New York Times,* 11 July 1987; Robert Jewett, "Zeal without Understanding: Reflections on Rambo and Oliver North," *Christian Century,* 9–16 September 1987, 755.

32. *New York Times,* 7 August 1987; *Harper's,* September 1988, 8; *Newsweek,* 20 July 1987, 19.

33. *New York Times,* 24 July 1987; David Denby, "Ollie North, the Movie: Hollywood Meets the Constitution," *New Republic,* 3 August 1987, 8, 9.

34. *Harper's,* September 1987, 8; *Washington Post,* 4 August 1987; 7 August 1987; *New York Times,* 18 July 1987.

35. *New York Times,* 10 July 1987.

36. *New York Times,* 18 March 1981; 9 August 1981; Michael Schudson, "Ronald Reagan Misremembered," in *Collective Remembering,* ed. David Middleton and Derek Edwards (London, 1990), 108–19.

37. Louis Harris, *Inside America* (New York, 1987), 382–83; Barry Sussman, *What Americans Really Think: And Why Our Politicians Pay No Attention* (New York, 1988), 219; Richard Sobel, "Report: Public Opinion about United States Intervention in El Salvador and Nicaragua," *Public Opinion Quarterly* 53 (Spring 1989): 125, 127.

38. Morley, "Paradox of North's Popularity," 122; *Washington Post,* 14 July 1987.

39. *Washington Post,* 31 July 1987; Bob Hill, column, *Louisville Courier-Journal,* 1 August 1987; *Bloomington Herald-Telephone,* 20 July 1987.

40. *New York Times,* 13 September 1987; Christopher Hitchens, "Olliemania Share Price Plummets," *New Statesman,* 11 September 1987, 13.

41. Mark Hertsgaard, *On Bended Knee: The Press and the Reagan Presidency* (New York, 1988), esp. pp. 4–9, chaps. 2–3, pp. 106–8; Tip O'Neill quoted in Lou Cannon, *Reagan* (New York, 1982), 407; "Comment: Swept Away," *Columbia Journalism Review* 26 (September—October 1987): 24.

42. Mark Crispin Miller in *New York Times,* 16 November 1988; *Newsweek,* 15 December 1986, 40; Hitchens, "Olliemania Share Price Plummets," 13. For a detailed account of how journalists allowed the Reagan administration to shape their stories, see Hertsgaard, *On Bended Knee.*

43. Sussman, *What Americans Really Think,* 246; *Nation,* 27 June 1987, 874.

44. *Iran-Contra Investigation* 1:6, 11, 16, 17, 19; *New York Times,* 3 May 1987; 26 April 1987.

45. *New York Times,* 27 November 1986.

46. Sobel, "Report," 124–25; Cohen and Mitchell, *Men of Zeal,* xxvi; Mayer and McManus, *Landslide,* 208–12.

47. North, *Taking the Stand,* 453, 454, 715. McCollum's reversal in response to Olliemania is described by Ben Bradlee, Jr., *Guts and Glory: The Rise and Fall of Oliver North* (New York, 1988), 522–23, and Theodore Draper, "Rewriting the Iran-Contra Story," *New York Review of Books,* 19 January 1989, 39.

48. North, *Taking the Stand,* 750–53.

CHAPTER THREE

1. Bill Moyers, *The Public Mind* (Journal Graphics transcript for 15 November 1989 telecast), 2.

2. For a discussion of how viewers have reacted to live coverage of such events differently from their usual dismissal of television as an escape from life, see Elihu Katz and Daniel Dayan, "Media Events: On the Experience of Not Being There,"

Religion 15 (July 1985): 305–14; Daniel Dayan and Elihu Katz, *Media Events: The Live Broadcasting of History* (Cambridge, Mass., 1992).

3. *Newsweek*, 10 August 1987, 8.

4. W. Phillips Davison, "The Third Person Effect in Communication," *Public Opinion Quarterly* 47 (Spring 1983): 1–15, gives this process a name.

5. Telephone, telegram, and correspondence logs of the Senate Select Committee on Secret Military Assistance to Iran and the Nicaraguan Opposition, 1987.

CHAPTER FOUR

1. Cohen and Mitchell, *Men of Zeal*, 172; interview with Matts, 30 September 1987; Congressional Mail Service (CMS) mail count as of 1 October 1987 for George Mitchell, provided by Mary Catherine Toker.

2. Interview with Matts, 30 September 1987; letter from Broomfield, 20 October 1987.

3. The total of 7,747 written communications to Cohen received by 30 September 1987 were sorted by Cohen's office staff and tabulated by the United States Senate Automatic Indexing System into categories for which he could send form responses. I base conclusions about the theme of each letter on the classification assigned it by Cohen's staff members as they determined which form response to send.

4. Milan Kundera, *Immortality*, trans. Peter Kussi (New York, 1991), 109–112.

5. Interviews with Matts, 30 September 1987; Dave Muha, 25 September 1987; Joyce Larkin, 30 September 1987; CMS mail count for Mitchell, provided by Mary Catherine Toker; letter from Broomfield, 20 October 1987; Cohen and Mitchell, *Men of Zeal*, 172.

CHAPTER FIVE

1. Michael Pertschuk and Wendy Schaetzel, *The People Rising: The Campaign against the Bork Nomination* (New York, 1989), is an excellent account.

2. *New York Times*, 24 July 1987; *Washington Post*, 26 July 1987; Richard Viguerie and Chip Heartfield, "Your Next Appeal Is Just a Headline Away," *Fund Raising Management* 18 (October 1987): 29, 32.

3. This conclusion is based on the names and addresses of people to whom Cohen's office mailed a CMS form letter tailored to answer the specific issues raised by the Christic Institute.

CHAPTER SIX

1. In a *Time* poll, 57 percent reported that the proceedings were "motivated more by politics than by the evidence" (*Time*, 20 July 1987, 15). Asked to pick a single characterization of the committee, 20 percent of respondents told the *Los Angeles Times* poll that the committee was "politically motivated" (*Los Angeles Times*, 15 July 1987).

2. *Washington Post*, 11 July 1987.

3. Letter provided courtesy of D. Sharon Matts in Brooks's office.

4. See chap. 7, for fuller analysis of this study.

5. In a *Time* poll, 84 percent believed North's actions were approved by higher-ups, and by a 58–23 percent margin they believed that Reagan knew about the deal (*Time*, 20 July 1987, 15). In a *Newsweek* poll, 19 percent believed North was telling the whole truth, 15 percent believed that he was withholding information to protect himself, and 53 percent believed that he was shielding others. In the same poll respondents by a 70–21 percent margin believed North had authorization from his superiors for "everything" he did (*Newsweek*, 20 July 1987, 18). Sixty percent told the *Post* that North was covering up for Reagan, and by a two-to-one margin respondents told the *Times* that North acted "with the knowledge and approval" of Reagan (*Washington Post*, 23 July 1987; *New York Times*, 11 July 1987).

6. In *New York Times* polls, 21 percent said the committees were too hard on North, 60 percent said they were fair, and 10 percent said they were too easy; a week earlier 27 percent had said the committees were too hard on North, 49 percent had considered the committees fair, and 10 percent had said they were too easy on him (*New York Times*, 11 July 1987; 18 July 1987). In a *Newsweek* poll, 48 percent said that the committees were harassing North and 23 percent said that North was giving uncooperative answers (*Newsweek*, 20 July 1987, 18). When asked to choose a single characterization of the committees in a *Los Angeles Times* poll, 8 percent called the committees "hostile to witnesses" and 6 percent considered them "fair" (*Los Angeles Times*, 15 July 1987).

7. Clifford Geertz, "Common Sense as a Cultural System," in *Local Knowledge: Further Essays in Interpretive Anthropology*, ed. Clifford Geertz (New York, 1983), 91.

CHAPTER SEVEN

1. Cohen and Mitchell, *Men of Zeal*, 66.

2. In Lou Harris polls in December 1986, 81 percent of Americans considered the Iranian government an enemy of the United States, and by an 82–12 percent margin Americans condemned Reagan for selling arms to Iran (Harris, *Inside America*, 384, 385). Although there were minor rises and falls in popular attitudes toward contra aid, there was little long-term change in general sentiment against it, as reflected in *New York Times*/CBS News polls (compiled in Sobel, "Report," 125): Do You Approve U.S. Military and Other Aid to Contras? (percentage of respondents)

	10/84	5/85	1/87	7/9/87	7/21/87	8/87	10/87	1/88	3/88
Approve	30	24	28	33	40	33	35	30	39
Disapprove	44	66	60	51	49	49	53	58	48
No opinion	26	11	12	16	12	18	12	12	14

3. William Safire observed that the collapse of the Soviet Union and the fear of spreading communism deprived the Right and Republicans of the basic cement that had held them together in the 1980s (*New York Times*, 18 October 1992).

4. Mary Matalin and James Carville, *All's Fair: Love, War, and Running for President* (New York, 1994), 19. In an interview on 22 June 1995, Carville emphasized the point that most Americans approached most issues with positions of their own.

5. The limitations of polls as indices to "public opinion" are illustrated by responses to questions about the hearings themselves. In a *New York Times*/CBS News poll, 82 percent said it was important to know what transpired in the Iran-Contra affair, 58 percent said they learned something new from the hearings, and 22 percent said the hearings were devoid of any interest (*New York Times*, 11 July 1987). By a 58–39 percent margin respondents told the ABC News/*Washington Post* poll that Congress had spent too much time investigating the affair, but by a 58–38 percent margin they believed that important facts were still not uncovered (*Washington Post*, 7 August 1987).

6. North, *Taking the Stand*, 342.

7. Peggy Noonan, *What I Saw at the Revolution: A Political Life in the Reagan Era* (New York, 1990), 238–40, describes support for the contras as a key division between pragmatists, who saw it as a losing issue, and conservatives, who saw it as a basic ideological commitment.

8. In a *Time* poll, 77 percent considered North "a scapegoat for higher-ups," 67 percent "a true patriot," 37 percent "someone we need in Government," 29 percent "a national hero," 26 percent "someone I would want to marry my daughter," and 15 percent "a reckless adventurer" (*Time*, 20 July 1987, 15). In a *Newsweek* poll, 65 percent believed he was "well meaning but he did things that were illegal" and 28 percent "would vote for him for public office" (*Newsweek*, 20 July 1987, 18). Asked to choose one trait, 37 percent of respondents told the *Los Angeles Times* that North was "dedicated," 27 percent that he "can get things done," 11 percent that he "can be bought," and 4 percent each considered him dangerous, a fanatic, and a hero (*Los Angeles Times*, 15 July 1987). Although 73 percent told the *New York Times* that North was a "real patriot," only 25 percent considered him a "national hero" (*New York Times*, 11 July 1987; 18 July 1987). In a direct referendum on his heroism, respondents by a 74–18 percent margin rejected the label. When asked by the *Washington Post* to choose whether he was a "hero," "victim," or "villain," 64 percent chose "victim," more than three times as many as chose hero (cited in Morley, "Paradox of North's Popularity," 122).

CHAPTER EIGHT

1. Cohen and Mitchell, *Men of Zeal*, 154, 157, 165, 155, 162, 168.

2. Cohen and Mitchell, *Men of Zeal*, 172; CMS mail count for Mitchell. In a telephone interview on 16 December 1992, George Mitchell recalled that in the middle of North's testimony, he, like others reported in this book, found a dramatic shift from support of North to opposition among the calls and letters he received from citizens. Mitchell recalled that an "impossible to quantify" number had supported both him and North. There were few letters to Hamilton that supported both the committee and North.

3. Telephone interviews with Mitchell, 16 and 17 December 1992.

4. Jack McLaughlin, ed., *To His Excellency Thomas Jefferson: Letters to President* (New York, 1991), xxi, xxii.

5. For a discussion of how Southern working-class women came in the 1930s to draw on the intimate relationships and conversations of their lives when they wrote to Franklin Roosevelt, see Hall, Leloudis, et al., *Like a Family*, esp. 309–10.

6. *Chicago Tribune,* 4 November 1988.

7. James Beniger, "The Popular Symbolic Repertoire and Mass Communication," *Public Opinion Quarterly* 47 (Winter 1983): 482; Walter Lippmann, *Public Opinion* (New York, 1922), 248.

8. Patrick Brantlinger, *Bread and Circuses: Theories of Mass Culture as Social Decay* (Ithaca, N. Y., 1983), pp. 55–56, 70, chap. 2.

9. Zgymunt Bauman, *Legislators and Interpreters: On Modernity, Post-Modernity and Intellectuals* (Ithaca, N. Y., 1987), 39, 46, 78; C. Wright Mills, *The Power Elite* (New York, 1956), 310.

10. Frederick W. Taylor's *The Principles of Scientific Management* (New York, 1911) remains the classic exploration of how modern management introduced a struggle between the "word of mouth" knowledge and codes of workers enforced by face-to-face mutuality and the centralizing ambitions of management that depended, at core, on new forms of surveillance. The classic shopfloor perspective on the introduction of Taylorism is David Montgomery, "Workers' Control of Machine Production in the Nineteenth Century," *Labor History* 17 (Fall 1976): 485–509. See also Daniel Nelson, *Managers and Workers: Origins of the New Factory System, 1880–1920* (Madison, Wisc., 1975), and for more recent developments David F. Noble, *Forces of Production: A Social History of Industrial Automation* (New York, 1984). IBM quoted in William H. Whyte, *The Organization Man* (New York, 1956), 276.

11. Selwyn K. Troen, *The Public and the Schools: Shaping the St. Louis System, 1838–1920* (Columbia, Mo., 1975); David Thelen, *Paths of Resistance: Tradition and Democracy in Industrializing Missouri* (New York, 1986), 108–16. Richard Sennett and Jonathan Cobb, *The Hidden Injuries of Class* (New York, 1972), explores how the same war continued in the 1960s and 1970s.

12. Susan Herbst, "Numbered Voices: The Rationalization of Public Opinion from the Greek City-States to Modern America" (Ph.D. diss., University of Southern California, 1989), 29–30, 34–37; Susan Herbst, *Numbered Voices: How Opinion Polling Has Shaped American Politics* (Chicago, 1993); Charles Tilly, "Speaking Your Mind without Elections, Surveys, or Social Movements," *Public Opinion Quarterly* 47 (Winter 1983): 461–78; E. L. Godkin, "The Growth and Expression of Public Opinion," *Atlantic Monthly,* January 1898, esp. 1; John Gilbert Heinberg, "History of the Majority Principle," *American Political Science Review* 20 (February 1926): 52–68; Wilhelm Bauer, "Public Opinion," in *Encyclopedia of the Social Sciences,* ed. Edwin R. A. Seligman (New York, 1934), 669–74.

13. See Benjamin Barber, *Strong Democracy: Participatory Politics for a New Age* (Berkeley, Calif., 1984), esp. chaps. 2–4, for the intellectual strands that came together to create representative government in the late eighteenth century. I am indebted to Rhys Isaac for suggesting points of overlap between perspectives of late-twentieth-century opinion management and late-eighteenth-century political thought.

14. Theodore Porter, *The Rise of Statistical Thinking, 1820–1920* (Princeton, N.J., 1986), esp. Introduction and chap. 1, esp. pp. 3, 5. See also Herbst, *Numbered Voices,* chap. 1.

15. James Beniger, *The Control Revolution: Technological and Economic Origins of the Information Society* (Cambridge, Mass., 1986), 20.

16. Donald Fleming, "Attitude: The History of a Concept," *Perspectives in American History* 1:287–365, quote from 360; Beniger, *Control Revolution,* 20.

17. Salvador Giner, *Mass Society* (New York, 1976), 57–62; Gregory W. Bush, *Lord of Attention: Gerald Stanley Lee and the Crowd Metaphor in Industrializing America* (Amherst, Mass., 1991), 80; Gabriel Tarde, *On Communication and Social Influence,* ed. Terry N. Clark (Chicago, 1969), 300.

18. Edward L. Bernays, *Crystallizing Public Opinion* (1923; New York, 1961 ed.), 105; Lippmann, *Public Opinion;* Adolf Hitler, *Mein Kampf* (Munich, 1934), 92 (for a more literal translation, see John Chamberlain et al., eds., *Mein Kampf* [New York, 1940], 108).

19. Otis Pease, *Responsibilities of American Advertising* (New Haven, Conn., 1958), p. 12, chap. 2, quote from p. 22; Philip Gold, *Advertising, Politics, and American Culture: From Salesmanship to Therapy* (New York, 1987), 10, 15.

20. George Creel, *How We Advertised America* (c. 1920; New York, 1972 ed.), and Committee on Public Information, *The Creel Report* (1920; New York, 1972 ed.), are the best primary accounts of wartime propaganda. See also Stephen Vaughn, *Holding Fast the Inner Lines: Democracy, Nationalism, and the Committee on Public Information* (Chapel Hill, N. C., 1980).

21. Hannah Arendt, *Totalitarianism* (San Diego, 1968), 6, 14, 16.

22. Lindsay Rogers, *The Pollsters: Public Opinion, Politics and Democratic Leadership* (New York, 1949), 17, 37–38, 45–51, 72–74.

23. Robert Griffith, *The Politics of Fear: Joseph R. McCarthy and the Senate* (Lexington, 1970); Robert Griffith and Athan Theoharis, eds., *The Specter: Original Essays on the Cold War and the Origins of McCarthyism* (New York, 1974); Jonathan Schell, *The Time of Illusion* (New York, 1975).

24. Michael Kelly, "David Gergen, Master of The Game," *New York Times Magazine,* 31 October 1993, 64.

25. Interviews with David Gergen and James Carville, 22 June 1995; Robert Darnton, *The Kiss of Lamourette: Reflections in Cultural History* (New York, 1990), chap. 5; Schudson, "Ronald Reagan Misremembered," 113–18.

26. The overall cost was estimated in Moyers, *Public Mind,* 2. For costs of hearings, see *Broadcasting,* 11 May 1987, 31, 32; *USA Today,* 9 July 1987; *New York Times,* 12 May 1987; 14 July 1987; 20 July 1987; Cohen and Mitchell, *Men of Zeal,* 140.

27. For an excellent account of how opinion marketers and campaign contributors came to shape debate and policymaking in the 1980s, see Bennett, *Governing Crisis.*

28. For a description of this transformation, see Kiku Adatto, *Picture Perfect: The Art and Artifice of Public Image Making* (New York, 1993), 88.

29. Kelly, "David Gergen," 64.

30. Joan Didion, *After Henry* (New York, 1992), 47, 49–50.

31. Johann Wolfgang von Goethe, "Study," *Faust,* pt. 1.

32. Samuel Schrager, "What is Social in Oral History?" *International Journal of Oral History* 4 (1983): 77.

33. Peter H. Rossi, *Why Families Move* (1955; Beverly Hills: Sage, 1980 ed.), 28, 31, 32; Stephan Thernstrom, *Poverty and Progress: Social Mobility in a Nineteenth Century City* (Cambridge, Mass., 1964); Peter J. Coleman, "Restless Grant County: Americans on the Move," *Wisconsin Magazine of History* 46 (Autumn 1962): 16–20; Bennett M. Berger, *Working Class Suburb: A Study of Auto Workers in Suburbia* (Berkeley, Calif., 1960), esp. chap. 2.

34. Ruby Jo Reeves Kennedy, "Single or Triple Melting-Pot," *American Journal of Sociology* 58 (July 1952): 55; Lydio F. Tomasi, *Italian Americans: New Perspectives in Italian Immigration and Ethnicity* (Staten Island, N. Y., 1985), 117, 118; James Stuart Olson, *The Ethnic Dimension in American History* (New York, 1979), 435. Charles H. Mindel and Robert W. Habenstein, eds., *Ethnic Families in America: Patterns and Variations* (New York, 1976), provides good maps of assimilation of different groups.

35. Irion, *Public Opinion and Propaganda*, 142; Charles W. Smith, *Public Opinion in a Democracy: A Study in American Politics* (New York, 1939), 110; Gary A. Steiner, *The People Look at Television: A Study of Audience Attitudes* (New York, 1963), 4, 21–22.

36. William Schneider, "'Off With Their Heads': The Confidence Gap and the Revolt against Professionalism in Politics," in *Reexamining Democracy: Essays in Honor of Seymour Martin Lipset*, ed. Gary Marks and Larry Diamond (Newbury Park, Calif., 1992), 316, 317, 326. For interpretations of the "legitimacy crisis," or "confidence gap," see Richard Flacks, *Making History: The Radical Tradition in American Life* (New York, 1988), esp. chaps. 2–3; Seymour Martin Lipset and William Schneider, *The Confidence Gap: Business, Labor, and Government in the Public Mind* (Baltimore, 1987); Mary Grisez Kweit and Robert W. Kweit, *Implementing Citizen Participation in a Bureaucratic Society: A Contingency Approach* (New York, 1981), chap. 2, esp. pp. 19–29, which sees it as a "participation crisis."

37. Yi-Fu Tuan, "Place and Culture: Analeptic for Individuality and the World's Indifference," in *Mapping American Culture*, ed. Wayne Franklin and Michael Steiner (Iowa City, 1992), 27, quote from Camus on 43.

38. Jane Addams, *Twenty Years at Hull-House* (New York, 1910), chap. 11; William I. Thomas and Florian Znanecki, *The Polish Peasant in Europe and America* (Urbana, Ill., 1984), pt. 1.

39. For an excellent summary of these studies, see Edward Shils, "The Study of the Primary Group," in *The Policy Sciences: Recent Developments in Scope and Method*, ed. Daniel Lerner and Harold D. Lasswell (Stanford, Calif., 1951), 44–69, esp. 47–51.

40. The classic study is Samuel Stouffer et al., *The American Soldier*, 2 vols. (Princeton, N.J., 1949), statistic from 2:109. Bradford Perkins remembers the war in these terms in "Impressions of Wartime," *Journal of American History* 77 (September 1990): 566.

41. Paul G. Cressey, "The Motion Picture Experience as Modified by Social Background and Personality," *American Sociological Review* 3 (August 1938): quotes from 518, 522. Elihu Katz and Paul F. Lazarsfeld, *Personal Influence: The Part Played by People in the Flow of Mass Communications* (Glencoe, Ill., 1955), chaps. 2–6, is the fullest review of how primary groups and interpersonal relations affect reception of mass appeals. Michael Schudson, *Advertising, the Uneasy Persuasion: Its Dubious Impact on American Society* (New York, 1984), esp. 96–99. I kept returning in this book to Robert Merton's *Mass Persuasion: The Social Psychology of a War Bond Drive* (New York, 1946) for good questions. The Lazarsfeld tradition of research also left classic studies of radio listeners (*Radio and the Printed Page* [1940; New York, 1971 ed.]; with Harry Field, *The People Look at Radio* [Chapel Hill, N. C., 1946]) and of voters in the 1940 election (Paul F. Lazarsfeld, Bernard Berelson, and Hazel Gaudet, *The People's Choice: How the Voter Makes Up His Mind in a Presidential Campaign* [New York, 1948]). John Fiske, *Television Culture* (London, 1987), chap. 5, surveys recent research on "active audiences" that has emphasized the contexts in which autonomous people interact as more basic

than the texts they encounter; for good examples, see Patricia Palmer, *The Lively Audience: A Study of Children around the TV Set* (Sydney, 1986); Dorothy Hobson, *Crossroads: The Drama of a Soap Opera* (London, 1982); Ang, *Watching Dallas*. These issues are put in wider frame by Daniel J. Czitrom, *Media and the American Mind: From Morse to McLuhan* (Chapel Hill, N. C., 1982). Cognitive studies of how people make meanings include W. Russell Neuman, Marion R. Just, and Ann N. Crigler, *Common Knowledge: News and the Construction of Political Meaning* (Chicago, 1992); William A. Gamson, *Talking Politics* (New York, 1992); David Morley, *The Nationwide Audience: Structure and Decoding* (London, 1980); Graber, *Processing the News*.

42. David Harvey, *The Condition of Postmodernity: An Enquiry into the Origins of Cultural Change* (New York, 1989), esp. chap. 3; Todd Gitlin, "Postmodernism: Roots and Politics," in *Cultural Politics in Contemporary America*, ed. Ian Angus and Sut Jhally (New York, 1989), 347–60; Bauman, *Legislators and Interpreters*, esp. chaps. 8–9.

43. Charles Horton Cooley, *Social Organization: A Study of the Larger Mind* (1909; New York, 1962 ed.), chaps. 3–5, quotes from pp. 23, 24, 27, 28, 30, 32, 33, 35, 36, 38–39, 40, 42, 43, 47, 48, 51, 54.

44. John Dewey, *The Public and Its Problems* (New York, 1927), 211, 212, 213.

45. Flacks, *Making History*, esp. chaps. 1–3.

46. Sigmund Freud, "Le Bon's Description of the Group Mind," in *Readings in Public Opinion*, ed. W. Brooke Graves (New York, 1928), 85–92.

47. Mary Daly, *Beyond God the Father: Toward a Philosophy of Women's Liberation* (1973), 189, quoted in Valerie C. Saiving, "A Feminist Appropriation of Process Thought," in *Feminism and Process Thought*, ed. Sheila Greene Daveney (New York, 1981), 13; Theodore M. Newcomb, *The Acquaintance Process* (New York, 1961), 260; Kurt Lewin, *A Dynamic Theory of Personality: Selected Papers*, trans. Donald Adams and Karl E. Zener (New York, 1935), esp. 171–79; Joseph de Rivera, *Field Theory as Human-Science: Contributions of Lewin's Berlin Group* (New York, 1976), esp. 44–50; William N. McPhee, *Formal Theories of Mass Behavior* (Glencoe, Ill., 1963), 80.

48. Maurice Halbwachs, *The Collective Memory*, trans. Francis J. Ditter, Jr., and Vida Yazdi Ditter (1950; New York, 1980 ed.), 22–49, esp. 121; Kim Chernin, *In My Mother's House: A Daughter's Story* (New York, 1984).

49. Jonathan Schell, *History in Sherman Park: An American Family and the Reagan-Mondale Election* (New York, 1987); R. Robert Huckfeldt, "The Social Context of Political Change: Durability, Volatility, and Social Influence," *American Political Science Review* 77 (December 1983): 929–44; Robert Huckfeldt and John Sprague, "Networks in Context: The Social Flow of Political Information," *American Political Science Review* 81 (December 1987) 1197–1216.

50. Jane J. Mansbridge, *Beyond Adversary Democracy* (New York, 1980), 34, 63. The classic study of how women's liberation emerged from the shared discovery by particular women of male domination of the New Left is Sara Evans, *Personal Politics: The Roots of Women's Liberation in the Civil Rights Movement and the New Left* (New York, 1979).

51. I am indebted to Doug Mitchell for directing me to Richard McKeon, "The Development and the Significance of the Concept of Responsibility," in *Freedom and History and Other Essays: Richard McKeon*, ed. Zahava K. McKeon (Chicago, 1990), 62–87.

52. Clifford Geertz, *Local Knowledge: Further Essays in Interpretive Anthropology* (New York, 1983), 151.

53. Patricia Meyer Spacks, *Gossip* (Chicago, 1985), 43, 57, 101, 172.

54. Addams, *Twenty Years;* Mary Kenny quoted in Allen F. Davis, *American Heroine: The Life and Legend of Jane Addams* (New York, 1973), 79.

55. Edward A. Ross, *Sin and Society: An Analysis of Latter-Day Iniquity* (Boston, 1907), 1, 11, 29, 86, 107, 109, 131.

56. Nelson Lichtenstein, *Labor's War at Home: The CIO in World War II* (New York, 1982); Clayborne Carson, *In Struggle: SNCC and the Black Awakening of the 1960s* (Cambridge, Mass., 1981).

57. Arlene Stein, "Sisters and Queers: The Decentering of Lesbian Feminism," *Socialist Review* 21 (January/March 1992): 33–55.

58. Wini Breines, *Community and Organization in the New Left, 1962–1968: The Great Refusal* (New York, 1982); Jack Whalen and Richard Flacks, *Beyond the Barricades: The Sixties Generation Grows Up* (Philadelphia, 1989), chap. 4, esp. pp. 116–20.

59. Todd Gitlin, *The Whole World Is Watching: Mass Media in the Making and Unmaking of the New Left* (Berkeley and Los Angeles, 1980), esp. pt. 2.

60. Whalen and Flacks, *Beyond the Barricades,* esp. chap. 5, on maintenance of continuity.

61. Interview with Gergen, 22 June 1995.

CONCLUSION

1. Quoted in Bennett, *Governing Crisis,* 105; Greider, *Who Will Tell the People,* 21–22.

2. Tim Wirth, "Diary of a Dropout," *New York Times Magazine,* 9 August 1992, 16–17, 26, 34–46, quotes from 34, 36.

3. *Chicago Tribune,* 26 November 1995; *Bloomington Herald-Times,* 8 December 1995.

4. *Chicago Tribune,* 8 December 1995.

5. Larry J. Sabato, *Feeding Frenzy: How Attack Journalism Has Transformed American Politics* (New York, 1993), Afterword, esp. 248–51, 262–96.

6. Tim Jones, Janita Poe, and Stephen Franklin, "The Faces of Change," *Chicago Tribune,* 3 September 1995.

7. Larry King with Mark Stencel, *On the Line: the New Road to the White House* (New York, 1993), 2.

8. *Talkers,* no. 58 (April 1995): 1; no. 59 (May 1995); Dan Nimmo and James E. Combs, *The Political Pundits* (New York, 1992), 130; *Chicago Tribune,* 6 February 1995.

9. First poll reported in *Norfolk Virginian-Pilot,* 20 May 1995; Rosenstone et al., American National Election Study. Participants in this sample had more faith that they could make a difference than Americans as a whole because 58 percent of them reported that they voted in 1994 while only 39 percent of eligible voters actually voted.

10. Interview with Gergen, 22 June 1995; *Los Angeles Times,* 26 August 1994.

11. I am indebted to Doug Mitchell for drawing my attention to a perspective on the forum that strongly influenced what follows: Manfred Stanley, "The Rhetoric of the Commons: Forum Discourse in Politics and Society," in *The Rhetorical Turn: Invention and Persuasion in the Conduct of Inquiry,* ed. Herbert W. Simons (Chicago, 1990), 238–57.

12. Stanley, "Rhetoric of the Commons," 255.

13. John Dingell quoted in John M. Barry, *The Ambition and The Power: The Fall of Jim Wright: A True Story of Washington* (New York, 1989), 314; *Chicago Tribune*, 10 November 1994.

14. Richard McKeon, "The Development and Significance of the Concept of Responsibility," in *Freedom and History and Other Essays: An Introduction to the Thought of Richard McKeon*, ed. Zahava K. McKeon (Chicago, 1990), 62–87, esp. 85–86.

15. Peter Kornbluh and Malcolm Byrne, eds., *The Iran-Contra Scandal: The Declassified History* (New York, 1993), 409–11.

16. *Chicago Tribune*, 24 August 1995.

17. *New York Times*, 30 July 1995.

18. Hertsgaard, *On Bended Knee*, chaps. 13–14, quotes from p. 316 or 341; Howard Kurtz, "Asleep at the Switch: How the Media Bungled the Story and Contributed to the S&L Crisis," *Washington Post National Weekly Edition*, 21–27 December 1992.

19. Jerry Mander, *Four Arguments for the Elimination of Television* (New York, 1978), is a provocative exploration of how experience and diversity can generate alternatives to what is presented and experienced from television. Harry Boyte, *The Backyard Revolution: Understanding the New Citizen Movement* (Philadelphia, 1980), chap. 1, surveys how corporate and political establishments built a counterattack that simultaneously silenced the democratic movements of the late 1960s and early 1970s and brought conservative issues to the media. Two important studies that trace how media presentation narrows the range of debate—Todd Gitlin, *The Whole World is Watching: Mass Media in the Making and Unmaking of the New Left* (1978; Berkeley, 1980 ed.), and Edward S. Herman and Noam Chomsky, *Manufacturing Consent: The Political Economy of the Mass Media* (New York, 1988)—both overestimate the willingness of Americans to believe what they see on television and understate how much journalistic narrowing represents self-censorship and fear of offending the powerful and failure to report deep popular suspicions individual reporters heard all the time.

20. Robert M. Entman made just this suggestion. See *Chicago Tribune*, 3 January 1994.

21. I am indebted to Nick Cullather for reporting his observations as a staffer for Lee Hamilton.

22. For an explanation of the universal principles Americans develop beneath differences in ways they apply those principles, see Paul H. Robinson's forthcoming *Justice, Liability and Blame* as previewed in *Chicago Tribune*, 8 February 1994.

23. Lincoln Steffens, *Upbuilders* (1909; Seattle, 1968 ed.), x—xi.

24. *Time*, 20 July 1987, 15.

25. Gallup poll in Austin Ranney, "United States of America," in Austin Ranney and David Butler, *Referendums: A Comparative Study of Practice and Theory* (Washington, 1978), 75; *Congressional Quarterly Weekly Report*, 5 November 1994, 3139. For a recent argument for wider use of initiative and referendum, see David Thelen, "Two Traditions of Progressive Reform, Political Parties, and American Democracy," in *The American Constitutional System under Strong and Weak Parties*, ed. Patricia Bonomi et al. (New York, 1981), 37–63.

26. I am indebted to Harry Boyte for recounting this story.

27. Whalen and Flacks, *Beyond the Barricades*, 100–105.

28. Barbara Boxer with Nicole Boxer, *Strangers in the Senate: Politics and the New Revolution of Women in America* (Washington, 1994), quotes from dust jacket and 40. I am grateful to Senator Simon and his courteous staff for permitting me to examine his incoming correspondence in November 1991 in his office. For a journalist's account that perceived that experience, not credibility, was what concerned viewers, see *Chicago Tribune*, 17 October 1991.

29. *Louisville Courier-Journal*, 31 January 1993.

Index

Westwood Friends Meeting, 92
Weyrich, Paul, 193
Wills, Garry, 113
Wilson, Pete, 195
Wirth, Tim, 193
World Economic Review, 113
World War I, 21, 23, 133, 152; and origins
    of opinion management, 164, 167, 173

World War II, 43; and origins of opinion
    management, 166, 174, 179, 189

Young Republican Club, 92

Zimmermann, Paul, 23
Znanecki, Florian, 178